Healing Your Family Tree

John H. Hampsch, C.M.F.

Queenship
**PUBLISHING
COMPANY**

P.O. Box 42028 Santa Barbara, CA 93140-2028
(800) 647-9882 • (805) 957-4893 • FAX: (805) 957-1631

COVER PHOTO: As an appropriate symbol of the family tree, the bristlecone pine is one of nature's oldest living entities. Some of these trees are now nearly five thousand years old — already centuries old when Abraham was born.

Braced against the harsh mountain elements at eleven thousand feet altitude, the bristlecone has an incredible survival capacity. The needles, with a thirty-year "generation" period, absorb sunlight, as persons within the family absorb life-giving grace and communicate it to the whole organism. Tree growth is sporadic — at most for forty-five days out of the year. Like present-day families, the upper parts of the bristlecone are sandblasted by the harsh environs, while the roots (much like the ancestors in one's family) continue to grow in the eternal subsoil, as if on the other side of death.

Constant healing counteracts the erosion of the tree itself, as if caressed by the tender hand of an ageless Caretaker.

* * *

PRINTED IN THE UNITED STATES OF AMERICA

TABLE OF CONTENTS

FOREWORD

From the growing repertoire of playground humor comes the quip: Confucius say, "He who studies math will have problems."

Acknowledging problems isn't a problem. Finding a solution to problems — that's the problem.

All puns aside, that touches on the very purpose of this book, which is to present a program of "something new and something old" (Matt. 13:52) from the storehouse of God's armamentarium of remedies — a healing program that has proven to be one with astonishing power.

All of our "problems" really started in the Garden of Eden (and if I may elicit from you another "pun-groan," it has been said that the problem back then was not the apple in the tree, but the "pair" on the ground). The "problem" of obeying God in the face of temptation was not solved properly, and this resulted in an outcropping of problems for all of us farther downstream in the generations of human history, as Paul reminds us in Romans 5:12.

"Adam ate the apple and our teeth ache from it," says the old Hungarian proverb. Our great tree of the human race became diseased because our protoparents didn't properly confront an option emblematized by another tree — "the tree of the knowledge of good and evil." The evil that has contaminated mankind ever since has taken many forms, including death itself: "When you eat of it, you will surely die" (Gen. 2:17).

But prior to this life-terminating experience of death, we all have life-weakening experiences of physical illness, pain, trauma, mental illness, etc., and also spiritual disorders ranging from apathy to the deepest malevolence. This started with the anti-life act of Abel's murder by Cain, an individual sin that became a kind of *societal* sin, whose malaise seeped into man's innermost being: "Every inclination of the thoughts of man's heart was evil all of the time" (Gen. 6:5) — "condemned clay" says Augustine.

Adamic sin did not destroy our intellect, it only obfuscated it (Job 24:16). Nor did it destroy our free will; it only debilitated it (Gen. 8:21). Subsequent contamination in Adamic family lineage has had its effect on each individual, and yet left each individual free to sin or to avoid sin and practice virtue, independently of the inherited sin in which each was conceived (Ps. 51:5; 58:3; John 9:34). As the ante-Nicene Church Father St. Clement of Alexandria phrased it (Sermon 55): "It is the freedom of *each one* that makes true goodness and reveals real wickedness."

This is an *intra*-personal option. However, by divine decree it has *inter*personal effects or sanctions. It is in this dynamic precisely that the small "household" unit of the human family tree can become contaminated: "He punishes the children and their children for the sin of the fathers to the third and fourth generation" (Exod. 34:7). (This decree is rephrased in many ways in many passages in both the Old and the New Testaments.)

The limited family tree (three or four generations — a "household" in terms of family life structure in the time of the early Jews) is a kind of familial microcosm of the larger family tree of the human race; and the ongoing contamination of "inherited" original sin finds its microcosmic replication in the three- to four-generation unit that can be influenced by non-original (personal) sin of one's ancestors.*

Sin is both contagious and hereditary.

Within the family tree it is contagious, inasmuch as the sin of one family member affects the whole family constellation. It is hereditary, inasmuch as it is affected by the ancestry and affects the progeny, as it moves through the genealogical lineage.

---

* An exegetical caveat might be appropriate at this point: it is possible that the oft-used phrase "to the third and fourth generation" may be the symbolic way of expressing a limited but indefinite process of inheritance just as its counterpart, "blessed to the thousandth generation," may signify a very prolonged but indefinite inheritance of blessings, including the "hundredfold" extended family given to zealous Christians in this life (Mark 10:30). Excessive literalism in the understanding of such phrases could lead to contradictions and confusion in the application of God's word.

Its contagion is "horizontal"; its heredity is "vertical."

Yet, it is not *really* correct to say that sin is contagious or hereditary. It is really only sin's *consequences* that are contagious or hereditary. These consequences are damages in the body, mind, or spirit of each "victim" of another's sin, compounding the same kinds of damage from one's own personal sin.

It is to these damages, in their kaleidoscopic forms, that healing is directed.

The whole dynamic of healing in this program consists essentially in bringing to fulfillment of God's plan of having each human family incorporated into God's spiritual family:

> See how very much our heavenly Father loves us, for he allows us to be called his children — think of it — and we really *are*! But since most people don't know God, naturally they don't understand that we are his children. Yes, dear friends, we are already God's children, right now . . . (I John 3:1-2 LB) . . . so that you may share the fellowship and the joys we have with the Father and with Jesus Christ his son (I John 1:3). . . .If we are living in the light of God's presence, just as Christ does, then we have wonderful fellowship and joy with each other and the blood of Jesus his Son cleanses us from every sin (v. 7).

Peter reaffirms this unitive and healing effect of immersing ourselves into the family of God more profoundly:

> May God bless you richly and grant you increasing *freedom* from all anxiety and fear . . . for it is his boundless mercy that has given us the privilege of being born again so that we are now members of God's own family . . . and God has reserved for his children the priceless gift of eternal life . . . (I Pet. 1:2-3 LB).

The progression in this healing process is described by Paul in Colossians 2:19 (LB): "Christ [is] the head to which all of us who are his body are joined . . . and we *grow* only as we get our nourishment and strength from God." Hence, our unity and our progressive healing and integrity of personhood is contingent upon our relationship with Christ, the head of his mystical body. This is reaffirmed by Paul's remarks to the Ephesians (2:19-22 LB): "You are members of God's very own family . . . and you belong to God's household . . . a beautiful and constantly *growing* temple for God . . . joined *with him* and *with each other* by the Spirit, and are part of the dwelling place of God."

In approaching this healing program it would be helpful, I think, to survey the overall "human problem" before specifying the methodology of this relatively new approach to the family tree healing.

One might visualize a polluted river flowing from Adam and Eve to us today. The fountainhead of the pollution was that original sin of disobedience — a diversion from God's will. Much farther downstream from the source, there are other effluents of pollution within this great polluted river. The smaller currents of pollution are caused by personal sins that leave a somewhat limited range of pollution within family groups "to the third and fourth generation" — to use the phrase so often found in Scripture. Sin causes both forms of pollution, the larger from the Adamic source, the smaller current from personal sources. The toxic effect of the Adamic sin includes death (Gen. 2:17), susceptibility to illness, ignorance, and weakness of the will experienced by all mankind (v. 5).

The toxic effect of personal sin (in at least some cases) includes countless specific ailments of body, mind, and spirit (I Thess. 5:23), such as cancer, arthritis, depression, anxiety, lust, perversion, rape, terrorism, alcoholism, drug addiction, and contamination by diabolic forces of evil in endless forms.

Thus, personal sin reinforces and specifies the effects of original sin, and like original sin it has an "inherited" component, though more limited—namely, to three or four generations.

All of this sounds very dark and foreboding. Yet, not all is bad. The first candle in the darkness was Noah (Gen. 6:8), with God protecting his little family tree: "Go into the ark, you and your whole family, because I found you righteous *in this generation*" (Gen. 7:1). Noah prepared the ark to save his family (Heb. 11:7). As a prototype of the future Messiah, he was the instrument of God's goodness to counteract the evil which affected not just Adamic descendants but also all of God's diseased creation (Rom. 8:22), including animals antonomastically salvaged in the ark riding above the flood of evil.

In restoring his fallen creation, God did not remove the stigma of death—only its sting, which was "swallowed up in victory . . . through Jesus Christ" (I Cor. 15:56-57). Nor did he abolish all sickness, pain, and suffering. But when "the perishable has been clothed with the imperishable, and the mortal with immortality" (v. 54) he will have made available to us "through the resurrection of Jesus . . . an inheritance that can never perish, spoil or fade — kept in heaven for you . . . until the coming of salvation . . . in the last time" (I Pet. 1:4-5).

Yet, there is more good news to offset the bad. God has provided solutions to the problem — for instance, "healing for every disease and infirmity" (Matt. 9:35). "Praise the Lord . . . who *forgives all your sins* and *heals all your diseases*, who redeems your life from the pit and crowns you with love and compassion" (Ps. 103:2-4). Even in this problem-laden life on earth, we have access to various benefits of redemption: grace-spawned fortitude, trust in God's loving providence, natural and supernatural healing of *every facet* of our personhood (since Christ came not only to save souls but persons in all their integrity of body, mind, and spirit) (cf. I Thess. 5:23). There was also the offer of God's grace to help us deal with prevention of sin "so that when you are tempted, you will find a way out" (I Cor. 10:13).

He also offers us a "cure" of sin by means of repentance (Luke 24:27). It is encouraging to know that we are not altogether helpless as "victims" of original sin: "His divine power has given us everything we need for life and godliness . . . so that you may participate in the divine nature" (II Pet. 1:3-4). "This promise is for *you and your children* and for all who are afar off" (Acts 2:39).

There is still more good news—highlights in God's love letter, the Bible: *Original sin* can be erased through baptism: "Putting off of the old sinful nature . . . having been buried with him in baptism and raised with him" (Col. 2:11-12; cf. Acts 2:38), with baptism symbolizing the redemptive death and resurrection of Christ (I Pet. 3:21). *Personal sin*, on the other hand, can be erased through repentance, which may be expressed in any of several ways, including love of God (Luke 7:47).

Healing Your Family Tree is written to help make use of all this "good news" to clean up the *effects* in our lives and the lives of our loved ones that result from these two sources of pollution.

The overall healing process really means attaining something new. We are a motley family of God, children and aged persons, pillars of the church and fallen-aways, kindly persons and crabby persons, saints and the martyrs who must live with the saints. Some older translations of the Bible call us God's "peculiar people," which is perhaps an apt description. We are strange in some way, yet we are Christ's body on earth.

Cardinal Ratzinger calls this an example of the "divine law of disguise"—God's divine ability to be present in what is weakest and least likely, so that holiness can shine forth for what it is, his own. As we are healed and our family is healed, our living members are integrated more in charity; deceased persons in our family attain a closer union with us in Christ, because they become closer to the God-presence and more fulfilled through this prayer. In this corporate familial healing God's glory is manifest abundantly, often dramatically.

The general format of this book is somewhat unique. Each chapter has its own content, of course, defined by the title; but this material is such that, when I have given it in lecture form, it has always given rise to a flurry of questions. Recalling many of these questions, culling some from my correspondence, and trying to anticipate others that are epilogic to the teaching content, I have arranged them, with my answers, as "mini-chapters." By this means I hope to "tie together the loose ends" of this very defusive topic *before* they get "loose," and at the same time help the reader to be more selective in perusing subtopics. The end result, which I think makes for easier reading, is a kind of written interview or exploratory dialogue about a somewhat new form of healing. Also, the question-and-answer format lends itself better to study and discussion group use.

I have made an exhaustive attempt to substantiate my observations by Scripture quotations or at least citations so that the more serious reader may confirm my remarks and have starting points for study clubs, for deeper research, etc. Scripture quotes are from the *New International Version* (NIV), with only a few from the *Living Bible* (LB).

I am grateful for the encouragement I have received both in person and by letter from Dr. Kenneth McAll, in England, who pioneered the resurgence of interest in this type of healing program with his popular book with almost the same title as this one — *Healing the Family Tree*.

Finally, I want to express my deepest gratitude to Erna Barr, whose extraordinarily dedicated efforts in producing this book can hardly be exaggerated. Besides her assiduous research, she has contributed her word processing and computer skills to the project, even to the point of providing the final typeset coding for the manuscript. Her personal interest in this endeavor and her deep prayer before each work session have, I'm sure, done more than anything to ensure that the reader will benefit from this book in a lasting way.

I urge you, my readers, to pray that Jesus, the Divine

Healer, may use this modest presentation to show you the wonders of his healing love.

John H. Hampsch, C.M.F.
Los Angeles, California
November 2, 1986
Feast of All Souls

(Note: This second edition, published in 1989, contains over a hundred minor revisions and an added index.)

Chapter One
HEALING
YOUR
FAMILY TREE
What Is It
All About?

Q **Why should I be concerned about a family tree
healing?**

A A cursory glance at your family history will undoubted-
ly reveal a long line of various problems and disorders if
your family is a typical one. I am reminded of a recent car-
toon in which the whimsical character Ziggy is shown
standing in a long supermarket checkout line, saying to
another: "I came from a long line of people who stand in
long lines." I guess we all wish inherited defects were
limited to something so insignificant as that. But for most
of us, our inherited defects leave little to laugh about. "Our
fathers sinned and are no more, and we bear their
punishment" (Lam. 5:7).

There are many people who recognize that they are in
bondage to sinful habits and negative behavior, and they
wonder if these might affect their offspring. Many persons
are afflicted with excessive fears and phobias or aversions,
rage, anger, resentment, outbursts of temper, pouting,
overwhelming sense of guilt feelings, addictions to drugs
or alcohol, many types of sexual perversions or sexual
drives that are very difficult to control, strong temptations
to infidelity and fornication, adultery, etc., many types of
relationship problems that affect deep levels of the psyche:
"A spirit of prostitution is *in their heart*" (Hosea 5:4).

One out of every five American youngsters under
eighteen has a serious mental health problem, according to

Behavior Today newsletter. Between ten and twenty percent of adolescents are problem drinkers (alcoholic or pre-alcoholic). In the first half of the 1980s, the number of adolescent psychiatric patients increased 350%. There is reason for concern even in the fact that researchers have found that the *average* life expectancy of a drug addict is 33 years; for an alcoholic it is 45 years. Their descendants might also expect to have shortened lives in many cases: "I will cut off the offspring and descendants of the wicked" (Is. 14:20-22).

The last place that most people would look for the cause of their various problems is in the sins of the ancestors — and in all honesty not *every* problem is rooted in that source. Yet, while God "does not leave the [personal] guilt unpunished, still he also punishes the children for the sin of the fathers to the third and fourth generation" (Num. 14:18 — a restatement of Exod. 20:5 and 34:7). This dictum given through Moses was soon dramatically punctuated by the miraculous extinction of the families and households of Korah, Dathan, and Abiram (Num. 16:27-34). Esau's "inheritance was left to the desert jackals" (Mal. 1:3). Eli's descendants felt the lasting effects of his neglect to restrain his recalcitrant sons (I Sam. 3:14). Samuel's unethical sons brought about a tragic change in the whole political structure of Israel (8:3-5). The effects of ancestral bondage reached beyond families to the destruction of entire nations, like the Amalekites (15:2). "Saul and his blood-stained family" sinned and brought a three-year famine on God's people. Again and again the principle was put into effect by God, with "the offspring of the wicked suffering for the sins of their forefathers" (Is. 14:21), for "God stores up punishment for a man's sons" (Job 21:19; cf. I Kings 21:22). A son may be punished but not blamed for his father's wrongdoing (*Summa Theol.* 1-2, 81.1).

Q How far-reaching are the effects of ancestral sin?

A Family tree experts (genealogists) think that there are

about three and one-half million people nationwide who directly descended from John Alden and Priscilla, of *Mayflower* fame, with their eleven children. It is awesome to think how far-reaching the effects of sin (or goodness) might be in multiple generations of the offspring of any one person or couple. Every person on earth is related to you more closely than a fiftieth cousin, say experts at Florida Atlanta University.

Israelite households were usually groupings of three or four generations; hence, a sinner would usually live to see the effects of his sin within that generational range, but the effects *could* reach farther. Theoretically, one person's sin could affect millions of descendants, especially if the ancestral bondage were (exceptionally) transmitted as far as the tenth generation, as it was in applying a sanction for illegitimate birth in Deuteronomy 23:2-3 (the number ten being symbolic of completeness or finality).

Q Can sin itself be transmitted, or only its effects?

A In the Lord's second apparition to Solomon (I Kings 9:6), he said, "If you or your offspring do not observe my commands . . . I will cut off Israel from the land, and they will reject this temple." We see in this passage that punishment, not guilt, can be generationally linked, since the offspring were "punished" for their ancestors' disobedience; however, their own guilt was a different kind of rebellion — rejecting the temple. Sinful parents often raise sinful children, but the personal guilt from sin depends on each individual's free will (II Kings 14:6). Pope John Paul II affirmed this while highlighting also the social dimension of sin (November 5, 1986).

Q Is suffering or sickness the result of personal sin?

A Many holy people have suffered, such as Job, who was truly righteous (Job 1:1, 8). Remotely, all suffering results from original sin, as is clear from Genesis 1:16-19. The existence of the freedom of the will to resist temptation resulting from original sin is patent from the Lord's challenge to Cain in Genesis 4:7. *Remotely, all* suffering, sin, and death result from original sin; but *proximately some* suffering results from personal sin. However, this may be either one's own personal sin or that of one's ancestors. Nongenerational disorders, in some cases, could include ignorance of health care, preventative medicine, environmental dangers, etc.; malice (crime, child abuse or neglect, etc.); demonic attacks (by, for instance, a spirit of sickness: II Cor. 12:7 and Luke 13:11).

Q This is my "afraid-to-ask" question: Isn't it unjust of God to make the offspring suffer for the sins of the ancestors?

A You're not the first to ask that question; it was asked by Job (21:19), and he complained about it elsewhere (5:4). David also asked the question in I Chronicles 21:17 and II Samuel 24:17.

The bottom-line answer is the one given by the Lord to Job (38:2): "Why are you using your *ignorance* to deny my providence?" or the reprimand to the house of Israel: "Are my ways unjust? . . . Is it not your ways that are unjust?" (Ezek. 18:29).

Yet, the word of God does provide us with some answers more in detail. Let me enumerate a few:

1. The apparently unjust policy of inherited guilt is only temporary, until the Second Coming, as Ezekiel (18:20) and Jeremiah (31:30) prophesy.

2. Original sin itself is an inherited sin (Rom. 5:15; Ps. 51:5). Persons who take that for granted do not always do the same with ancestral sin.

3. We take for granted that the innocent suffer for the guilty in everyday events: shame comes to the family of a criminal; families are impoverished by the extravagance of one member or by fines imposed on one delinquent member; parental neglect causes untold suffering in children in

countless ways; children suffer from their parents' divorce; spouses suffer from their partner's infidelity, etc. Ancestral sin has a similar spinoff effect; is it therefore unjust? (cf. Num. 16:22).

4. Inherited suffering may be discipline for one's own sins, so "victims" of ancestral sin can't always claim "innocence" (I John 1:8). To claim this would be to claim that human nature itself was "innocent." "No one is good — not one in all the world is innocent" (Rom. 3:10, quoting Ps. 14:3; cf. Eph. 2:3; Rom. 5:12).

5. Not every inherited defect is necessarily all bad. For instance, a retarded child has an above-average love capacity and less-than-average capacity for sin.

6. God's love and mercy can work through inherited defects, for "He knows what is best for us at all times" (Eph. 1:8 LB), and ultimately "All things work together unto good for those who love him and are fitting into his plan" (Rom. 8:28).

7. Countless acts of heroism and charity are practiced toward those who are suffering from inherited defects; this practice of virtue (patience, fortitude, charity, compassion, etc.) glorifies God, and occasions great reward for those who practice these virtues (Rev. 22:12).

8. People with inherited handicaps are often outstanding inspirations to others, such as Helen Keller and those who taught her (cf. I Cor. 11:1; Phil. 3:17; II Thess. 3:7; Titus 2:7; James 5:10, etc.).

9. Is it necessarily evil to have been born weak instead of strong, poor instead of rich, etc.? The poor, for example, are spared temptations to a life of luxury and often consequent profligacy (I John 2:15-17).

10. Punishment "to the third and fourth generation" can't be compared to the blessings "to the thousandth generation" as ancestral reward. God's mercy overshadows his justice; "where sin abounds, grace abounds all the more" (Rom. 5:20). Our complaint about the bad often eclipses the gratitude we should have for the good effects that we enjoy from our ancestors. We complain about a

headache and never thank God for the marvelous gift of a brain; we complain of disease and never thank God for our marvelous immune system.

11. It can't be proved that those who inherit their ancestors' guilt-effects are worse off, *on the whole*, than those more exempt. God's view ranges farther than ours, as the Lord reminded Job (40:1), to which Job apologizes: "I spoke of things I did not understand" (42:3). "My ways are not your ways, says the Lord. As the heavens are higher than the earth, so are my ways higher than your ways, and my thoughts than your thoughts" (Is. 55:8-9).

12. God gives inner resources to counteract inherited defects. Disorders like alcoholism, depression, anxiety, etc., can be dealt with, through many means, such as free will, the immune system, support by friends, a spurt of courage, the will to live, and various organizational supports.

13. Modern remedies and technology can alleviate and cure disorders: biogenetics, pharmacology, surgery, psychiatry, etc. These are all special gifts from God to help cope with the effects of an ancestral sin.

14. Many who complain about the "injustice" of ancestral sin ironically are often the ones who bring harm on their own progeny (cf. Jer. 7:26), by drug or alcohol abuse, infidelity, selfishness, and countless other sins.

15. Suffering for others' sins (vicarious suffering) couldn't be all bad, for we have Jesus himself who "bore our iniquities" (Is. 53:4; I Pet. 2:24, Matt. 8:17, etc.). His example sets the standard for non-complaining endurance. "The Lord has laid on him the iniquity of us all . . . yet he did not open his mouth" (Is. 53:6-7).

16. Experiencing inherited punishment in ourselves can be a deterrent to sin, as we anticipate the effects of our sin in our progeny.

17. We don't claim God is unjust when we see one person's sin affecting many, outside of the ancestral sin dynamic; for example, Hitler and the Holocaust; serial murders; dangerous toxic waste disposal ordered by unscrupulous executives; terrorism; taxpayers suffering from

politicians' graft; consumers paying more because of shoplifting losses, etc. If God's justice is not challenged in these things, why is it challenged with regard to ancestral sin's transmission?

18. As a Protestant scholar, Gleason Archer, writes in *Encyclopedia of Biblical Difficulties*, God killed David's illegitimate baby (II Sam. 12:15-23) "because the people needed this rebuke as a reminder that God's children, *even though forgiven*, must bear temporal consequences of their sin, and patiently endure them as an important part of their repentance." (Incidentally, this is the Catholic rationale for purgatory.)

19. Family punishment for sins of one member was not *always* regarded as unjust, for Mephibosheth (grandson of Saul) admitted that he "deserved" to be put to death for Saul's sins, though he was spared by David (II Sam. 19:28).

20. The threat of generational bondage is tempered by the offer of God's mercy. Jesus excoriated the Jews, calling the "blood of Abel to Zechariah on this generation," but followed it with the gentle remonstrance, "I would gather your children to myself . . . but you would not; . . . so your house will be left desolate" (Matt. 28:36-37). "You will not come to me that you may have life" (John 5:40). Thus, we suffer much needlessly because we don't turn to God. There are many peace marches but few prayers for peace; much marriage counselling, but few sincere attempts to "love one another with tenderhearted love" (Col. 3:12). He would "gather us" (as in a Eucharistic community) "but you would not." "Are my ways unjust?" asks the Lord. "Is it not your ways that are unjust?" (Ezek. 18:29).

21. Ignorance-induced suffering cannot rightly be blamed on God, so why should sin-induced suffering? For instance, many babies suffer some degree of brain damage from pregnant women consuming alcohol, even in cough medicine; thalidomide babies suffered from the results of pharmaceutical ignorance; children living with smokers, even unborn babies, can experience respiratory damage even from "second-hand" smoke (as do pets). Should we

blame God for such tragedies? There's less reason for blaming him for ancestral sin's effects than for ignorance-spawned effects.

22. There are hints that inherited suffering is only part of God's permissive will, not his positive will, with words like "punishment will be visited" rather than "I will punish"—at least in some passages that refer to ancestral sin.

23. Ultimate *family* good may be in the providential design of God for the suffering caused by members of the family tree, as in the case of Joseph. His brothers' murderous plans (Gen. 37:19) circuitously redounded to the saving of the Israelites from starvation (Gen. 45:7), and gave a new unity and direction to the whole family tree (45:10). We are all co-responsible.

24. The righteous suffer with the wicked in this life, like the wheat grown with the weeds: "Let both grow together until the harvest" (Matt. 13:30). The separation comes later (Matt. 3:12). This indiscriminate presence of suffering in the world may be to make everyone, good and bad, aware of God's absolute sovereignty over evil.

Besides these twenty-four reasons why it is not unjust for God to allow the progeny to suffer for the ancestor's sins, I'm sure there are other reasons that my readers may think of; these are the only ones I can think of. There may be any number of reasons that we will know only in eternity, when we will appreciate more the marvels of God's loving providence. (See the first question on page 46.)

Q What is the role of original sin, and the role of personal sin in generational bondage?

A Just as original sin is the origin of physical death (Rom. 5:18), so personal sin is the origin of spiritual death (Rom. 8:13). They both can be transmitted in some way. Original sin can be transmitted by a spiritual heredity, but although personal sin itself cannot be transmitted, its effects can be (for example, Num. 14, 18), and the spiritual death is what we deal with here in the breaking of the bondage of transmitted effects of personal sin. Original sin is dealt with through baptism.

Contravening those two kinds of death is a statement of Christ from John 10:10, "I have come to give you *life* and life more abundantly" — as opposed to the Evil One, "the thief, who comes only to destroy and kill" — to undermine life.

A simple epigrammatic poem expresses the generational succession, the needs for healing that it carries with it, and the effective release that can be had through the power of prayer:

"Out of the seed the flower, out of the flower the seed; out of the need the power, out of the power the deed."

Q **I have always regarded grace and sin as something personal between me and God; but some say grace and sin are transmissible. Have I been theologically in error about this?**

A "My people perish from lack of knowledge" (Hosea 4:6). As we learn more about the nature of generational sin and its transmission, we come to understand something of the communitarian nature of grace as well as sin, the societal functions of the spiritual factors in human existence. Pope John XXIII once said, "We humans are saved and sanctified in clusters, like grapes." As we pray together we reinforce each other in holiness by community prayer. If we sin together (for instance, in adultery, gossip-spreading, and team theft) we reinforce each other in evil by bad example and cooperation in sin. For instance, in gang activities bad influence is obviously contagious, and, conversely, the infectious good influence is found in prayer communities.

The communitarian nature of grace and the communitarian nature of sin are something we usually don't give enough thought to, until we consider the consequences of ancestral sin with its sequential effects on others, and present sin with its contemporaneous effects on others.

Living family members can be contaminated or enriched as a group, but also even the descendants and those as yet unborn can also be affected favorably or unfavorably. The communitarian element extends itself not only horizontally but also vertically from past ancestors to future descendants. Truly, there is a "clustering" of good and evil, like good or rotten descendants (to extend the analogy of Pope John XXIII).

Likewise we suffer in clusters, like grapes that are crushed, not one at a time, but many at once. I can hardly conceive of any kind of human suffering that doesn't have some bearing upon those around us. An alcoholic may be suffering from the driving force of the compulsion to drink, but the whole family also suffers. A government study found that a high percentage of juvenile delinquents come from broken homes and half had another family member who had been imprisoned. Could some non-biological (spiritual) factor possibly be involved?

Someone has said, "No one goes to hell alone"; the damned person always drags others to hell with him. But neither does anyone go to heaven alone, but by goodness, one influences others to move heavenward. This is especially true of parents influencing their children for good, but it is also a worker influencing a co-worker for good, or a parishioner influencing a fellow parishioner. The power of good example can hardly be overestimated. If we were to see the communitarian dimension of grace and how deeply involved we are in this network of grace, we would be awestruck with our great responsibility.

Think for a moment about the nature of sin in its interpersonal dimension, and you will see the truth of that adage. A rapist is hell-bound, but so is the unforgiving victim. A person who commits adultery leads the partner to commit adultery. A person who commits fornication cooperates with a partner in the sin. A person who therefore sets up his own damnation, especially under the false name of love, and leads another person to damnation, still calling it love, is a very twisted person. We can be the cause through bad example of others' damnation—which is why Jesus said, "Woe to those who scandalize. . . . It is better for such a person to have a millstone hung about his neck and be cast into the depths of the sea" (Luke 17:2). This societal dynamic becomes especially meaningful in the healing of generational sin and its effects that otherwise would infect future generations.

Q How can generational bondage within the family tree be recognized?

A In Luke 6:44, Jesus says, "Each tree is recognized by its own fruit." That is meant to be more than a family tree pun based upon a scriptural pericope. Both negative and positive patterns show up in family trees in many forms; you can recognize the (family) tree by its fruit. The children are the "fruit" of the parents' union; likewise the children's behavior, good or bad, is the fruit of the parents' behavior in many ways — not just in the children's moral behavior, but also in physical and mental health status.

In the scriptural and theological perspective, which we are considering mainly in this book, the question may be asked whether these predispositions might not be only the matrix within which divine providence works to engineer the transmission of the effects of ancestral sin. Divine providence may allow the offspring to be predisposed toward a problem ("bad fruit" of ancestors) without causing that problem.

Q Are there unrecognized effects of ancestral sin?

A Yes, especially in the sense that the suffering is recognized, but it is not recognized as inherited punishment.

The morally infected family lineage is often submerged and not recognized until it surfaces by happenstance. Jesus made it a point to stress that delayed punishment is "now hidden from your eyes" (Luke 19:42-44). It then is often shown to be true that "Even from birth the wicked go

23

astray; from the womb they are wayward" (Ps. 58:3).

There was a young man a number of years ago who approached his father and said that if he didn't get help, he was going to commit suicide. The father, who had been interested only in making money, continued to neglect the son until the young man contracted a social disease. The father eventually sent the son to an institution for treatment. After a year of therapy, the son married a beautiful girl, who died in childbirth. Having lost his wife, he was further overwhelmed with grief when he found out that the baby was physically and mentally deficient. In desperation he committed suicide.

The story didn't end there. The mentally and physically deficient baby lived. One day in Buffalo, New York, he was waiting in line to shake hands with the President of the United States, William McKinley. As he grasped the hand of the President, he drew a gun and assassinated McKinley. Shortly after that, this man himself was executed. It is a tale of tragedy that moves from a materialistic father through the symptoms of suicidal tendencies in the son, the son's profligate life, venereal disease, the death of his wife in childbirth, the deformity of the grandson, and that grandson's own crime of assassinating a president and finally his own execution.

If every crime that makes headlines were investigated in terms of family lineage, I daresay we would find a rather consistent pattern of defects and evil and weaknesses running through the family lineage. It's only when we look at that from the viewpoint of possible ancestral sin that we become aware of any kind of hurt beyond our immediate present sufferings.

The purpose of this program is not to simply look at our own ailments that need healing now, but the healing of the entire family tree. "Weep for yourselves and your children," Jesus said (Luke 23:28).

Q **In what way are physical ailments subject to healing in this family tree healing program?**

A The most common concern of most people who learn of ancestral contamination is *physical* illness, with less concern, unfortunately, for *spiritual* weaknesses they may have inherited or will transmit to their offspring. Hence, to teach the heinousness of sin, God has emphasized its physical effects: "If you do not obey the Lord . . . the fruit of your womb will be cursed. . . . The Lord will plague you with diseases . . . and strike you with wasting disease, with fever and inflammation" (Deut. 28:15-21; cf. Lev. 26:16, 39). The healing of many physical diseases is contingent on the healing of the spiritual disease called *sin*: "He who forgives all your iniquities also heals your diseases" (Ps. 103:3). In forgiving ancestral iniquities, physical outcropping of such sin is also healed. This seems to be the underlying dynamic of the healing of the family tree program, and accounts for the astonishing testimonies of physical healings that are reported as a result of this program, as well as emotional and interpersonal healings. A fourth of all physical ailments are genetic.

Q My father, as his father before him, saved his money and spent little so that I would have a comfortable inheritance. Would this fact augur for good or for bad for our family tree?

A Some wag expressed epigrammatically a worldly-wise truth: "A miser isn't much fun to live with, but he sure makes a wonderful ancestor."

If holiness is to be preferred to wealth, then one could say it is better to have a saintly ancestor than to have a miserly one who might provide a substantial material inheritance. In general, the holier your ancestors, the less intergenerational healing you will need, and by consequence the holier you are, the less intergenerational healing your children, grandchildren, and great-grandchildren will need, according to the promises of God's Word (Exod. 20:6; 34:7).

The pursuit of material goods is less frenetic in godly

people, for "Those who reverence the Lord will never lack any good thing. Sons and daughters, come and listen and let me teach you the importance of trusting and fearing the Lord"(Ps. 34:10-11 LB).

Q Do all offspring suffer the same kind of punishment?

A Not always. Sometimes the descendants' disorders are highly variegated. But frequently they are "patterned." As an example, Kurt Koch once wrote that he had talked to the granddaughter of an atheist living in Switzerland. This atheist grandfather had written a book of great contempt of Christianity. None of this man's descendants were normal. His children were either born with crippled legs or they were accidentally crippled later in life or became crippled as the result of illness or accidents. Some of his children were mentally retarded and some of his grandchildren have had the same affliction. In all of his descendants, there appears to be a moodiness, and they seem to suffer from depression, and all of them have become professed atheists. Such consistent patterns are often found among descendants of a person who has put himself into the hands of the enemy of God. Forces of evil then take over the person's life. The pattern sanction is quite common. To explain such patterns as mere coincidence would ignore the fact that such disorders are statistically related to the immoral behavior or perverse belief of an ancestor. The pattern sanction is repeated with great consistency, not just in a few family trees, but in thousands upon thousands. The case for the intergenerational bondage theory becomes very tenable, almost irrefutable, just on the basis of statistical probabilities.

Q How can there be financial effects of ancestral sin?

A Loss of prosperity is a common punishment for ancestral sin. The age-old practice of voodoo (as in Haiti) impoverishes subsequent generations. God threatened this form of sanction on numerous occasions, among a litany of other punishments (cf. Deut. 28:15-68).

As an example, some years ago in New York state, there was an outcast girl by the name of Mag, one of thousands on welfare. Alienated from her family she turned to prostitution and a life of profligacy. Ultimately, the expense to the state of New York went far beyond state-financed hospitalization, food, etc. When her family tree was studied by some sociologists, they tried to approach the genealogy from a financial point of view. She had, during seventy years, approximately 1200 descendants. As far as these sociologists were able to trace her genealogy, they found 280 of these descendants were state-supported paupers and 148 were jailed criminals. In measuring the costs of the criminals, their housing and jail, the amount of money that they stole, the cost of the injuries that they caused, etc., they figured it was, conservatively, $1,308,000, a considerable amount at that time — the early 1900s. This may not be as significant as the toll of human tragedy that resulted from this type of ancestral sin (cf. I Kings 22:52), but there are people who cannot be impressed by moral arguments, only by financial statistics.

Q Is there a scriptural basis for ancestral sin and its effects?

A The classic quote (with many parallels, such as Num. 14:18 and Jer. 32:18) used as the nucleus of this whole book is Exodus 20:5-6: "I the Lord your God . . . punishing the children for the sin of the fathers to the third and fourth generations of those who hate me, but showing love to a thousand generations of those who love me and keep my commandments." In verse 6, the word "hate"or "love" used in that passage indicates either a rejection or loyalty to the covenant of God. So it is a very basic position of for-or-against. That basic double option that ethicians call "synderesis" was simply articulated by Jesus: "He who is not with me is against me. He who does not sow with me scatters" (Matt. 12:30).

In this passage, "the sins will be visited," the word "visited" in Hebrew is *paqad*. The main denotation means to visit, but it has many connotations or derivative meanings and they include: avenge, charge, count, due-judgment, hurt, punish, or reckon. If all of those were transposed for the word "visit" in that passage, "visited upon the children" — that would perhaps make the passage more clear. Punishment in such connotative contexts could better be seen as a function of God's permissive will rather than his positive will.

Q Is the punishment always "to the third and fourth generation"?

A Not always. The principle is so all-embracing that it can reach back farther than the fourth generation, as Jesus seemed to imply when he said that the sins of the Jews from the time of the murder of Abel to the murder of Zechariah would come upon that generation (Matt. 23:36); therefore, though the sanction may be limited to three or four generations in terms of the more deleterious effects, still there could be a more extensive contamination, by way of exception. Ancestral sin can be punished even to the tenth generation, as stated in Deuteronomy 23:2-3.

In praying for *healings*, ask that they be just as extensive as the *prevention* of disorders mentioned in Exodus: to the thousandth generation. In other words, the normal limits of punishment or reward are to the third and fourth generation, but there are exceptions. The more "remote" punishment may be less severe, and the "remote" reward may be less manifest. The principle applies when counting backward in ancestry (living or dead), or forward in progeny (living or as yet unborn).

Q I would like very much to participate in the fami-

ly tree healing program. How exactly is the program conducted?

A In the family tree healing service, each person should engage in a kind of individualized private prayer, even though it may be done as a group service. It could be a simple prayer like: "Do not hold against us the sins of our forefathers" (Ps. 79:8). Or, "Punish me not for my sins . . . nor for those of my forefathers" (Tobit 3:3).

It is helpful, but not necessary, to outline one's family tree by using a structured genogram (see sample, pages 296-297) showing one's family tree, listing in particular any living or deceased persons who may have strongly influenced the family members in a hurtful way causing emotional, physical, or spiritual problems ("a man's enemies are the members of his own household" [Micah 7:6]). This listing could include persons with ongoing psychosomatic disorders that may have in some way been "absorbed" by a kind of *spiritual* heredity which may have been superimposed upon components of their *physical* heredity.

In this process the persons going through the healing should consider in a very special way anyone who may have had a need of an added prayer at the time of the person's death. This includes situations like infant deaths in abortion and miscarriage; also sudden deaths of victims of murder, fire, drowning, earthquakes, crashes, etc. For those persons who at the moment of death perhaps were not completely aligned with God's will, there may be a need for a healing, even after they have crossed the threshold of life into eternity.

Normally, the healing program concludes with a Eucharistic service in which prayers are offered to God to cut any negative bondage between ourselves and past generations, and between presently living generations and future unborn generations. The participants in the program are encouraged to offer prayers of real forgiveness for those who have offended them, living or dead, since your own resentment will induce a curse on your own offspring

(Job 5:2-4). It is important to extend — like the father of the prodigal son — unconditional love for family members and any other close relatives, and even friends and associates, employing the broadest use of the term "family."

We have to keep in mind that the persons included here must be not only those who are alive, but also those who are deceased. We pray that each person related to us, proximately or remotely, be brought into God's light and love; requesting and receiving forgiveness for our own sins by repentance, asking pardon for neglect and for not adequately putting forth the effort to change negative behavior, or for not depending upon God's help in the past to change that behavior.

To assure the success of this healing program, we must surrender in deep humility, in dependence on the Lord to do the healing, while acknowledging our own helplessness to cope with the situation. That sense of dependence touches upon the very essence of religion itself, the "binding" of creature to creator. *"Religo"* (binding) is the root word from which we get the word religion. While relinquishing any *binding* to evil practices, we bind ourselves to God in a bond of love. Thus, bonding replaces bondage. That is the essence of divine healing. It will be successful in proportion as we seek humbly to undergo that reversal or "metanoia," as the Greek Fathers so aptly phrased it. Loving surrender to God's love in the program of healing the family tree elicits the love that binds us to God, and it is the same "love that binds us all together in family unity" (Col. 3:14).

In the concluding part of the healing service, the eternal sacrifice of Calvary is relived and "proclaimed," as Paul says in I Cor. 11:26: "Every time we eat the bread or drink the wine, we show forth the death of the Lord." We symbolically reenact the sacrifice of Calvary with the *real* body and blood of Jesus (John 6:55). At that time each person is encouraged to pray that the blood of Jesus which was shed on Calvary will now be applied to that person's own bloodline — the lineage of the living and the dead respectively;

and praying also that anything that is preventing one from a healthy or holy life, or an emotionally stable life, would be removed.

As the bondage is cut from the past and future generations, each one is encouraged to pray that the control of these things be now transferred to Jesus, the Lord of the universe, the King of creation, the One who is really in control. We must submit to that control, allowing him to take complete mastery of our lives and the lives of our loved ones, "no longer controlled by sinful nature, but by the Spirit of God" (Rom. 8:9), "living in the Holy Spirit's power and following the Holy Spirit's leading in every part of our lives" (Gal. 5:25). We can take heart, in the midst of our personal and family problems, with the words of Jeremiah (31:16-17): "Stop your weeping, dry your eyes; your hardships will be redressed . . . there is hope for your descendants."

Q **How can the healing program, for instance, help parents who have lost an infant in death?**

A With the use of mental imagery, the prayer can become more meaningful as the person doing the praying — the mother or the father—can open her or his arms to "receive" from Jesus the child that he has taken to himself. He allows the parent or parents to hold the child and express love as if the child were truly alive and in their arms. With Jesus to speak to the child, the parents wish and pray for all the things that they would like to have done for the child even belatedly, and to ask Jesus to inform them what needs to be done in the future to deepen and make more meaningful the relationship with the deceased child in the context of the doctrine of the "communion of saints" in the mystical body of Christ.

One who engaged in this prayer might visualize Jesus holding the baby and confronting the parent, whose anger against God for taking the child is released, with the Lord responding that he is the author of life and death and that the child belongs to the Lord, and was only loaned for a while to the parents, whether within the womb or whether for a short life after birth; that God had numbered the days of the child and made plans for his life (Ps. 139:13-18). Or a simple Scripture meditation, appropriately chosen, could be used:

> You made all the delicate inner parts of my body and knit them together in my mother's womb. Thank you for making me so wonderfully complex. It is amazing to think about. Your workmanship is marvelous and how well I know it. You were there when I was being formed in utter seclusion. You saw me before I was born and scheduled each day of my life before I began to breathe, every day of my life was recorded in your book. How precious it is, Lord, to realize that you are thinking about me constantly. I can't even count how many times a day your thoughts turn towards me" (Ps. 139:13-18 LB).

Q There seems to be a "genealogy explosion" these days. Why is there such widespread interest in "family trees" at this time?

A The significance of the family tree to the average man on the street seems to be reflected in the Bible itself. Mention of the first parents in the very first book of the Old Testament is the most fascinating part of that first chapter. And in the New Testament the very first words (in Matthew's gospel) are: "A record of the genealogy of Jesus Christ, the son of David, the son of Abraham. . . ."

The reasons for interest in the family tree might be as predictable as just plain curiosity, or as specialized as a need for medical history. The Church of Jesus Christ of Latter Day Saints (Mormons) has the largest collection of genealogical information in the world, established because of their unusual rituals that require identifying *deceased* ancestors for the "baptism of the dead" (a custom that Paul referred to in I Cor. 15:29). Whatever the individual motivations, they have bred 1800 genealogical societies nationwide in the United States, including more than a hundred in California alone.

There has been a kind of renewed media focus on genealogy in recent times because of the rededication of the Statue of Liberty and its relation to Ellis Island, through which forty to forty-five percent of this county's population can trace its heritage, since over 17,000,000 immigrants passed through that tiny island between 1892 and its closing in 1954. Many people feel the insecurity of a detached isolated existence in modern society; we have lost our roots, the kind of roots we had when we grew up surrounded by an extended family, as people did in agricultural days when there was a strong sense of history and tradition. Most of us today aren't surrounded by our extended family, and we are searching for roots to give us a sense of our place in the history of the human race. In the highly mechanized society and highly mobile society, we may start to feel like detached molecules floating around in space. This hunger for knowing one's roots was stimulated by the *Roots* miniseries, which set new TV ratings records and caused many people to become interested in genealogy.

Perhaps all of this was a sociological framework within which God chose to stimulate interest in the effects of ancestral sin and virtue, with their respective consequences on the offspring as mentioned in Scripture, the basis for the relatively new family tree healing program.

Thus, we see today a revived interest in anything that links us spiritually to our predecessors. Sermons and seminars are focusing on pericopes like Exodus 20:5-6, "the sins of the parents are visited upon the children to the third and fourth generation, but showing love to a thousand generations of those who love me and keep my commandments."

Q **How much of the deeply-ingrained effects of ancestral sin are really within our ability to change or control?**

A The handicaps like weak eyes, poor teeth, bad backs, and other traits many times are handed down from one generation to another, sometimes as a fulfillment of the prophecy of the "sins of the parents" being punished in the lives of the children. Also, personality traits — that is, psychological disorders — are often passed on to the children and the grandchildren and great-grandchildren. Deuteronomy 28:18 says, "The fruit of your womb will be cursed" (referring to those who do not obey the Lord). The tenacity of sickness, problems, etc., makes that curse appear to be almost irreversible.

Nevertheless, we need not live under a curse. When persons give their lives over to God and repudiate the sin in their lives, they can dispose God to break that curse, and in the place of that, the blessing of the Lord is manifested. In Exodus 20:6, it says that God will show mercy "to thousands of them who love me and keep my commandments." (An alternate translation is "showing love to a thousand generations of those who love me and keep my commandments.")

This passage referring to the love we should have for the Lord makes use of the treaty language used in the ancient Near East. The word "love" meant that kind of love that was owed to a king — a conventional term for total allegiance and implicit trust expressing itself in obedient service. It is that kind of love for God which can break the transmission of disease, neurosis, etc., and reverse the process by giving blessings and other benefits. As a result, thousands of our descendants are blessed when we decide to live godly lives (or repair the damage when we have not lived godly lives).

But, *healing of inherited hurts often requires more than living godly lives.* Sometimes it requires prayer for the healing of those inherited hurts and a breaking of a remnant bondage or "contamination" derived from our ancestors because of their sin. This prayer dimension of the healing process is maximally effective when it is exercised in the context of the Eucharist, as twenty centuries of experience attests. That is the core of the program of healing the family tree.

Q Do all forms of suffering and sickness result from ancestral sin?

A No. The disciples asked, when Jesus cured the man born blind, "Who has sinned, this man or his parents that he was born blind?" (John 9:2). Jesus answered: "Neither this man nor his parents have sinned, but this happened so that the work of God might be displayed in his life."

This probably went directly in the face of the opinion held by the Jews, who attacked the blind man after his healing by saying that he was steeped in sin at his birth (John 9:34).

Jesus' disciples and the Jews were operating under the presumption that *all* forms of sickness were the result of ancestral sin. The rabbis had developed a principle that stated: "There is no death without sin, and there is no suffering without iniquity." Some even thought that it was possible for a child to sin in the womb, or that its soul may have sinned in a preexistent, preembodied state. They also held that terrible punishments came on people almost exclusively because of the sins of the parents. Jesus disabused them of that *universal* conclusion by pointing out that in this case, and implicitly in other cases, the cause of the suffering was to manifest divine providence. In this case the providential act was to display the miraculous power of God through Jesus.

The gospel of Luke reaffirms the truth that not all suffering is the result of sin, even personal sin; much less can we say that all suffering is the result of ancestral sin. Jesus spoke about the Galileans whose blood Pilate had mixed with their sacrifices. . . . "Do you think that these Galileans were worse sinners than all the other Galileans because they suffered this way? I tell you, no! . . . Or those eighteen who died when the tower of Siloam fell of them. . . . Do you think that they were more guilty than all the others living

35

in Jerusalem? I tell you, no!" (Luke 13:1-4).

In the time of Jeremiah and Ezekiel (sixth century B.C.) the belief was very strong in the teaching that all suffering was the result of ancestral sin, but these prophets foretold of the end-times when ancestral effects of sin would be abolished (Jer. 31 and Ezek. 18). Until that time, we, like Josiah, recognize that "great is the Lord's anger . . . because our fathers have not obeyed" (II Kings 22:13). But like him, we can divert God's anger. As king of Judah he conducted one of the first "programs" for healing the family tree and, as a result, was blessed abundantly, along with his people (vv. 19-20).

Q **In spite of countless genetic disorders, humans have survived very well. Is genetic lineage "self-cleansing"? If so, trying to heal or "clean up" the genetic debris could be superfluous, like cleaning a self-cleaning oven.**

A By his divine providence, God has arranged for the majority of the human race to be healthy. In a sense, this involves the application of the survival of the fittest, not in terms of Darwinian evolution, but in the sense of keeping the stream of life, that is, the DNA (deoxyribonucleic acid), intact. As one generation follows another, the sperm or the eggs with the damaged DNA are unlikely to fertilize or be fertilized. If they are fertilized, spontaneous abortion is likely. Stillbirth is the next natural consequence. And, finally, if the child is not stillborn, the damaged DNA lineage is often spontaneously terminated, or sometimes death occurs before the age of reproduction.

One wonders whether this couldn't place a societal connotation in Romans 8:13: "If you live according to the sinful nature, you will die, but if by the Spirit you put to death the misdeeds of the body you will live, because those who are led by the Spirit of God are the sons of God." By analogy, the death of the individual results from certain physical defects, but also the death (termination) of defective elements in the lineage damaged in its DNA components. In this sense, we would see how, in this biological "cleansing," in some way things could "work together unto good," as God over a long period of time would tend to make the race, as a whole, healthier, while some individuals would experience premature death — premature by "average" standards of life duration.

Q **Ezekiel predicted a discontinuance of the proverb that the "fathers eat sour grapes and the children's teeth are set on edge," and that "the son will not share the guilt of the father." Hasn't that phophecy been fulfilled already, with our redemption through Christ?**

A That would *seem* to be true from the parallel phrase of Jeremiah 31:29. Yet both Ezekiel and Jeremiah speak of the cessation of this ancestral bondage as a future event and indicate that it is not at the time of Christ's first coming, but in the *fullness* of the time of his new covenant, that is, at the parousia or second coming of Christ. The reason for this is that it will coincide with a time when "they will all know me, from the least to the greatest" (Jer. 31:34) (obviously not at the present time). This is confirmed by Hebrews 8:11 and 10:16. It will occur when he "makes all things new" (Rev. 21:5). St. John refers to that time when all will know the Lord, namely, "When he appears, we shall see him as he is" (I John 3:3; cf. Ps. 17:15).

So, for the present, we are still subject to ancestral bondage. Jesus himself, in his parable of the unmerciful servant, referred to the accepted belief of generational punishment: "The master ordered that *he and his wife and children* and all that he had be sold to repay the debt" (Matt. 18:25). But because of Christ's death, we can avail ourselves of the liberation from bondage that he offers: "If the Son sets you free, you will be free indeed" (John 8:36). We still suffer from inherited sin's effects, but we can break free from them by this liberation Christ offers. The healing of the family tree program facilitates our acceptance of Christ's freeing, healing power.

Q **Scripture mentions sins of fathers. Do mothers convey sin's effects to their offspring?**

A Excessive literalism in interpreting Scripture can cause much confusion. "Fathers" in this context means forefathers or ancestors, male or female. Most genes are transmitted through the cell nucleus inherited from *both* the father and the mother. However, there is a type of gene that occupies tiny suborgans called mitochondria, which are located within the cells but outside the nucleus. Each of us, men and women, get our mitochondria DNA *only* from our mothers, and she from her mother, etc. If it is true that genes are the vehicle for both physical and emotional characteristics, we may suspect that certain types of characteristics could be transmitted only through the mother by means of the mitochondria. Fathers cannot transmit mitochondria DNA genes to their offspring. Hence, we might find a certain type of characteristic or a series of characteristics that correspond more frequently to ancestral sin and its consequences *only* in the lineage of our mothers and grandmothers, great-grandmothers, etc. This ancestral sin *could* include, for example: moral weakness leading to prostitution, abortion, lesbianism, etc. Mother-to-daughter transmitted evil tendencies are hinted at in Ezekiel 16:44.

Q **I'm sure that illness is not always a punishment for sin, either personal or ancestral. What other reasons could there be for sickness?**

A St. Basil the Great, bishop of Caesarea (A.D. 330-379), suggested that there are six explanations of illness in God's economy.

First, it may be for our correction and discipline even when, and perhaps especially when, we see that it is transmitted because of our transgressions to our progeny.

Second, for our punishment — and this, too, in light of its possible effects on our progeny.

Third, from natural physical origins, such as poor hygiene and neglect on our part.

Fourth, it could be sent by Satan, as in the case of Job (1:12).

Fifth, to allow the faithful to serve as models of fortitude for spiritually weak persons who quail at illness.

Sixth, as it was used by Paul, to keep us from becoming conceited (cf. II Cor. 12:7). He also advocated the proper use of medicine and medical resources as gifts of God to be used when necessary (cf. Sir. 38).

Q How are the effects of sin transmitted?

A We understand environment to be not simply chemical environment but spiritual environment. If "the sins of the parents are visited upon the children to the third and fourth generation," it may well be that God would use the genetic structure, or "bad blood," with its defects as the basis for transmitting a disorder. Consequently, the disorder that would only be latent where sin would not be transmitted would become patent where sin was to be transmitted, and it would simply be the *spiritual environment* that would give the added element to make the disease-prone genetic factor become activated.

For instance, there are many kinds of deteriorative or "wasting" diseases, such as AIDS, cancer, tuberculosis, and cirrhosis. "Because of their fathers' sin they will waste away" (Lev. 26:39; cf. Deut. 28:15-21). This could include "wasting diseases that will destroy your sight and drain away your life" (Lev. 26:16).

Untoward deaths in the family, especially of children, could well be part of the effect of bad "spiritual environment" induced by ancestral sin: "For the sins of their forefathers . . . I will cut off the offspring and descendants" (Is. 14:21-22). Sometimes specific ailments are assigned to specific sins; for example, the offspring of adulterers are often infertile or die young (Wis. 3:16), and the descendants of those who practice bribery often have defective eyesight (cf. Job 17:5). Troublemakers cause family alienation among their descendants (Job 4:8-11). Adulterers' offspring will suffer (Gen. 20:7).

Q Can you briefly outline the principles of genetics?

A Messages of heredity in all living things are carried in the chemistry of deoxyribonucleic acid, or DNA. The long twisted strands of this master chemical of heredity are made up of four different subunits repeated in combinations, thousands and even millions of times (and these combinations constitute the universal code for the regulation and production of every subunit the cell makes). The subunits are abbreviated "A," "G," "C,"and "T" — the letters of the genetic alphabet; the genes and the amino acids for which they are blueprints might be thought of as the paragraphs, and the genetic information on each of the twenty-three pairs of chromosomes are the chapters of the encyclopedia of each person's heredity (genome).

Altogether, the human genetic apparatus is an immense archive of about three billion subunits of DNA, and just one error among the three billion can produce all the symptoms and biological derangements of the disease such as muscular dystrophy or thalassemia.

Many diseases are "recessive," a term that means the faulty gene must be inherited from both parents for the disease to occur. A person who has only one copy will be a carrier but ordinarily will not develop the symptom of the disorder. Cystic fibrosis is typical of this type of disease. Other diseases such as Huntington's Chorea are "dominant" genetic disorders in which it takes only one copy of the misspelled gene to produce the problem.

Q Doesn't this prayer-approach to healing do a dis-

service to the dedicated men of science striving to help suffering mankind, through medicine, surgery, genetic engineering, etc.?

A In no way would we want to retard the marvelous advances of science or research into genetic technology, because God can use natural means to heal as well as supernatural means. This principle is valid, even aside from the consideration of ancestral sin. We find that cancer can sometimes be cured by surgery or chemotherapy or radiation. We find also that it can be cured by prayer, as has been done in countless cases without reference to any ancestral sin. But, as we discover a spiritual contamination *in the lineage*, we find that a spiritual approach to the therapy can be effective, but less so in the situations that do not involve ancestral sin.

Diagnoses are becoming ever more available through laboratories that analyze a fault in one or another single gene among the fifty thousand to one hundred thousand that each human possesses. Even prenatal detection of the classic form of hemophilia has become possible since 1985, and also cystilemma fibrosis and fairly accurate detection techniques for muscular dystrophy. At least fifty genetic diseases could be detected and corrected by genetic engineering prior to 1986.

In the future there may be the possibility of having comprehensive genetic profiles for each person showing, for instance, exceptional risk for heart disease, diabetes, and schizophrenia. There are genetic components in these diseases. The key point here, however, is that in most cases these components constitute part of a *predisposition* based on the combined effects of several genetic, environmental, and spiritual factors.

It is those spiritual factors that we are *primarily* concerned about here, which are the focus of our control through prayer, repentance, and reverence for God by persons seeking to heal members of their family tree. This in no way does a disservice to science.

Q Doesn't the science of genetics make ancestral sin transmission look like just superstition, especially when genetic disorders are labeled "demonic"?

A The bottom line of the evaluation of all the scientific data about the diagnosis, and even treatment of genetic disorders, is that experience has shown that all of the genetic disturbances that are observable could be the *substructure* for intervention of possible demonic forces. Physical and emotional abnormalities can certainly be transmitted genetically, but I think it is significant that there is a *much higher ratio* of physical and emotional problems when there is a history of occultism within the family lineage.

A remarkable example, recently headlined in newspapers, is that of Alletah Ngako, an African woman who at the age of thirty-three has revealed the incredible secret that for the past four years she had had a horn growing out of the top of her head, an inch and a half long when it was examined by doctors. It is a pointed sharp horn, still growing and causing agonizing headaches. She revealed that her great-great-grandfather was a witch doctor who also had, according to her family history, a horn on his head. Witchcraft has been common in her family lineage. She is a devout Christian who preaches against witchcraft, but regards her disfigurement as an inherited curse from her non-Christian ancestors. At the time of this writing, the doctors are exploring the possibility of removing the horn surgically.

Many freakish physical anomalies like this are found in families where there is a history of occultism or witchcraft — a much higher percentage than in families in which there is no history of witchcraft or occultism.

There seems to be some strong pastoral and clinical experience that indicates that the presence of evil in the family lineage can be somehow involved in producing defective genes, or at least activating a defective gene to provide what we might call a spiritually negative environment, which results in the disorder being transmitted. The reason for maintaining this position is simply an experiential one; for prayer, especially within the context of the Eucharist, or deliverance prayer, has been shown with remarkable consistency to alleviate disorders that appear to have a genetic basis. The medical use of recombinant DNA can change the material substructure, but the use of prayer and repentance for one's own sins and for those of the ancestors (Lev. 26:40) can bring about an interruption in the overall *transmission* of the disorder to oneself and one's offspring. The healing effect of this family healing prayer is even more dramatic when it cures otherwise intractable disorders.

Q **When Jesus called down the blood of their ancestors on the Pharisees, he seemed unduly stern. Can you put this in perspective so that is doesn't eclipse the idea I have of a loving, healing Christ?**

A When Jesus, speaking to the Pharisees (Matt. 23:27), compared them to "whitened sepulchers . . . full of dead men's bones," he could well have been hinting at the inherited sins ("dead men's bones") of dead ancestors that infected the Pharisees with hypocrisy. Stepping on a grave made one ceremonially unclean; hence the graves were whitewashed to make them easily visible at night. Thus, the Pharisees were regarded as making themselves particularly "visible" in their good works; so Jesus called them "whitened sepulchers."

He quotes them as saying, "If we had lived in the days of our forefathers, we would not have taken part with them in shedding the blood of the prophets" (v. 30). Jesus shows that they acknowledge that they are the descendants of murderers, but they refused to accept any of their transmitted guilt. Jesus says disgustedly, "Fill up then the measure of the sin of your forefathers." In this, Jesus paralleled the mandate of Ezekiel 20:4 by confronting them with the "detestable practices of their forefathers," as God did with the people of Judah (II Kings 22:17). Because of their hypocrisy, Jesus called down upon them "all the righteous blood that has been shed on earth from the righteous Abel" (Gen. 4:8) "to the blood of Zechariah" (II Chron. 24:20-22, which is the last book of the Old Testament in the Hebrew arrangement). Thus spotlighting the first and last Old Testament martyrs, Jesus summed up the history of martyrdom in the Old Testament and imputed an inherited guilt of these murderous ancestors to those who were so hypocritically self-righteous that they claimed superiority over their forefathers.

Jesus then responds with a prayer that *shows that he wants to interrupt the flow of ancestral guilt*: "Oh, Jerusalem, Jerusalem, you who kill the prophets and stone those sent to you, how often have I longed to gather your *children* together as a hen gathers her chicks under her wings, but you are not willing. Your house [household, progeny, family] is left to you desolate." As the forefathers were unrepentant for stoning the prophets, Jesus was hoping that their offspring ("children") would submit to his sovereignty and forgiveness. This reflects God's loving desire to have us open to the interruption of the transmitted effects of guilt. His compassionate desire in turn offers us hope, as reflected in Jeremiah 31:16-17: "Stop your weeping, dry your eyes, your hardships will be redressed . . . there is *hope* for your descendants."

Q **Should we just pray for our family members, or can we administer healing to them? If so, how is healing administered?**

A Of course you can "ask and you will receive." But also we should "pray for one another that you may be healed" (James 5:16). The healing itself can be administered in several ways. First, it can be done by a prayer of authority. Jesus told his disciples to go out and heal (Mark 5:41). Jesus used the authoritative prayer: "Get up, little girl . . ." (Mark 5:41; Luke 8:54); or in another situation, "Get up, take your mat and go home" (Matt. 9:6); "Young man, I say to you, get up" (Luke 7:14). We can pray "in the person of Jesus" (John 14:14), as long as we seek his will for the sick person (I John 5:14).

To exercise the prayer of authority, one first must have the *rhema*, or the prophetic word, from God to the healer in such things as commanding the person to get up and walk from his stretcher or wheelchair. Without having heard this word from God, there could be great damage in using the prayer of authority; it would not be under the direct bidding of the Holy Spirit in such cases, and this could lead to "prayer failure." For using the prayer of authority, we must "wait patiently for the Lord" (Ps. 37:7) to tell us to pray in that particular way.

A second form of prayer is also a prayer of words. It is a prayer of entreaty. Something will happen on some level; when we pray in the spirit and mind and emotion and the body, we put ourselves in the posture, as it were, of a little person, and our prayers can be very simple, such as "Lord, take care of my sick friend here; please heal him." This prayer is quite different from the prayer of authority. We just ask and leave the results to Jesus. There is no need to strain or raise our voice in this form of prayer for ourselves or our family members. This type of prayer is very powerful, particularly when the one who is praying has a degree of spiritual maturity. In James 5:16, it says, "The prayer of a *righteous* man is powerful and effective."

The third type of prayer is the prayer of touch mentioned in Mark 16:17, where we are told that our touch (laying on of hands) will heal, as Jesus' touch did. The closer we are to Jesus, the more of his life is in us, and the more it can be communicated by touch. But it can also be communicated effectively by his directly touching us in the Eucharist at Communion time. This type of prayer is especially effective in praying for difficult cases, such as for children with long-term illness, mental retardation, cancer, or people in intensive care. If we lay hands upon the sick, we should try to be prayerfully conscious of the life and healing love of Jesus' pouring *through us* into the sick person. This is sometimes called "God's radiation treatment."

Q Of all the Old Testament personages who experienced punishment from God for their ancestors' sins, were there any who challenged it as unjust?

A Moses first asked this obvious question: "O God, will you be angry with the entire assembly when only one man sins?" (Num. 16:22). God, in a way, answered his question by showing the power of Moses' intercessory prayer to limit the effects of sin.

The question was asked by Job (21:19) and David (I Chron. 21:17 and again almost verbatim in II Sam. 24:17), and by Ezekiel (18:29). We see David questioning the justice of God in slaughtering the 70,000 people of Israel for his sin by sending the plague upon Israel. "David said to God, I am the one who has sinned and done wrong, these are but sheep, what have they done? Oh, Lord my God, let your hand fall upon me and my family, but do not let this plague remain on your people."

It is interesting that David acknowledged that there could be a punishment for himself *and his family*, but he tried to diminish the extent of the punishment to those outside of his family, the 70,000 people of Israel who were suffering from the plague. He was suggesting that a certain amount of corporate punishment would be expected, but his prayer was to diminish the widespread effect to less than God planned it originally. With that prayer God stopped the plague. David had already seen the effect of his sin upon his descendants because of his adultery and murder of Uriah; David's own illegitimate child died after seven days (II Sam. 12:18). Twice he had questioned and yet acknowledged the truth that his sin could be visited upon his children and family.

Q The word "bondage" is often used in reference to

ancestral guilt. Where, precisely, is there any "bondage" or "binding" effect?

A In speaking of bondage we do not mean to indicate that the person is bound to an ancestor in some way, but the person may be bound up with his or her own ailment (physical or moral defect), and that "bondage" may be further activated by an evil spirit where it is resident — a demonic spirit that may have obtained access through the weakness inherited because of the sin of the ancestor. The offspring only very indirectly could be said to be bound to the evil spirit or the evil spirit bound to him or her (except by rare cases of diabolic possession).

The bondage is primarily the restriction occasioned by the defect itself. Demonic forces seek the weakest link in the chain, and the weak link in a person's personality *could* be the inherited defect. By the permissive will of God (as illustrated in Job 1:12), the demonic force could infect the individual or a series of individuals in the lineage by any of six forms of influence: possession (rarely), obsession, oppression (as, for instance, by a spirit of infirmity), depression, infestation (poltergeist phenomena), or simply by temptation.

Q **When healing takes place, is it usually instantaneous?**

A No. That is the most infrequent modality of healing, in healing the family tree or any other kind of healing. There are five modalities of healing:

1. Instantaneous healing (rare).

2. Gradual healing (over a period of time from minutes to months). An example is Hezekiah, who was not able to go up to the temple of the Lord for three days after his miraculous healing from terminal illness (II Kings 20:5).

3. The phase-in healing, or healing in steps, such as Jesus' healing of the blind man in two phases (Mark 8:25).

4. Delayed healing, where there is a delay between the

positing of the claim and the removal of the symptoms, analogous to the act of Jesus cursing the fig tree and its withering from the roots recognized a day later (Mark 11:20).

5. Recurrent healing, where after remarkable healing takes place, the effects may last for quite a period of time, even years, and then a relapse may occur. The point being, that God wants us to pray for a permanent healing based on the faith that is engendered from witnessing the temporary healing. And this prayer at the point of relapse, if intense enough and faith-filled enough, brings about a permanent healing.

Q **How much of my suffering is caused by the effects of original sin, from Adam and Eve, and how much from my own sins, and finally how much from the sins of my ancestors?**

A The disruption of our God-designed integrity is the result of original sin; the transmitted disorders that we experience in life find their ultimate cause in the failure of our protoparents, Adam and Eve. However, that inheritance of hurt, ignorance, and spiritual weakness finds a more proximate cause in our personal sin, as distinguished from the original sin that we "inherited." Not only our personal sin, but the personal sins of our ancestors, particularly within the "third or fourth generation," which Scripture refers to so frequently, have left their negative impact upon us.

Expressed another way, our contamination with original sin (or only its effects, after baptism) is a *predispositional* cause for disorders. Personal sin, on the other hand, is a *precipitative* cause for our disorders, that is, it precipitates what we are already predisposed for by inherited Adamic sin.

This distinction is carried farther in the family tree healing program, inasmuch as we recognize that the personal sin that precipitates our problems need not be our own personal sin, but it is often the personal sin of our ancestors, especially "to the third and fourth generation." An infant that is blind, paralyzed, or retarded obviously has committed no personal sin to cause such disorders. But *perhaps* the personal sin of adultery, witchcraft, theft, etc., on the part of the grandmother or great-grandfather induced the infant's suffering. I say *"perhaps"* because it can happen, as Jesus pointed out in the case of the man born blind, that the disorder was not connected with either his personal sin nor that of his ancestors, but was to provide an occasion for God to be glorified by a miracle (cf. John 9:3).

Q **Moses and Daniel and other Old Testament persons prayed for their people, relatives, and ancestors with great benefit. Can't we expect even greater benefits in our time, since we now have Jesus, "who always lives to intercede for us" (Heb. 7:25)?**

A We have now in this New Testament period a particularly powerful access to the mercy of God in Jesus, for there is "no other name under heaven given among men by which we must be saved" (that is, attain the fullness of salvation, including integrity of health: Acts 4:12); "No man goes to the Father except by me" (John 14:6). We know that Jesus, the Good Shepherd, comes to protect and "lead them out" (John 10:3). I have come that they may have life and have it to the full" (John 10:10).

Moses acknowledged in Numbers 14:18 that "the Lord is slow to anger, abounding in love and forgiving sin and rebellion; yet he does not leave the guilty unpunished; he punishes the children for the sin of the fathers to the third and fourth generation." Still he prayed that the Lord's strength would be displayed (v. 17) asking that "in accordance with your great love, forgive the sin of these people" (v. 19). If our prayer parallels that of Moses for the people and their ancestry, we too will witness great miracles. This is particularly true today, in the new dispensation, when we can invoke the name of Jesus to break the bondage.

Hebrews 3:5 shows the superiority of Christ over Moses by two comparisons : (1) Moses was God's servant, Christ is God's son, and (2) Moses was in God's family, whereas Christ is *over* God's family. Hence, since we now have a great "high priest" who can "sympathize with our weaknesses . . . we can receive mercy and find grace to help us in our time of need" (4:14-16).

Q **Does Jesus really want to heal us? Wasn't his main interest in teaching and preaching? It seems that he healed people to "convert" them. I'm already "converted" as a Christian, so I wonder if he really wants to heal me?**

A Jesus understood the very basic fact that although people were desirous of knowledge, they were far more desirous of comfort. They wanted to be relieved of their pains and sufferings and hardships as the most urgent need for them personally; consequently, Jesus worked the miracles of healing as the attraction to lead people to his teachings. They didn't come to hear Jesus talk, they came to him because he healed (cf. Matt. 12:15). His healing ministry was associated with the teaching and preaching ministry; Jesus' threefold ministry is stated in one sentence (Matt. 4:23): "He went about all of Galilee *teaching* in their synagogues and *preaching* the gospel of the kingdom and *healing* every disease and every infirmity among the people." Jesus recognized that we tend to separate God from his actions, and his words from his deeds. For instance, we speak of God as "all powerful," or "almighty"; yet we need to *experience* this truth as a living power in our lives.

The integration of *body, mind,* and *spirit* referred to by Paul in I Thessalonians 5:23 clearly corresponds to Jesus' threefold ministry of *healing, teaching,* and *preaching.* What Jesus did twenty centuries ago, he still wants to do today, for he is "the same yesterday, today and forever" (Heb. 13:8). He really wants to heal us and complete us physically, mentally, and spiritually.

Q Some families show inherited defects more clearly than others. If defects aren't easily recognized, does it mean that we just haven't looked closely enough for them?

A One recent scientific study has shown that a man is three times as likely to become an alcoholic as an average person, if his grandfather (not necessarily the father or mother) was a heavy drinker. This example shows the subtlety of the transmission. Furthermore, this *particular* form of alcoholism is apparently not reflected in the genetic structure; it seems to be something transmitted through the human spirit, and can be healed only by God. That may be why the Bible commands us in Leviticus 26:40 to confess not only our own sins, but the sins of our forefathers. In confessing the "sins of the fathers" we can dissolve aberrant tendencies that are passed down from generation to generation (even though defects sometimes "skip" a generation or two).

It is possible through prayer, especially Eucharistic-centered prayer, to bring wholeness to the victim of such bondages, even the more subtle ones. When we touch the problem in its root cause rather than in its mere symptoms, we "take the axe unto the root of the tree" (Matt. 3:10). Then in spite of poor ancestral material, wholesome offspring can be formed: "Even from stones God can raise up children" (v. 9).

We have learned to live with and accept our idiosyncracies and problems as part of our nature, not recognizing that some of these are inherited tendencies and are very destructive. Many are plagued with mental illness, depression, extreme nervousness, critical or negative attitudes, anger, bitterness, vicious tempers, sexual deviations, alcoholism, drug addiction, marriage conflicts, etc., and take for granted that such defects are just "part of being human." In reality they are often rather "part of being a human in this particular family." A closer look at the family tree could reveal some surprising bits of information — hidden "skeletons in the closet." However, even things that remain hidden after a thorough search are not hidden to God. In fact, most ancestral sin is unknown to us, but known to God (Job 20:27; Luke 12:2). That doesn't interfere with the healing prayer; it only makes our prayer *intentions* a bit more diffused.

Q My mother and father both died of cancer, and I am fearful that I might get the same disease. Is it appropriate to pray to be kept safe from disease, or is this program intended only to heal disease?

A The mercy of God in giving us abundant life (John 10:10) can be manifested in either of two ways: by preventative healing or by therapeutic (that is, curative) healing. The former is to be preferred, though it is often less appreciated. In answer to the simple question "Which would you prefer: health or healing?" most would admit that to have no need for a healing is a better state than to experience a healing. The blessing of normal eyesight, taken for granted by most people, is a far greater gift of God than the healing of blindness.

In any healing program, therefore, as much emphasis should be placed upon preventative healing (praying for continued good health and functioning of the immune system, etc.) as for restoring good health (accelerating the healing processes of the body or mind). The Lord offers this double alternative to us within the context of the "family tree" overview. He points out the need for healing of transmitted defects from "the sins of the parents"; but on the other hand, there is his great gift of the *prevention* of defects through his bestowing his "blessings upon a thousand generations of those who love me and keep my commandments" (Exod. 20:5-6; cf. Exod. 34:6-7).

Q How is the devil involved in all the process of

trans-generational sin, sickness, etc.?

A The enemy, the thief, tries to "steal, destroy and kill" (John 10:10) — that is, to interfere with life especially in its generational transmission, by diminishing the quality of life — if not removing it completely through promptings of suicide, abortion, murder, etc. He can diminish the *quality* of life in countless ways: through emotional and physical ailments, poverty, unemployment, crime, divorce, etc.

The anti-life thrust of the enemy, where present, can be counteracted by a deliverance prayer, among other means, beginning with the prayer that Jesus taught us in the last phrase of the Lord's Prayer: "deliver us from the evil one." The healing of the family, in my opinion, is essentially but not exclusively a prayer for deliverance from the power of evil. Satan and his minions can damage or perhaps even lodge in the "bloodline" or genetic structure of a person; and by God's implicit permission (Job 1:12), demonic forces are allowed to harass successive generations within the family tree.

Our ancestors, by their sin, have set our family tree, to some extent, under the control of the devil. As St. John says: "He who does what is sinful is of the devil" (I John 3:8). Yet, for our encouragement, John adds, "The reason the Son of God appeared was to destroy the devil's work."

He then speaks about transposing our family ties into God's family as the first step toward a sin-free lineage: "No one who is born of God will *continue* to sin because God's seed remains in him." (The seed [Greek: *sperma*] bears the life principle and transfers the paternal characteristics.) "He cannot go on sinning because he has been born of God" (v. 9); that is, he will not have a life *characterized* by sin, though not totally sinless. This would seem to imply that not only personal sin but also *habits* of sin can be broken, as we disengage ourselves from the enemy's contamination and attain to the immunity provided to those who affinitize themselves totally with God's family.

Q Precisely how can sin be transmitted through generations?

A To understand this, it is first necessary to understand how sin is ultimately tied in with the correlation of authority and responsibility.

The first man was given authority over all material creation — beginning with the "authority of taxonomy," or nomenclature (providing names for the animals and plants). They were given to him by God (Gen. 1:28) so that he could be an agent of God in bringing out the potential betterment of creation. But correlative with this God-given authority was a responsibility to the same God. Neglect of that responsibility would undermine his right to the authority. Because he sinned, those things under his authority began to suffer and continue to do so to the present (Rom. 8:23).

By the same dynamic, a parent who neglects parental responsibility causes suffering in the children; a teacher who neglects responsibility as a teacher causes defects or limitations within the pupils; a pastor who neglects his parishioners will cause harm to them (Jer. 23:1). In other words, when responsibility is neglected, persons who are subject to that responsibility suffer. This is the basis for original sin having its effect upon us, the "subjects," the offspring of the protoparents, Adam and Eve.

As vice-regent and plenipotentiary of God, Adam might have been called the "prince of this world," but in surrendering to Satan he abandoned his responsibility to God; he forfeited it, along with that authority to Satan, who then became "prince of this world" (John 12:31; 14:30; 16:11) — "the spirit who is now at work in those who are disobedient" (Eph. 2:2) holds them in bondage.

Once Adam and Eve had sinned, the immediate effect was manifested in the next generation, with the first personal sin — Cain's murder of Abel. As St. Thomas Aquinas pointed out, Adam disengaged himself from God's authority by disobedience. His offspring subsequently were disengaged from Adam's authority. Once the first link in the chain was broken, the rest of the chain fell off or "fell short"—the first meaning of the word "sin" in Romans 5:12 (*hamartia* in Greek)—"we have fallen short." This is distinguished from the word for sin or transgression as used in verse 14 (*parabasis*), which means the violation of a specific command. The "falling short" state of sin is transmissible as a result of an original *specific* sin or transgression. This is how the family tree of human society in general in contaminated. The specific violation of God's law—the other meaning of sin—was that which inchoated the transmissible sin.

To say that "all have sinned" is to say that our sins are derived from the first sin, the original sin that has gone before us. Adam's offspring inherited this lowered standard and transmitted it to others, their own descendants. Transmitting or passing on sin is equivalent to putting a kind of "curse" on one's descendants. The personal guilt (imputable malice) is *not* transmitted, however—only its effects; this is true whether considering original sin, transmitted through all generations, or personal sin, transmitted through three or four generations.

Q Healing one's family tree emphasizes the negative inherited traits in a family. What about inherited positive traits or "blessings" that are not material for healings?

A Just as evil can be "inherited" so can the "gift of justice" be inherited; and just as sin can be in some way universal, so can holiness be made universal to those who are in Christ, for "In Christ we who are many, form one body, and each member belongs to all the others" (Rom. 12:5). In Jesus we can have a new life and "propagate" that new life. Several Fathers of the Church claimed that as we were made in the image of God, we were remade (reformed) in the image of Jesus. Through him we have available to us a healing, a restoration from inherited weaknesses, such as violent temper, lust, physical illness, and depression, as part of his redemptive benefits. In the words of St. Augustine quoted in some Easter Vigil liturgies, *"O felix culpa"* ("O happy fault"), that provided the world with a redeemer. From the evil of sin at the beginning of man's creation came a restoration through the second Adam, Christ.

Consequently, either good or bad can be transmitted to the offspring, and we, because of the goodness of Christ, can divert the bad effects and absorb the good effects. This can be done by us personally and claimed for our descendants because of that same "Adamic" principle, often referred to as the "corporate personality of society."

Just as a violation of God's norms had brought serious diseases on Pharaoh and his household (Gen. 12:17), and infertility on Abimelech's household (Gen. 20:18), so also God could provide that *good* would be manifested to a household when his commands were fulfilled. Abraham was rewarded in his offspring by numerous descendants through his sons, Isaac and Ishmael (Gen. 21:12-13). As a reward to righteous Noah, the new father of the human race (Gen. 6:17-18), God promised never to destroy man and the earth until his purposes for creation would be fully realized. God established his covenant with Noah and with his descendants after him (Gen. 9:9).

The double direction of sanctions even in the same family tree is possible, as seen in the fact that Ham was cursed with his son Canaan into slavery by Noah, while Ham's two brothers, Shem and Japheth, were blessed with extended territory. Both reward and punishment participate in the principle of corporate personality.

In the mystical body of Christ "if one part suffers, every part suffers with it; if one part in honored, every part rejoices with it" (I Cor. 12:26), for we are all "members together of one body and sharers together in the promise in Christ Jesus" (3:6). Yet, even our inherited suffering, when it is used "redemptively," can be an advantage, as Paul's suffering was adjunctive to the redemption, but not essential to it: "I fill up in my flesh what is still lacking in regard to Christ's afflictions, for the sake of his body which is the church" (Col. 1:24). He was "filling up" Christ's afflictions by experiencing the added sufferings necessary to propagate the message of redemption; he suffered afflictions by experiencing the added sufferings necessary to propagate the message of redemption; he suffered afflictions in preaching the good news of Christ's atonement, as he extended Christ's "family."

God's parental concern for us offers a restoration for parental neglect that may have had its deleterious effects on the offspring. "Can a mother forget the baby at her breasts? . . . though she may forget, I will not forget you" (Is. 49:15). "Though my father and mother forsake me, the Lord will receive me" (Ps. 27:10).

Not only in spite of the parents' neglect, but also because of the same parents' goodness, God will reward the offspring, thus showing the two aspects of his beneficence in terms of the lineage receiving the effects of God's mercy. Solomon was rewarded by God because of his father, David (I Kings 3:6). Isaiah reported the word of the Lord to Hezekiah (II Kings 19:34) that the city of Jerusalem would be saved from desolation "for the sake of David my servant."

Q What is the "anthropological echo" that is spoken of in family healing services?

A This is a term used sometimes by Scripture scholars to summarize St. Paul's references to inherited sin and its accumulated effects.

In Romans 3:23, when Paul says, "All have sinned," that refers to personal sin, whereas in Romans 5:12, when he says, "All have sinned," that does not refer to personal sin but the Adamic sin (original sin), which involved all of subsequent mankind in condemnation, as referred to in verses 18 and 19: "Just as the result of one trespass was condemnation for all men, so also the result of one act of righteousness was justification that brings life for all men

... so that just as sin reigned in death, so also grace might reign through the righteous to bring eternal life through Jesus Christ our Lord" (v. 21 reaffirms v. 15).

To show how the mercy of God overshadows the justice of God, Paul reminds us (Rom. 5:16) that "the judgment followed *one* sin and brought condemnation, but the gift followed *many* trespasses and brought justification."

But in Galatians 3:22, he reminds us that we have a means at hand to break through this imprisonment of ancestral bondage: "The Scripture declares that the whole world is a prisoner of sin, so that what was promised, being given through faith in Jesus Christ, might be given to those who believe." We no longer need to be under the bondage (cf. v. 25). Belonging to the family of God through faith in Jesus Christ by means of baptism, we are clothed with Christ now (v. 26) for we now "belong to Christ . . . are Abraham's seed and are heirs according to the promise" (v. 29). We now have access to a new supernatural family tree of the Trinity "Because you are sons, God [the Father] sent the Spirit of his Son into our hearts, the Spirit who calls out 'Abba, Father.' So you are no longer a slave but a son; and since you are a son, God has made you also an heir" (Gal. 4:6-7).

Our victory and ability to break through the bondage then is based on the fact that we have access through faith and baptism into the family of God as part of his family tree, which when fully operative does not displace our own human family tree but purifies it. "In all these things we are more than conquerors through him who loved us" (Rom. 8:37).

The method of reaching this great victory in Christ as the people of God is spelled out in considerable detail in Colossians 3 and in II Peter 1:5-11. Peter reminds us (v. 9) that if we do not pursue holiness seriously, then we have forgotten that we have been cleansed from past sins and released from our sin bondage.

If we totally accept our position in the family of God as his children, then we can share in the victory with Christ.

This is articulated by St. Paul in Romans 8:17. "Now, if we are children, then we are heirs — heirs of God and co-heirs with Christ. . . ." Instead of inheriting the defects of our ancestors, we can inherit "a share in his glory."

Q **In attaining a healing of our family tree, does the healing involve some radical change on our part?**

A In some ways, yes. Healing the family tree is, in a sense, a transplanting of the tree from a "toxic dump site" to rich, productive soil. Or, to use another analogy, it is a "grafting" of our family tree into the healthy stock of God's great "family tree." St. Paul expresses zeal for the great family tree of God, within which the individual family trees are meant to be incorporated: "I pray to the Father of all the great family of God — some of them already in heaven and some down here on earth. . ." (Eph. 3:15 LB).

Essentially, the *healing* of the family tree involves the *deepening* of the incorporation of our human family (living and dead) into God's family. In doing this, we can dissolve any remnant of "infection" which, by God's *permissive* will, may be controlled by the devil or his minions who infect the human family tree. In the *Living Bible*, I John 5:18 tells us: "No one who becomes a part of *God's family* makes a practice of sinning, for Christ, God's son, holds him securely," and "the devil cannot get his hands on him." Demonic control or bondage is thus broken. The remainder of that passage is pertinent: "We know that we are children of God and that all the rest of the world around us is under Satan's power and control, and we know that Christ, God's son, has come to help us understand and find the true God, and now we are in God because we are in Jesus Christ, his son . . . dear children, keep away from anything that might take God's place in your hearts" (vv. 19-21).

From this we can see that although contamination surrounds us and may permeate our family tree, we still have access to a healing and to the saving presence of Christ. The means by which we access that saving and healing power is through faith in the person of Jesus.

We know from I Thessalonians 5:23 that the integrity of the human personality implies a tripartite approach, "body, mind and spirit." Therefore all healing eventually must be a physical healing or a psychological healing or a spiritual healing. However, in the spiritual order, the defect may be intrinsic (sin or guilt) or extrinsic (demonic forces); correspondingly, we can avail ourselves of a spiritual healing of sin through repentance, and a spiritual healing of demonic interference through deliverance ("deliver us from the evil one" [Matt. 6:13]).

Q **I have heard a preacher say that if we are suffering, it is only because of sin. This left me feeling guilty and discouraged in my efforts to pray for my healing. Does the family tree healing prayer offer anything to encourage me?**

A It is true that sin is the ultimate source of suffering, in the sense that Adam and Eve by their sin introduced suffering into a world that otherwise would be free of it. But besides that, other sin can be one of the possible causes of suffering, whether it is the sin of the individual himself or that of his ancestors, just as personal sin can cause suffering in our descendants (cf. Lev. 26:16, 25; Deut. 28:20-22, 35, 58-61). In contrast to the morbid thought of all these things that could happen to us because of sin, we should "consider the great love of the Lord" (Ps. 107:43). His healing love is offered to us who foolishly bring upon ourselves sin-spawned suffering.

As that same Psalm says: "Some became fools through their rebellious ways and suffered affliction because of their iniquities; . . . they drew near the gates of death. Then they cried to the Lord in their trouble, and he saved them from their distress. He sent forth his word and healed them, he rescued them from the grave" (107:17-20).

Q **I don't feel that I have much prayer power, when**

I see so many of my prayers go unanswered. Will I find more "prayer power" in the prayers for healing my family tree?

A The healing we pray for in ourselves and our loved ones within our family tree is one of the favored works for which God created us, since we were "created in Christ Jesus to do good works which God prepared in advance for us to do" (Eph. 2:9-10). The power that God has placed in our hands is overwhelming: "His incomparably great power *for us* who believe . . . is like the working of his mighty strength, which he exerted in Christ when he raised him from the dead" (1:19-20).

Q **Will science some day be able to "heal the family tree" by genetic engineering, or will there always be a need for prayer to do this?**

A As long as you eschew the pitfalls of secular humanism, it is not wrong to hope that modern science and technology — itself a gift from God to our society — will find cures for inherited defects. In fact, much has already been done in this regard, identifying not just causes of disease, but even codes of individuality.

Locked within the spiral rungs of the DNA molecule in the form of a double helix are the genetic codes that govern life and the identity of each person with their respective characteristics. By means of a "gene probe," a ribbon of chemicals that binds to a specific part of the DNA molecule, it is possible for researchers to create "genetic fingerprints" that could yield incontestable proof of a person's identity, far more complete and accurate than any other identification system, including fingerprinting.

Toward the outset of this new science in 1985, within less than one year, more than fifty genetically transmitted diseases were identified. As researchers continue to investigate the genetic structure, it has become possible to identify specific characteristics, especially behavior characteristics, and even to change the molecular structure of the defective components ("genetic engineering").

Some of these defects in the DNA *could* be caused by God as a punishment for ancestral sin. However, over and above this, there is a kind of "spiritual heredity" (dealt with elsewhere in this book) which does not lend itself to corrections by genetic engineering. This is in the order of grace — the bestowal or withdrawal of grace from persons because of their predecessor's sins. Only repentance and prayer for healing the family tree can correct defects from the "spiritual heredity." And, of course, from the positive side, we should thank God for the benefits and blessings that could also come from such "spiritual heredity."

Q What defects should I look for in my family tree?

A Potentially, there are thousands of kinds of defects that one could look for. Generically, these can be classified into groups of disorders:

1. Inherited spiritual defects — anything from prayerlessness to atheism.

2. Inherited physical defects — anything from dandruff to diabetes.

3. Inherited emotional defects — anything from shyness to suicide tendencies.

4. Inherited psychosocial defects — anything from poor inter-spouse communication to psychopathic murder.

5. Inherited societal defects (defects common to entire families, and even nations or ethnic groups) — anything from in-law aloofness to Mafia families.

The use of a genogram will be helpful in this review of your family tree (see sample, pages 296-297). As you write down the names or initials of persons, their illness or tendencies will come to mind for each.

Q Is it enough simply to repent of sin, and to encourage my family members to do the same, in order to "cleanse the bloodlines" of our family?

A It is of critical importance to understand that there are two kinds of evil that could be involved in infecting the family tree, one interfacing with the other very often. The first kind of evil may be called intrinsic evil, or sin. In the Lord's Prayer, we refer to that with repentance in the prayer "forgive us our trespasses." The second kind of evil mentioned in the last part of the Lord's Prayer is extrinsic evil, which includes all evil forces — devils, demons, and evil spirits that may attack us from without, which we deal with in the phrase "deliver us from evil"— that is, from the Evil One.

Wherever there is any attachment to sin (intrinsic evil) there is usually an attempt of the extrinsic forces, demonic forces, to lodge within those areas. But Jesus, who says, "The prince of this world has no power over me" (John 14:30), should be called upon to cleanse the bloodlines of the family tree, both living and dead, of anything of evil that may block the healthy state of the individuals within that family. Through Jesus' power we can break any inherited curses or hexes that may have been transmitted through the generations, and cast out any evil spirits that may harass the living members of the family. In this, we are simply obeying the Lord's injunction not merely to heal, but also to cast out the Evil One (Mark 16:17-18). The fact that this is most effectively done within the context of the Eucharist is emphasized by Paul in I Corinthians 10:21: "You cannot drink the cup of the Lord and the cup of demons too; you cannot have a part in both the Lord's table and the table of demons.

In taking the "cup of the new covenant" (I Cor. 11:25 and Luke 22:20) we should intend to break any "old covenants" with the Evil One as we enter into a new covenant with the Lord.

Q How much of my suffering, and that of my family, comes from the devil?

A All sin is an invitation for the intromitting of demonic forces in one's life. In the epistle to the Romans and elsewhere, Paul seems to describe sin as a repressive force that prevents fullness of integration into God's plan in body, mind, and spirit (cf. I Thess. 5:23). James reaffirms this (3:15): "When we were children, we were in slavery under the basic principles of the world" (also translated: "under the influence of *elemental spirits* of the world" [Gal. 4:3]). "You were slaves to those who by nature are not gods" (v. 8; cf. Matt. 5:37).

These evil influences of the world headed by the "prince of this world" are negative powers that can be marshalled by occultic practices; witches elicit these evil entities to serve their perverted purposes and are aware of the forces that they wield. It is these same forces of evil that contaminate or repress the body, mind, or spirit with their respective disorders. But with the power of Jesus we can suppress these negative forces. He taught us to pray a deliverance prayer: "Deliver us from the evil one" (Matt. 6:13); it is within our authority, when that authority is exercised in the name of Jesus (Mark 16:17).

A predisposition for exercising this deliverance power — "a sign that the kingdom of God has come to you" (Luke 11:20) — is repentance (I John 4:4; 5:18), being reborn in God's family. This enables us to come against the negative family traits that have been transmitted to us, and to prevent the transmission of our own negative traits to our offspring. This is simply applying one's own "baptismal rights" to restore the life of God to the deadened areas of the family tree. (The baptismal right is that by which we have access to God's family, for in baptism we become "children of God" and part of his family tree.) James succinctly formulates the strategy: "Submit yourselves to God. Resist the devil and he will flee from you. Come near to God and he will come near to you" (James 4:7-8).

Q **My sister and her daughter both say they occasionally hear strange voices in their rooms and sometimes are frightened by "apparitions." Could**

this be caused by deceased relatives?

A An astonishing number of mental patients suffer from the presence of "spirits" or the intrusion of "voices" which appear to them to be from another world, audible only to themselves. Psychiatrists not familiar with demonology usually dismiss these phenomena as expressions of insanity, and in *some* cases they are correct. However, some of these "spirits" seem to be demonic entities educed as the result of occult practices, especially séances. Other voices, sometimes with apparitions also, seem to be neutral and harmless, often begging for help. And, a third category of this phenomenon includes voices or appearances of persons who appear to be one's recently dead relatives.

Whenever there is an oppressive bondage relating to a dead person who is unknown, an effort should be made by the counselor to identify the controlling force. Frequently, the phantom voice or image is that of a member of one's own ancestry. By drawing up a family tree (genogram — see pages 296-297) one can better recall whether there have been any obvious behavioral problems or serious known sin on the part of the deceased person, which requires prayer for them (Dan. 9:8; Lev. 26:40). Perhaps there is a need to ask the deceased person for forgiveness, and/or extend forgiveness to him or her, in and through the presence of Jesus.

If it is truly demonic forces that are active, they may not always manifest themselves directly by voices, etc., but they may lodge in the genetic material that is transmitted through the generations and hence less directly affect the living. It is not inconceivable that they may even be able to modify the genetic components for transmission from generation to generation, which by scriptural implication could go on for three or four generations, perhaps skipping one or another generation. If the bondage is truly a controlling bondage, as in the case of obsessions and some cases of depression, the controlling spirit should be consigned to Jesus, and the patient himself must submit to Christ's control. This is especially effective in Eucharistic celebration, where the release may occur immediately or possibly after some delay. The Eucharist is the single most powerful exorcistic prayer available to us. If possible, the patient should attend the Eucharist offered for the healing, and also receive Communion worthily (cf. I Cor. 10:21).

Q Can the family healing principles be applied to other groups besides families?

A The principles of healing the family tree may be applicable in a more diluted sense to what could be called "extended families," such as religious communities, parishes, even neighborhoods, especially where for instance there appears to be a rash of crimes, divorces, suicides, murders, etc., related to a given "familial" environment. An extended family may have many advantages in cultivating holy fellowship, but it may also be the matrix of contamination in a given location or among a given group of persons. It is in the understanding of this concept of extended family, designed to enhance spiritual unity under headship, that the custom has arisen among Catholics, Anglicans, Espiscopalians, and Orthodox of calling their priests "Father" as a title of address.*

---

*This has led to some resistance on the part of persons of fundamentalist persuasions. The excessively literal interpretation of Christ's command (Matt. 23:9) to "call no man father or teacher or rabbi" was contravened by Paul's assuming of the role of "spiritual father" ("you are my children" — II Cor. 12:14 LB). He claimed a "spiritual fatherhood" as "life conveyor" by his conveying the life of the gospel message to his "children": "I am . . . writing to warn and counsel you as beloved children . . . remember that you have only *me as your father,* for I was the one who brought you to Christ when I preached the gospel to you" (I Cor. 4:14-15 LB). "I speak to you as my children" (II Cor. 6:13). And to the Thessalonians: "We dealt with each of you as a father deals with his own children" (I Thess. 2:11). John in his first and third epistles uses the phrase "dear children" or "my dear children" repeatedly as he assumes the position of spiritual fatherhood in guiding those to whom he writes. Paul refers to Timothy as being like a "son" (I Tim. 1:2). A spiritual fatherhood or parenthood is not something outside of God's will, for he has promised "spiritual children" (Is. 54:1-3), and "foster fathers" to his chosen ones (Is. 49:23).

Q **I know that healing is conditioned on repentance. But how can I know if I'm sorry enough for my sins?**

A Sin is an offense against God that produces a condition of guilt by which the sinner is estranged from God and, to some extent at least, deprived of his grace and friendship, incurring a debt of punishment by this transgression. When the sinner repents, the sin is forgiven and the sinner is totally reconciled to God, though not necessarily all of the *punishment due* to that sin is remitted; that depends on the degree of love-motivated contrition.

Although there are several ways sin can be forgiven by God, the universally necessary condition of forgiveness from God is contrition or sorrow for sin. This sorrow for sin must involve some element of love for God, not merely shame. For instance, a man who has remorse for getting drunk the previous night "because he made a fool of himself" does not have true contrition. It is not directly or indirectly God-related but only emotion-related; it regards only a sense of embarrassment. Without some element of love for God, it is impossible for a sinner to be restored to a right relationship with God.

Moreover, this "readiness to love God" cannot exist unless the sinner is prepared also to love other children of that same heavenly Father, as St. John clearly teaches (I John 4:20-21). This Christian love (*agape*) must extend not only to God's people at large, but in a very special way to one's own family as specifically designated within the general family of God for this individual. Therefore, the individual's willingness to forgive injuries done to him by anyone, but especially by members of his own family, is an accurate test, easy to apply, of the sufficiency of his own dispositions to receive God's forgiveness himself. The word of God is uncompromising on this point (cf. Matt. 6:14-15; 18:21-35; Mark 11:25-26).

Q **Should I expect a "miracle" healing in the family healing prayer, or does God more often heal in-**

directly, by providential events?

A A woman who was attending one our family healing services with a healing Mass prayed for her son who had been on drugs. Upon returning home from the service, her son (she later learned) had received a call from a girl in France whom he had met over there previously. She had asked to come and visit him.

When the mother declined permission, her son begged her to change her mind, promising that he would give up drugs completely if the girl would be allowed to visit him. He kept his promise faithfully and has not returned to the use of drugs since. The mother felt that this was a direct answer to her prayer for his healing because the call came in at the very time the Mass was being celebrated for the healing of the family tree.

This incident illustrates how sometimes the healing of the family tree program produces effects in very oblique ways.

Q **Do more serious sins result in more serious effects in one's offspring?**

A Some sins have more serious effects than others on one's descendants. Stealing, lying, and sacrilegious abuse of sacred objects (Josh. 7:11) brought horrible death to all of Achan's family, household, and even his cattle (vv. 24-25). Devil worship and occult practices have far-reaching consequences. "I will set my face against that man and his family, and will cut off from their families both him and all who follow him" (Lev. 20:5). Hence, occultism (even practicing astrology) often results in family disintegration, feuds, divorce, separation, etc. Divorce and depression are extremely common among those who practice astrology, or among their offspring.

The Lord commanded Ezekiel to confront the elders "with the detestable practices of the fathers" (Ezek. 20:4). Jesus himself did precisely this in Matthew 23:30-32 and even more emphatically in Luke 11:47-51: "You say if you had lived in the days of our forefathers, 'we would not have taken part with them in shedding the blood of the prophets'; so you *testified against yourselves* that you are the descendants of those who murdered the prophets; *fill up* then the measure of the sin of your forefathers." Paul's remarks paralleled those of Christ (I Thess. 2:14-16), indicating that the sins of the past are continued in the present, for "those who killed the Lord Jesus and the prophets and also drove us out . . . heap up their sins to the limit" ("fill up the measure of the sin of the forefathers," to use the words of Jesus).

Those who disclaim the guilt of their ancestors — "we would not have taken part with them" — admit in some way their inherited guilt by the very act of trying to disclaim it, if at the same time they didn't do anything to avoid the sin themselves. In this way they "fill up the measure of the sin of the forefathers." "And so upon you will come the righteous blood that has been shed from the blood of righteous Abel to the blood of Zechariah, the son of Berekiah whom *you* murdered between the temple and the altar" (Matt. 23:35). The reason for Jesus using the second person "you" in referring to the series of crimes is described in the next sentence, "I tell you the truth, all this will *come upon this generation.*"

Jesus was summing up the history of martyrdom in the Old Testament from the murder of Abel (Gen. 4:8) to that of Zechariah (II Chron. 24:20-22 — the last book of the Old Testament according to Hebrew arrangement). In referring to the whole history of martyrdom and the sin that caused it in the Old Testament, Jesus was saying that those of that generation, because of their plan to "kill and crucify and flog in their synagogues," would suffer the ongoing effects of the past generations.

To interrupt the flow of evil requires a total conversion as described in Ezekiel 18:14. "This man has a son who sees all the sins that his father commits, and though he sees them, he does not do such things."

Q **Didn't Ezekiel mention the discontinuance of the principle of inherited punishment?**

A Yes, but only as something in the future "day of the Lord"; in foretelling the future eradication of the use of the proverb "The fathers eat sour grapes and the children's teeth are set on edge" (Ezek. 18:2-3), Ezekiel did not mean to imply that there was no such thing as inherited punishment.

In giving a description of three men standing for three generations who break the three- to four-generation pattern, he was showing something that would be *universally* true in the *future* (the "Day of the Lord," 30:3).

We know that the idea of corporate punishment was not obliterated because within the same book (Ezek. 30:13-19) we find clear examples of corporate punishment for the sins of individuals.

Moreover, when the same attempt to reverse the proverb is made by Jeremiah, we see it as *within the context of the future* (Jer. 31:19): "*In those days,* people will no longer say the fathers have eaten sour grapes and children's teeth are set on edge. Instead everyone will die for his own sin. Whoever eats sour grapes, his own teeth will be set on edge." The futuristic dimension of this is also clear from verses 27 and 31. (Verse 34 makes it clear that it is not to be accomplished in New Testament times but in the post-parousia period — after the second coming of Christ — after the "Day of the Lord.") "The son will not share the guilt of the father nor will the father share the guilt of the son. The righteousness of the righteous man will be credited to him and the wickedness of the wicked will be charged against him" (Ezek. 18:20). The same is true of the sincerely repentant sinner. "None of the offenses he has committed will be remembered against him" (v. 22).

The whole first twenty verses of Ezekiel 18 indicate that the chain of inherited punishment can be broken — followed by the teaching that the personal guilt accumulated within a person's life can be overcome. This is essentially a scriptural basis for the program for healing of the family tree. The secondary benefits involve the removal of the effects of the corporate guilt — that is, the removal of pain, sickness, depression, fears, compulsions, perversions, etc.

On the other hand, if a righteous man backslides into evil, "none of the righteous things he has done will be remembered. Because of the unfaithfulness he is guilty of, and because of the sins he has committed, he will die" (Ezek. 18:24). It is this latter aspect that "causes some to say, 'the way of the Lord is not just.' Are my ways unjust, O house of Israel? Is it not your ways that are unjust?" (v. 29). The bottom-line requirement for bringing about the interrupting of inherited punishment and its effect, that is, for healing the family tree, is given at the close of that chapter: "Repent, turn away from *all* your offenses; then sin will not be your downfall. Rid yourselves of all the offenses you have committed and get a new heart and a new spirit" (vv. 30-31).

Q Do the "thousand-generation" blessings from our virtuous ancestors come to us automatically or must we do something ourselves to appropriate these blessings?

A The Pharisees appreciated the goodness of some of their ancestors perhaps because they wanted to reap the rewards that had been earned by them (Exod. 20:6). Their appreciation was expressed, as Jesus acknowledged (Matt. 23:29: "You decorate the graves of the *righteous*"). They of course wanted to inherit the benefits of the righteous ancestors while repudiating the guilt of the evil ancestors (v. 30). However, they sought these benefits *without changing their own hearts*. In excoriating the Pharisees for this, Jesus showed that we can abort the benefits that would otherwise accrue to us from our virtuous forefathers.

Q Besides sickness or health, in what personal ways

does God reward or punish the descendants for the sins or virtues of the ancestors?

A The sanctions can be exercised by uplifting the repentant sinner, by hardening the unrepentant sinner, sanctifying further the fervent person, and by gradually deserting the careless believer; also by destroying sin, purifying what is imperfect, perfecting what is good, and thus separating those who will respond to him from those who refuse to do so.

Scripture makes it clear that God's sanction falls not only on individuals as such but also on societies. In countless places in the Old Testament it is shown that a man's faithfulness or unfaithfulness had its corresponding repercussions upon his descendants. Both groups and nations were condemned or rewarded by God for their corporate actions (cf. Ezek. 30:13-19).

All this is a very important consideration in understanding God's action toward his creatures, but it is equally important to understand that he has given his creatures the freedom to reverse the mode of sanction, that is, reward or punishment. In that option resides the opportunity for the healing of a communal disorder or a transmitted disorder as in the healing of one's family tree.

Q Besides families, are there other groupings of people that inherit punishment or reward from predecessors?

A This corporate sanction may be found not just in families and nations, but also even in the church, the people of God, which as a corporate society may suffer or be rewarded in accordance with the behavior of both its leaders and its members, for the Church is called to prove itself loyal to the covenant God has made with it in the blood of his Son. Hence, for example, it is not incongruous that the Catholic Church at Vatican Council II expressed repentance and asked pardon for the faults of an earlier generation of Catholics that had contributed to the disunity of the church ("Decree on Ecumenism," art. 7).

Civil society is also an instrument of divine providence in this regard. Occasionally, a natural disaster or widespread prosperity can reflect the judgment of God favorably or unfavorably, as seen often in the Old Testament; but *normally* the judgment of God will be seen in what directly touches the *inner* well-being of society itself, such as the presence or absence of tranquility, opportunities for personal development, observance or violation of human rights, respect for law and order, confidence in the government, and regard for the rights of others.

A very important observation derived from Scripture is that to the extent that a citizenry willingly conforms to God's manifest will, to that extent the society will experience that "tranquility of order" — St. Augustine's definition of peace. But where selfish aims are present in leaders or members of society, to that extent that society or institution is on its way to failure and dissolution, as historically reflected in the Roman Empire, the Greek Empire, etc.

Q It never occurred to me that families as such, not just individuals, have such a great responsibility before God — until I attended a family healing program. How can we cultivate this sense of responsibility in our family?

A Families are the building blocks of society; as basic natural social clusters they have a very special place in God's plan of corporate sanctions. Because families are constituted by the sacred union of matrimony, they fall in a special way under his sanctions. The frequent blessings in the Old Testament on God-reverencing families make this clear with regard to *external* things such as wealth, social status, and even health. But even more importantly, the things that are *internal* to the family reflect the family members' allegiance to God and his law. Thus, when a family strives to live together in unselfish love and to worship God together in praise and thanksgiving and trust, its members will know contentment and harmony. If they are negligent or disobedient in these areas, they will experience God's judgment negatively by the presence of domestic strife, jealousy, infidelity, suspicion, unhappiness, marital discord, broken marriages, etc.

Later generations may experience the full force of the judgment of God upon the corporate actions of an earlier generation. If the subsequent generations choose by their free will to repeat patterns of their parents or ancestors, they assume the responsibility not only individually but corporately of what had been done earlier (Lev. 26:38).

In obeying or rejecting God, these sowing-reaping patterns are not just a personal, but a trans-generational, phenomenon. Generations are so knit together that one generation sows and another reaps — sometimes slow-growing or even "skipping" a generation or two. "They that sow trouble reap it . . . and their children shall be scattered" (Job 4:8-11).

Hosea 10:13: "You have sowed wickedness, and you have reaped iniquity, therefore shall a tumult arise among your people . . . the mother dashed in pieces upon her children" (cf. Hosea 8:7). Some of the earliest and most dramatic occasions of this imprecation are found in Numbers 16:21-34 — Korah, Dathan, and Abiram and their families; the tragedy of Achan in Joshua 7:24; and the corporate progeny of the rebellious Israelites: "Your children will be shepherds here for forty years, suffering for your unfaithfulness" (Num. 14:33).

Isaiah 1:4: "What a sinful nation, a seed of evildoers loaded with guilt, their fathers before them were evil too."

Isaiah 14:20-21: "The seed of evildoers shall never be renowned. I will cut off . . . his children and his children's children."

Keep in mind that good seed, too, is available for sowing, and the fruits of it are a delight to the Lord (cf. I Cor. 3:6; Matt. 13:37).

Q It is well known that physical illness is often related to mental illness (emotional disturbances). Besides these types, are there other kinds of illness that can be helped by healing the family tree?

A Yes. Ultimately there are four kinds of healing available to us. A few words about this would be helpful.

Following the Neoplatonists such as St. Augustine, and most especially following the scriptural outline of St. Paul in I Thessalonians 5:23, we know that there are three main divisions of human personality that are subject to disorder and consequently subject also to healing. They are the body, the mind, and the spirit — the body being of course the material aspect of the human, the mind being the mental and emotional (psychological) dimension of the personality, and the spirit being that area that relates to God in prayer and grace and spiritual activity. The spiritual dimension can become disordered in two ways — both of which are mentioned in the Lord's Prayer. There is an intrinsic spiritual evil called sin that involves moral guilt ("forgive us our trespasses"), and an extrinsic form of spiritual evil — demonic forces, devils, demons, and evil spirits requiring a deliverance, referred to in the last part of the Lord's Prayer ("deliver us from the evil one"). With the third dimension having been thus divided, ultimately we see there are four ways in which the human person can become disordered.

They are: *first,* the body in physical sickness or injury; *second,* the mind in emotional disorders; *third,* the soul disordered by sin; and *fourth,* the soul afflicted with a demonic interference disorder. Corresponding to these four types of disorder, there are four categories of healing: *first,* the physical healing by natural or supernatural means; *second,* the emotional healing or psychological healing, again by natural or supernatural means; *third,* a spiritual healing from the disease of sin through repentance; and *fourth,* a deliverance healing or decontamination from forces of evil: devils, demons, or evil spirits.

All four of these types of disorders may blend and interact, and any — even several of these forms of disorder — can be manifested simultaneously so that it may be quite difficult without an exquisite degree of discernment to know which of the forms of disorder are operative at any given time, and how many of them. For instance, alcoholism may be regarded as a *physical* defect similar to an allergy based upon a physical or genetic component that provides the physical tendency toward that disorder. But it also involves, at least in the later stages, an *emotional* deterioration from the "pre-alcoholic personality" to the alcoholic personality with its commonly recognized "denial syndrome" by which the afflicted person lacks the sense of reality to perceive his own disorder. But it may also involve a *spiritual* or moral sickness, the sin of drunkenness, or a cognate sin — drunken driving, for instance — endangering one's own life and the lives of others, or the sin of extravagance that may impoverish one's family through the expenditures on alcohol, etc. Finally, the same disorder may very well *in some cases* involve the *demonic*, a spirit of addiction or a spirit of alcoholism superimposed on the other dimensions of that disorder. Thus, it can be seen that all four types of disorders may converge on a single problem area; one or a combination of several of the disorders may be involved.

Q **Many of my problems (pains, anxiety, frustration, etc.) have to do only with myself. But other problems (feeling rejected, misunderstood, etc.) have to do with my relationships with others. Are both of these types of problems dealt with in this healing program?**

A Yes, Many problems may be said to be intra-personal — that is, within the person himself or herself. But, I think most human suffering arises not so much from intra-personal disturbances, as from interpersonal ones. However, most often the two types of problems interface. For instance, the conflicts in marriage may be related to problems of alcoholism; the marriage conflicts are *inter*personal, the alcoholism disorder is *intra*-personal. The sociopathic personality involves himself in situations that are interpersonal, though his own emotional disturbance is intra-personal.

Even with physical disorders, such as rheumatoid arthritis that may carry with it a type of depression, both the physical and emotional components could interact with other persons within the same environment, and the problem then becomes also interpersonal. Once a problem becomes manifested as interpersonal — almost every problem ultimately does — the healing approach needs to correspond to that. Hence, we can speak not only of healing persons, but also healing relationships between persons: husband-wife, parent-child, neighbor-neighbor, pastor-parishioner, employer-employee, etc.

Once we are working within the interpersonal relationship, we find that there is a need to deal primarily with forgiveness, receiving and giving *forgiveness* — receiving forgiveness from God to remove guilt, and from our fellow man to remove rejection; and giving forgiveness to remove resentment, bitterness, antipathy, hostility, etc. Thus, the psychological as well as the psychosocial and psychospiritual aspects of the healing may be contingent basically upon the ability to give and receive forgiveness. Ultimately, this is a two-dimensional forgiveness, *receiving* it from God as the one ultimately offended by our neglect, and *giving* it. "Forgive us as we forgive those who trespass against us."

Q **Can individuals contaminate their own immediate family or even larger groups that they belong to, independently of any ancestral sin?**

A Certainly. Evil spawns its own contagion. Once when I was participating in a large prayer meeting in San Francisco, the flow of grace was deep and palpable, with abounding joy — until a woman came in and stood at the back of the auditorium. Suddenly the flow of prayer strangely ceased. It was only later that we understood why. She was a Satanist witch who came in to mock our praying. Her very presence cast a pall over the prayer meeting. The words of Deuteronomy come to my mind: "Make sure there is no man or woman or *family* among you today whose heart turns away from the Lord our God . . . make sure there is no root among you that produces such bitter poison" (Deut. 29:18). All of Judah suffered because of the sin of Manasseh (II Kings 23:26; 24:3), just as Israel suffered because of the sins of Jeroboam (17:22-23).

Among any grouping of people, there are different levels of proximity of persons that correspond to different levels of co-responsibility for each other's welfare. This is true within the church itself. "If anyone does not provide for his relatives, and especially for his immediate family, he has denied the faith and is worse than an unbeliever" (I Tim. 5:8).

We are members of a larger spiritual family: "Being born again, we are now members of God's own family" (I Pet. 1:3 LB). But there can be contamination within God's family by members not living up to their call — for they are "called to be holy together with all those everywhere who call on the name of our Lord Jesus Christ" (I Cor. 1:2). Paul told the elders at Ephesus that savage wolves would come among the flock, the family of God. To prevent this contamination at the church at Ephesus, he committed them to God and to the Word of his grace, "which can build you up and give you an inheritance among all those who are sanctified" (Acts 20:32). For Paul himself had a commission from the Lord to cleanse God's family: "I will rescue you from your own people. . ." (Acts 26:17).

Q I know a family with two sons, one very pious, and one living a worldly, dissolute lifestyle. Since both have the same ancestors, why is there this difference?

A Some persons seem less subject to generational or familial spirits than others. Some seem to be almost immune, or they have the grace to overcome the onslaught of these forces; but everyone is hindered in some way and to some degree from entering into the fullness that God wants us to have as members of his family. Besides, each person has a free will as far as moral decisions are concerned, and is able to reverse any evil tendency (Ezek. 18:14).

Frequent reference in Scripture to the enemy's involvement in generational bondage or corporate contamination reminds us that generational spirits (familial rather than familiar spirits) are constantly looking for the weak spots, unique to each individual, in which they might lodge to produce physical, psychological, or moral deformity.

Through generational healing, the Lord enables us to move toward the time when we "will be his people and God himself will be with us, and be our God; he will wipe away every tear from their eyes, there will be no more death or mourning or crying or pain, for the old order of things will have passed away" (Rev. 21:4). We must begin now in this life to "make everything new" (v. 5) by availing ourselves of the healing power that the Lord offers us, beginning with deep and total repentance for our own sins, no matter how susceptible we are in absorbing the effects of the sins of our predecessors.

Q Can our heredity really affect our spiritual life? If so, how can this be proved?

A The dictionary definition of hereditary is: "passed down from an ancestor; designating a characteristic transmitted from generation to generation." But the secondary meaning is: "an emotional *attitude* passed down from ancestors or predecessors." This double meaning of heredity embraces not only hereditary *diseases* such as proneness to alcoholism and cancer, but it could also include inclinations to *behavior patterns* such as an inclination to cursing, fornication, adultery, stealing, murder, lying, and hatred.

79

Through divine revelation, we are aware of still another factor operative in heredity, namely, the fact that the sin from past generations can provide a hereditary punishment to the offspring, whether this be an actual defect or a potential defect or weakness. The ultimate cause could be the sins of the ancestor which opened the descendants to the patrimonial bondage.

The weakness or potential weakness is the area in which demonic forces (familiar spirits) seek to intervene. In many cases, the generational spirit is very evident in blood-natural families and the influence is quite visible, while in other families it is more subtle. As one begins to deal with disorders from the generational perspective as described in Scripture, it is more clearly seen that ancestral sin is the root cause of many of the problems experienced in the progeny. This becomes especially evident when making amends for ancestral sins results in relief or cure of the symptoms in the offspring.

Some of the transmitted characteristics are simply replications of the defects in the ancestors. Thus, the Israelites were punished for their sins because "they would not listen and were as stiff-necked *as their fathers* who did not trust in the Lord their God" (II Kings 17:14). By perpetuating the sins of the forefathers, they brought disaster upon the whole nation, for the Lord "tore Israel away from the house of David" (v. 21).

But other defects — less obvious — are weaknesses or characteristics which are not duplications of behavior in the parents or ancestors but are the *effects* of that aberrent behavior.

Thus, often a child or a grandchild of a drug user will experience sleep abnormalities such as apnea and nightmares without necessarily being attracted to the use of drugs himself.

Q When we don't know of any sins of our ancestors, how can we inherit the consequences of their sins? And, if we don't know that our own sins could affect

our children, how could the effects of our sins be transmitted to them?

A In many disorders — physical, emotional, and spiritual — it is noteworthy that the knowledge of ancestral sin is not essential to the inheriting of its effects. A person may be totally unaware of sins of the ancestors and still suffer the effects of that sin, just as anyone may be unaware of the virtues of their ancestors and still reap the benefits of their virtue — God's special blessings — often unacknowledged.

On the other hand, a person who sins while being conscious of the fact that that sin may affect his or her descendants would have a greater guilt because of that awareness. It would be even more serious if that person would knowingly lead the offspring, the child, into sin. "If anyone causes one of these little ones to sin, it would be better for him to be thrown into the sea with a large millstone tied around his neck" (Mark 9:42).

Q Is ancestral inherited punishment the same as "blood guilt"?

A The tendency toward sin, as well as the effects of sin that are inherited, is often referred to as "blood guilt." Generational blood guilt was recognized by the chief priests and elders who with the people said, "Let his blood be on us and on our children" (Matt. 27:25). The full application of the blood of Christ to remove this blood guilt will be completed in the end-times, when he will "turn the hearts of the fathers to their children and the hearts of the children to the fathers" (Mal. 4:6). Pilate tried to disown the blood guilt with the words, "I am innocent of this man's blood" (Matt 27:24). This blood guilt was hinted at in Jesus' words to the women who wept for him on the road to Calvary, "Daughters of Jerusalem, do not weep for me, weep for yourselves and for your children" (Luke 23:28). And yet, significantly, this blood guilt is removed by the application of the blood of Jesus spilled for us on Calvary, and the blood that is symbolically shed in the Eucharist. "This is my blood which is *poured out* for many for the forgiveness of sin" (Matt. 26:28).

The Lord will not ignore our fervent prayer, especially as we pray at the Eucharistic service for the removal of the so-called "blood guilt" with the Psalmist, "Do not hold against us the *sins of the fathers*. May your mercy come quickly to meet us for we are in desperate need . . . deliver us and forgive our sins for your name's sake . . . then we, your people, *from generation to generation* will recount your praise" (Ps. 79:8-13).

Q When I sin I don't think about possible consequences for my children and grandchildren. How extensive is the damage that I might cause them?

A The passage referring to the iniquity of the fathers visited upon the children in no way has to do with determining their eternal salvation or damnation directly. It speaks of only a temporal form of punishment, for some day in the end-times this whole norm will be changed (cf. Ezek. 18:3 and 20; Jer. 31:29).

Another important consideration is that frequently God will refrain from visiting the punishment upon the children unless they imitate their ancestor's sins. Hezekiah, Josiah, and many other pious men were children of exceedingly wicked parents, but as they repudiated the sins of their fathers and became devoted to God, they enjoyed his blessings and favor in a high degree.

Nevertheless, even pious children can suffer from the effects of sinful parents. Children will suffer poverty from the sins of an extravagant or compulsive gambler. They may suffer the ravages of incest from the perverted parent or relative, and of course children trying to be holy and virtuous may find it very difficult in the presence of the bad examples of parents. Children will neglect church attendance and reception of Communion as their parents' example would lead them in that direction. Even good will on the part of children can be overwhelmed by bad example of parents, which shows a terrible responsibility on the part of the parents. "Woe to those who scandalize these little ones" (Luke 17:3; Matt. 18:6). (The young — "little ones" — may be immature in age or in faith.) The mandate of God to avoid transmitting evil effects to the offspring is an appeal to the human affection of parents for their children; it is presented as a deterrent to sin by the assurance that the posterity will suffer for that sin.

Q What is God trying to teach us by the spiritual heredity of ancestral sin?

A The recognition of the heredity principle shows:

First, the duty which every reformer or preacher has to protest against the sin of individuals, since ultimately they do not affect only the individual sinner.

Second, it shows the solemn responsibility of the vocation of parenthood.

Third, it shows that the best way to purify the human race of its contamination is by the training of the young, and emphasizes the exquisite responsibility involved in that.

Fourth, it serves to give us a better understanding of the origin of sin and the rationale behind our experience through the ages of its effects.

Fifth, it gives a different dimension to the understanding of Christ's suffering for a kind of "inherited sin" that he didn't commit himself. Since "he himself took upon himself our weaknesses and sins; he took up our infirmities and carried our sorrows . . . by his wounds we are healed" (Is. 53:4-5). "God made him who had no sin to be sin *for us* so that in him we might become the righteousness of God" (II Cor. 5:21).

Q Where should I direct my primary concern in praying for a healing in my family?

A The concern for members of our family tree should begin with our ancestors, especially parents, living or dead ("Honor thy father and mother") as Paul was addressing the adult offspring when he wrote: "Children and grandchildren should learn first of all to put their religion into practice by caring for their own family and so repaying their parents and grandparents, for this is pleasing to God . . . if anyone does not provide for his relatives and especially for his *immediate family*, he has denied the faith, and is worse than an unbeliever" (I Tim. 5:4-8). This is a more explicit formulation of Paul's words regarding the concern we should have for the broader family of God in Romans 12:13 (LB): "When God's children are in need, you be the one to help them out."

Q How much is included in the term "family tree"?

A The broader meaning of the "family tree" includes: *first*, all ancestors back to Adam and Eve; *second*, all descendants including those not yet conceived or born; *third*, close associates or friends who have left either a negative or positive impact on our lives, especially those who have injured us or given a bad example; *fourth*, even the "offspring" or "descendants" of sterile persons or celibates who have "children" by virtue of any spiritual authority (II Cor. 6:13; I Cor. 4:15), or correlative responsibility toward others, such as teachers, pastors, supervisors, mayors, and governors.

Thus, the family tree in these broad usages of the term could be occasions for lesser degrees of contamination than would be in the family tree in the strict sense, and yet would be subject to healing by the same process. These persons should be kept within the general ambit of our prayer during the healing of the family tree program, particularly during the celebration of the Eucharist.

The most neglected aspect of the prayer for healing the family tree is the part that relates to our deceased ancestors or family members. The prayer to break the trans-generational bondage must not only interrupt the "flow" of that deleterious effect, but also must go farther than that and release the very *persons themselves* — not only those who are alive, but also and especially those who are deceased — in the event that they may be in need of a deliverance from any lingering effects in themselves of their own sins.

The needs that these persons sometimes have can come to us in indirect ways, such as through dreams or through an awareness of a disquieted spirit in our environment, even by apparitional phenomena (somewhat rare), or it may be by a simple spiritual intuition of a deceased person's need in one's family background.

Q Can you give me a step-by-step program for a private form of a healing prayer for the family tree?

A The following step-by-step program may be helpful, especially when the Eucharistic part is not available:

First, recognize as many of the problems as possible in yourself and your family whether they be physical, emotional, spiritual, or interpersonal.

Second, repent of all failures on your part while confessing your sins.

Third, give forgiveness to all members of your ancestors (Lev. 26:40; Neh. 9:2; Ps. 106:6: Jer. 3:12-15, etc.). This induces an openness to *receive* God's forgiveness.

Fourth, give forgiveness to all the members of your family tree, living and dead, in the deepest possible act of forgiveness for any hurt they may have caused you or may have caused other members of the family.

Fifth, pray the prayer of deliverance: "deliver us from the evil one" over the entire family tree, coming against all the forces of evil that may have contaminated the family through the generations, using the Lord as the power behind the deliverance (Mark 16:17). Ancestral contamination is accomplished mainly through the work of the devil, for whom the door is opened by means of sin. But, Jesus came into the world precisely to destroy the devil's work (I John 3:8); hence, Jesus is the great Deliverer.

Sixth, destroy by transformation: "Do not conform any longer to the pattern of this world, but be *transformed* by the renewing of your mind. Then you will be able to test and approve what God's will is — his good, pleasing and perfect will" (Rom. 12:2). Essentially, this means being: (a) informed (of our inherited weakness), (b) transformed (in our thinking), and (c) conformed (to the perfect will of God).

Seventh, appeal to God to have the "angels of the Lord camp around those who fear him, and he delivers them" (Ps. 34:7), for angels are sent to serve us (Heb. 1:14), to guard us "in all our ways" (Ps. 91:11).

Eighth, place the cross of Jesus between each of the generations and over the head of each member of the family that comes to mind. Ask Jesus to pour his precious blood through each stratum of the family tree to dissolve the bondage that has been transmitted, and to link all the members of the family tree in a powerful bond of love to replace the bondage of sin and its effects. Humbly ask Jesus to destroy the negative patterns that have passed through the generations, with a total and complete destruction — patterns of adultery, alcoholism, drug addiction, depression, suicidal tendencies, etc.

Ninth, when the fallen angels are evicted, invite the holy angels to stand guard over the restored family.

Tenth, perseverance in prayer and sometimes with follow-up counseling and Christian fellowship; the perseverance in prayer (Luke 18:1) may be simply a periodic repetition of the family tree healing program and repeated participation in the celebration of the Eucharist with ever-deepening fervor and faith to clear up any remnant defects and to prevent relapses, consolidating the acquired healing. The perseverance in prayer and the repetition of the healing program gives a deeper assurance of prevention of damage to future generations within the family.

Q I would appreciate knowing whether the healing

always take place suddenly, during the family tree healing service.

A In the healing of the family tree, as in other forms of healing, we find five different modalities:

1. Instantaneous healing, which is almost of the order of a miracle by which a healing of tumors, cancer, arthritis, etc., occurs in a matter of moments or hours. This is the most dramatic of all forms of healing but the least frequent.

2. Gradual healing, which usually begins at the time of the prayer and continues over a period of days, weeks, and sometimes even months. This is the most common type of healing.

3. Phase-in or "spurt" healing in which a person has a series of partial healings at often irregular intervals — a kind of stair-step healing. An example of a "two-step" healing is Jesus' healing of the blind man from Bethsaida whom he touched twice to restore his sight (Mark 8:25).

4. Delayed healing, where nothing seems to happen at the time of the prayer or Eucharist celebrated for the healing, but often with a remarkable improvement or total healing after a delay, but in such a way that one can see the connection between the prayer for healing and the healing itself. An example of delayed effect of released power is seen in Mark 11:14-21, where it is recorded that the withering effect of Jesus' curse on the fig tree was not observed until a day later.

5. Recurrent healing is a type in which there is often a remarkable healing that lasts for an extended period, perhaps even several years, of serious disorders such as cancer, alcoholism, and homosexuality, followed by a relapse that gives the appearance of a merely temporary healing. This often causes discouragement when people do not apply the faith that they have received through that temporary healing to get them through the relapse into a "permanent" healing that God usually intends. (The only absolutely permanent healing is the most beautiful one, namely death, to be followed by a "super-perfect" healing

in the rapture or resurrection of the body [I Cor. 15:34-55; I Thess. 4:15-18].)

Of these five modalities of healing, the second and the third (gradual and phase-in) are the most common, perhaps because the Lord wants us to reinforce our prayer with continuity: "We should always pray and not give up" (Luke 18:1); "always keep on praying" (Eph. 6:18; I Thess. 5:17).

PERSONAL NOTES

PERSONALS NOTES

Chapter Two
HEALING
LIVING MEMBERS
OF YOUR FAMILY TREE
What Does It Mean
for My Family?

Q Should our healing prayer be directed more to our offspring or our ancestors?

A Don't neglect either. But your influence will be more obvious on your offspring. The book of Proverbs, often called a manual on parenting, has assigned 205 out of its 913 verses — almost one-fourth of the book — to the subject of rearing children. Adhering to the principle given there is one of the best ways of intercepting generational contamination for one's descendants. It was Homer Phillips who said: "The time to start correcting your children is before they start correcting you." Part of the purpose of the healing of the family tree program should be a preventative form of healing rather than a curative form; in that aspect we would put more emphasis on the descendants than on the ancestors. In either case, looking back or looking forward, looking up or looking down, looking toward the root system or toward the outer branches of the family tree, we should keep in mind that, in general, the major target area for healing is, as Scripture keeps reaffirming, "to the third and fourth generation," even though that healing process may skip a generation or two, just as the disorder itself may skip a generation or two. The disorder may perhaps not be found in this or that individual in the lineage. In the words of Jesus, "Now it is *hidden* from your eyes. But the days will come when you will be dashed to the ground and your children within you because you did not recognize the time of God's coming to you" (Luke 19:42-44).

We cannot change our ancestors, but we can do something about our descendants. We can change our ancestors to some extent, by breaking any existing bondage through the spiritual techniques that this book will outline, but we can do much more about the descendants.

I am reminded of the case of Coleridge. He was once talking with a man who told him that he didn't believe in giving little children any kind of religious instruction or direction, but that the child should be allowed complete freedom in religious training or absence of religious training until he came to the years of discretion, and then he could choose his own religion and religious opinions for himself. Coleridge took him out to the garden where the man was surprised to find that only weeds were growing. The visitor said, "This isn't a garden; there is nothing but weeds here." Coleridge answered, "Well, you see, I do not wish to infringe upon the liberty of the garden in any way; I was just giving the garden a chance to express itself and choose its own way of growing." Coleridge thus conveyed to this visitor the absurdity of the position that we shouldn't have instructional control over the children.

Q **The more I hear about the healing of the family tree program, the more concerned I become about the welfare of my children and grandchildren than that of my parents and ancestors. How can I best use this program to help them?**

A Some insightful writer once quipped, "Middle age is the time in life when you stop criticizing the older generation and start criticizing the younger one." As part of the program of healing of the family tree, parents in a special way should pray that the Lord would give his angels special charge over their children and their grandchildren and great-grandchildren, including those still unborn, for: "The children are the heritage from the Lord, and the fruit of the womb is his reward. As arrows are in the hand of a mighty man, so are children of the youth. Happy is the man that has his quiver full of them" (Ps. 127:3-5). An often-neglected duty of parents is to pray for the physical safety and welfare of their children. "Lift up your hands to him, for the lives of your children" (Lam. 2:19). Scripture reminds us of the availability of angelic support and guidance in Psalm 91:11 and Psalm 34:7 (cf. Heb. 1:14). They can do much to preserve everyone, especially children, from the effects of this transmitted bondage that otherwise might contaminate them. So that, when they are old, "they will not depart from the Word of God" (Prov. 22:6).

It is also suggested that parents pray for the Holy Spirit to be poured out upon their children, for the promise of Scripture is that our offspring will be "called" to be filled with the Spirit and blessed. Acts 2:39: "The promises to you and to your children and to all that are afar off in distant lands, as many as the Lord our God shall *call*."

Besides the general obligation of providing for one's children's material needs (II Cor. 12:14), parents should also ask to receive wisdom and counsel in bringing up their children in the discipline and the instruction of the Lord. With Paul, "ask God to help us understand what he wants us to do and to make us wise about spiritual things" (Col. 1:9 LB); "fathers telling their children about your faithfulness" (Is. 38:19; cf. Deut. 31:13).

"He commanded our forefathers to teach their children . . . even children yet to be born, and they in turn would tell their children . . . so they would not be like their forefathers" (Ps. 78:5-8; cf. Deut. 4:9; 6:7; 6:20; 11:19). But even the Lord failed to convince the Israelites not to be like their forefathers (Ezek. 20:18). Only great drought and defilement of the land brought their descendants to confess their own sins and those of their ancestors (Jer. 3:2-3; 2:25).

On the other hand, the imitation of godly parents carries with it its own blessings, as seen in the examples of Jehoshaphat, Uzziah, etc. (II Chron. 17:3; 23:3).

Twice Paul urges parents not to scold their children so much that they become discouraged or depressed with negativism in the family (cf. Col. 3:21; Eph. 6:4). The prayer should include the intention that the children experience emotional security from unity in the family, "with sympathy toward each other, loving one another with tender hearts and humble minds" (I Pet. 3:8).

Q **Arguments are common in our family, as I suppose they are in most families. Does this mean there is need for a family healing? Is ancestral sin the root of this problem?**

A Family conflicts are often the effect of ancestral sin, but more often they are the cause of it. In almost every record of family conflict mentioned in the Bible, there are clear indications of general unhappiness and multiple aftereffects reflected in problems in the offspring. Readers with time and interest to study this pattern might begin with a few Old Testament family squabblers as paradigms: Sarah and Hagar (Gen. 16:5); Rebekah and her daughters-in-law (Gen. 26:34-35; also 27:46); Jacob and Esau (Gen. 27:41); Moses and Aaron and Miriam (Num. 12:1); David and his wife (II Sam. 6:16); David and his household (II Sam. 12:11); Ahasuerus and Vashti (Esther 1:12).

In these conflictual situations, God showed his displeasure, and in some cases he intervened to restore family harmony (for example, by an angel sent to Hagar). He showed often that *intra*-personal healing was needed before the *inter*personal healing (Rom. 12:17-18; Titus 3:9-11; II Tim. 2:14; Heb. 12:14; Prov. 15:1, 20, 22; Sir. 10:6).

Q **Can you give me some practical suggestions for dissolving disharmony in the family? It's our greatest family need at the moment.**

A Dick Elliott once made a statement that touched on the root cause of disharmony and underscored a neglected dimension of love: "Problems between people are caused not so much by the difference as indifference."

Peter tells us to pray for peace in the family and to really work for it (I Pet. 3:11). In a devout family, that prayer for peace is powerful, "for the eyes of the Lord are focused on the righteous and his ears are open to their prayers" (v. 12).

Prayer for the family should be *sustained* as part of the healing program. It must not be limited to just one prayer appeal (Luke 18:1), or one prayer of healing, or one Eucharistic assembly but must become a habit, an attitude, an ongoing practice of cultivating, of what Peter calls "tenderhearted love for one another in the family."

St. John addressed three generations of family members about love: "I write to you fathers . . . to you young men . . . to you children" (I John 2:2-3). Paul instructs Titus (2:3-4) to have older women teach younger women to love their husbands and children. Many family problems, from teenage suicide to divorce, could be prevented if the biblical injunctions on family love were followed, "living in harmony with one another" (Rom. 12:16; I Pet. 3:8).

Yet love does not preclude discipline of youngsters. The father must "manage his own family well and see that his children obey him with proper respect" (I Tim. 3:4; cf. 3:12). One-fourth of the book of Proverbs deals with disciplining young people—for example, 13:24; 19:18; 22:15; 23:13. Too much love is impossible, but there are two kinds of love that are destructive to a child: overprotective love, and overpermissive love. Overprotective love causes rebellion or a sense of inadequacy, and overpermissive love causes selfishness or self-will in the child's behavior, producing a "spoiled child." These untoward behavior problems in turn can enormously complicate the family healing attempt.

Bad parental example, like neglect of church attendance (Heb. 10:25), family quarreling (Eph. 4:31), and bad language (4:29), will *prevent* the child from coming to the Lord. "Let the little children come to me" (Matt. 19:14). As John the Evangelist tells us in his gospel (21:15), Jesus is

95

concerned about his lambs as well as his sheep.

Q **Can parental neglect induce a generational bondage in the offspring?**

A Without a doubt. One of the causes of family bondage is simply negligence. It isn't *mis*informing, but rather *un*informing children; it isn't causing direct damage but indirect, through negligence. Youngsters can be damaged in any one of three ways: (1) directly attacking the child via such things as incest, injustice, and physical abuse; (2) personal sins committed by the parents, such as the sins of adultery, fornication, or abortion, that have a negative effect upon the child; (3) simple neglect of training, the absence of proper formation. Because Eli failed to restrain his sons, God imposed an unatonable bondage on his family (I Sam. 3:13-14).

The effects of sin are deeper and more far-reaching when parents, not only by bad example but by direct prompting, lead their children into sin as when the daughter of Herodius (Salome, according to Josephus) was persuaded by her mother to request the decapitation of John the Baptist (Matt. 14:8). "Ahaziah did evil in the eyes of the Lord, because he walked in the ways of his father and mother . . . and provoked the Lord to anger just as his father had done" (I Kings 22:52; II Chron. 22:3).

Some parents are concerned about just the misery (such as anxiety and depression) that may come as an end result of ancestral sin; some parents consider the disorders (such as physical or mental disease) that may directly or indirectly be the result of ancestral sin; still other parents are concerned merely about the financial effects of transmitted sin (usually not recognized as such).

Q **What is the effect of parental neglect within the family tree?**

A St. James says (4:17), "Anyone who knows the good he

ought to do, and doesn't do it, sins." That is called a sin of omission.

In archaeological digs in the ruins of Nineveh, there was discovered a library of plaques that contained the laws of the realm. One of those laws reads, in effect, that anyone who was guilty of neglect would be responsible for the result of that neglect, and specifically neglect to teach one's child to obey would put a burden of guilt on the parents, and an obligation to restore any property rights that were violated as a result of neglecting to train one's child. This is child-to-parent punishment, rather than parent-to-child — the effects of the child's sins. However, the very failure of the child may result from the sin of neglect of the parent.

We find therefore a two-direction impact of the family tree pattern. The child has an effect upon the parent (at least in this case legally, and in God's eyes perhaps morally), but more important, the parent has an impact upon the child, legally and morally. With regard to the *good* effects of non-negligent parents upon their children, we don't have to look far to find statistics for that, and also clear examples from everyday life, as well as many scriptural examples, such as II Timothy 3:14-16.

A survey sought to find the greatest influence in determining the vocation of 158 missionary doctors; it concluded that parental influence was the greatest factor — and this has been found to be true in the case of most religious vocations. The family of South Africa's saintly Andrew Murray included eleven children who finally reached adulthood. Five of the sons became ministers and four of the daughters became ministers' wives. The generation after that had an even more striking record. Ten grandsons became ministers and thirteen became foreign missionaries. The environment of the Christian home certainly had a lot to do with that, but we would tend to ask, how much influence is natural and how much supernatural, by the providential grace of God?

Considered negatively, we can ask the same question regarding the family tree that has been infected with evil:

How much results from a natural factor of environment caused by the parent and provided by the parents, and how much is simply the result of simply the absence of grace, where the sins of the parents are visited upon the children? It is very difficult to know exactly, from a sociological point of view of course, how much belongs to these causative categories, but in a multiple case study, one is almost forced to conclude that environment alone could not be the sole cause. There must be another factor involved in the transmission of good or bad qualities through the generations, as the Word of God indicates.

A classic study was done with the famous Jukes family — a well-known criminal family, where there was found a consistently high level of profligacy and insanity, as well as much professional prostitution, and an enormous amount of alcoholism. Out of the 1200 known descendants in the Jukes family, a very prolific family, 400 were physically self-wrecked by disease, injury, and mutilation; 310 became professional beggars; 130 became convicted criminals, 60 of whom were habitual thieves and pickpockets while 7 were convicted murderers, and out of the whole 1200 descendants only 20 ever learned a trade. Of those that did, half of them learned it in prison. Once again we see the connection between the sins of the parents and the effect upon the offspring.

Q I feel a deep concern and love for my children and grandchildren. Doesn't this assure me that I am not guilty of parental neglect?

A Loving parents can still be inconsistent in exercising their love for their children. They may refuse to let a reckless youngster drive the car, but allow him to neglect church attendance, prayer, etc., or allow him to choose unsavory companions, drink, take drugs, etc. Concern for physical welfare may be eclipsed by unconcern for spiritual welfare. Paradigmatic in this regard was David's concern for his son Absalom (II Sam. 18:29).

While president of Princeton University, Woodrow Wilson decried the difficulty of educators in coping with youngsters whose parents had been overpermissive during the formative years, and of the subsequent generations adversely affected by replicated patterns of parental neglect. Loving concern for spiritual needs is most effective in the malleable period of a child's life; the clay must be shaped before it is kiln-hardened (cf. Prov. 29:15).

Studies at the University of California at Davis and at Pitzer College have disclosed new data on parental influence. Some findings include:

1. Younger parents are *usually* more influential than older parents in exciting youngsters' latent abilities and ideals.

2. Firstborn and only children *usually* receive more attention and are thus more impacted by parents' aspirations and ideals.

3. A parent's death makes *some* children achievement-oriented and ideal-sensitive as a way of coping.

4. Parental conversation, religious role-modeling, and affirming family traditions tend to impact children subtly but deeply.

Q I regard myself as a good Christian, but not a really "devout" one. What bearing will this have on my descendants?

A At a Rotary meeting in Illinois, Gypsy Smith was giving a talk in which he asked the question of his audience, "How many of you can recall a saintly mother or a godly father who loved the Bible and read it and lived it and allowed its effects to seep into you as a child?" Almost every hand in the audience went up. Then quietly Gypsy swung home the idea that he was trying to convey. "With all your influence today, how many of *you* are so living that *your* children will remember you for the faithfulness to God's Word?" That was quite a tense moment. No hands were raised in answer to that question. We must keep in mind that the providing of a good or bad spiritual environment for one's children is a free choice for parents. When there is parental neglect, that could be called a sin (James 4:17) — a sin of omission in not providing good environment; and that "*sin* of the parents is visited upon the children."

In New England prisons, a study was made of 600 imprisoned teenagers. They were asked why they thought they were there as an ultimate cause of their crime. Six out of ten said that they had fathers who drank to excess. Many had mothers in the same condition. Three-fourths said that they were granted too much freedom, to come and go as they pleased without parental guidance and supervision. Seven out of ten had homes where there were no group or family activities or group prayer, even at mealtime and in *every* case there was no family room or place or time for a scheduled family prayer.

On the other hand, the statistics regarding good spiritual environment are truly astonishing. In a study from the University of Michigan it was determined that while approximately one out of two American marriages ends in divorce, only *one out of five hundred* American marriages ends in divorce where there is family prayer and Bible reading every day. Thus, when we choose to provide a good religious environment, God places his blessings upon the children from that environment. "I will bless those who reverence me, to the thousandth generation." Furthermore, the family tree program, as most forms of healing, provides a means by which God is glorified in restoring broken and weak persons to the fullness of health and vitality, in compensating for poor spiritual environments in childhood. In my own healing ministry, I have seen countless examples of this.

In one of the cathedrals I visited in England, there is a beautiful stained-glass window. As the sunlight streams through it, it displays the stories of the Old and New Testaments, and the glorious truths of doctrine in Christian revelation. But this window was fabricated by the artist only out of broken pieces of glass which had been discarded

100

by other artisans. I think that God delights in taking the discards of society and making something truly beautiful out of them. That for us is the basis for our hope and trust in God as we seek a healing, whether through the family tree program, or through whatever means the Lord provides. It's part of the divine ingenuity that he can make, with our cooperation, something beautiful out of something ugly.

A friend of John Ruskin's approached him with a very costly handkerchief in which a blot of ink had been spilled. He complained that nothing could be done with this very expensive piece of fabric. Ruskin took the handkerchief and after a time he brought it back; to the great surprise of his friend, it could hardly be recognized because of the very skillful way Ruskin had changed that blot into a design that he painted on the handkerchief in India ink. The handkerchief now was more valuable than ever. The work of the genius of Ruskin is reflected time and time again in the genius of God in taking the blots of our life and transforming them into beautiful artistic productions, since "he who began a good work in you will carry it on to completion" (Phil. 1:6).

God sees potential good in wickedness and weakness. Analogous to this, there is a story of Agostino D'Antonio, a sculptor of Florence, Italy, who, after trying to sculpt a large piece of marble into a statue, finally gave up because the marble seemed to be defective. Other sculptors tried to take up where he left off, and they too gave up the task. The stone was discarded and lay in the rubbish heap for over forty years. One day Michelangelo was out strolling past the area, where he saw the stone; his creative genius saw the latent possibilities in it. He brought it to his studio, began work on it, and ultimately his vision and work were crowned with success. From a seemingly worthless stone, he carved one of the world's masterpieces of sculpture, the statue of David.

The Lord is the master sculptor who can take any defective stone, whether damaged by one's own negligence or by a transmitted effect of sin from one's ancestors, and can reshape it into a masterpiece. This is one of the most beautiful expressions of God's condescending love for us.

In this program of the healing of the family tree, we find one of the most astonishing and remarkable means God has chosen in modern times to express his goodness, his healing power in making good from evil. In the words of Paul, "Where evil abounds, let grace abound all the more" (Rom. 12:21). In paraphrase, "Where weakness and sickness and disease abound, let health and goodness and wholesomeness abound all the more" through the goodness of God.

Q **Can ancestral sin work backwards? That is, can children induce the effect of their sin into the parents, grandparents, etc.?**

A An often overlooked aspect of the family healing program is the fact that children can be a source of damage to their parents, as well as parents being a source of damage to the children. Such defects are picked up, not by "inheritance," but by familial "infection" as exemplified in Proverbs 28:7 and 29:15, with children bringing "disgrace upon the parents" (cf. Deut. 21:20; 27:16; Prov. 15:20; 30:11; Micah 7:6; II Tim. 3:2).

Q **Since unborn children are part of the family tree, how can I convince my "pro-choice" daughter not to contaminate our family tree by aborting her child?**

A Deuteronomy 30:19 says: "Choose life, so that you and your descendants may live in the love of the Lord your God." The conclusion from this is that there are not "pro-choice" Christians — there are only "pro-life" Christians because we are commanded to choose life, and that means there is no choice but one for a God-oriented person.

Q **What are some of the psychological benefits of**

the healing program for persons who have been involved in attempted abortion?

A It has been shown a number of times that attempted abortions that are unsuccessful, fortunately leave the child alive but unfortunately damaged psychologically, to the point that there may be suicidal tendencies that reflect, in timing and in method, forms of inducing death that were parallel to the mother's intent to induce abortion.

The child, we know from the studies of embryonic psychology, responds in the most dramatic way to the parents' relationship to each other. The commonly recognized statistic established by Dr. D. H. Scott, is that there is a 237% greater risk of having a child with physical and emotional handicaps if the mother is in a stormy relationship or unsettled marriage during the time of pregnancy.

When the child dies by miscarriage or is stillborn, the intensity of grief, both conscious and subconscious, will have its effect upon the mother in most cases, almost as measurably as if the child were an adult who died. Often there is a phenomenon called "shadow grief," which may be reflected in depression, anxieties, fears, phobias, or other psychological problems. There could be either a temporary or a permanent type of grief affecting the mother, with its psychosomatic effects, back problems, fatigue, loss of appetite, psychological problems, episodes of rage, guilt complexes, etc.

Q In the context of ancestral sin, can we say that some children are born criminals — born to be criminals?

A No. However, if you were to ask, "Are some born with a greater predisposition to crime than others?" the answer is yes. At least that seems to be the conclusion of the massively documented book *Crime and Human Nature*, by James Q. Wilson and Richard J. Herrnstein (Simon and Schuster, 1985). The authors, after a highly disciplined investigation and research, have determined that there is no such thing as criminal genes; however, persons who commit frequent crimes are likely to display certain common characteristics early in life.

The *average* criminal tends to have an IQ of about 92, eight to ten points below average, makes poor scores in communication fluency and tends more often to have (with plenty of exceptions) a rather athletic build with an overweight tendency. (This particular build does not cause crime, but is often associated with an aggressive temperament, which could be a factor predisposing to crime.)

Criminals are often hyperactive, exceptionally impulsive, and tend to discount future unpleasant consequences of any social acts that provide immediate gratification. They are abnormally aggressive, are often problem children at school by the time they are eight or nine years old, have difficulty establishing strong emotional attachments, and overwhelmingly they are male. All of these qualities, contend the authors, are related in some degree to genetic inheritance.

One very impressive bit of evidence is the fact that biological parents who are criminals tended to produce children who, even when adopted out early in life, displayed the same sort of criminal tendencies; and, on the other hand, adoptive parent criminality has little apparent effect on the adoptee's tendency to break the law.

The factors that might be called environmental which counteract criminal tendencies (except in the case of psychopathic personalities) are *first*, parental affection, that is, frequently manifested love from the parents or parent figures; and *second*, receiving *consistent* discipline, whether severe or mild, with prompt rewards for good behavior and penalties for untoward behavior. To a lesser degree, coming from a two-parent family will protect against criminal tendencies. Bad peer influence may be a significant factor in the casual low-rate offender, and less for the continuing high-rate criminal.

Criminals typically seek immediate rewards and have

a short "time-horizon." It is questionable whether television stimulates significant and lasting aggressive behavior. However, TV addiction may well predispose the viewers to seek immediate gratification, which is a quality associated with criminal attitudes. The defective environment, particularly within the family context, certainly is to be presumed as a possible avenue through which ancestral sin can be transmitted. We must not discount the fact that God does not distribute talents or opportunities equally, as illustrated by the parable of the workers in the vineyard (Matt. 20).

Q Do separated twins, in separate environments, show equal risk of criminal tendencies?

A Studies of twins and adopted youngsters are the best evidence of a genetic basis for the precursors of criminality. Criminality is much more highly correlated among identical twins than among fraternal twins, and that is significant because identical twins are *genetically* the same while fraternal twins are no more alike genetically than ordinary siblings.

Adoption studies that parallel those of Dr. Sarnoff Mednick make the conclusion that if the biological parents of an adopted boy were criminals, he is more likely to be a criminal himself than if his parents were not criminals even though he never knew them or was raised by them, and this is the case regardless of what his adoptive parents were like.

It should be stressed that we are talking only about genetic *predispositions* toward criminality. This is similar to a predisposition to alcoholism or Alzheimer's disease. With the proper care and nurture and with some degree of luck, these children need never become criminals. Nobody is *predestined* to become a criminal. Moreover, *some* of the biological precursors may not be genetic at all. For instance, they can result from birth defects or poor prenatal care.

Q I have a number of relatives whose spiritual life is far from ideal. I'm really concerned about their spiritual needs (and to a lesser degree their other needs). Some have given up going to church, some are into drugs or alcohol abuse, some are practicing adultery, homosexuality, etc. What can I do to help them? Is it enough to include them in my prayer intentions in the family healing program?

A It is good that you have the zeal for the welfare of family members that Paul recommends (I Tim. 4:4-8).

The first thing we have to realize is that it is not up to us, but to God to draw people to himself through the Holy Spirit, as Jesus said (John 6:44). Secondly, we can pray that God will send some event or person across the path of the negligent relative to harvest that person for the Lord. Matthew 9:38: "Pray therefore the Lord of the harvest, that he will *send forth* laborers into his harvest."

There are no particular rules that would apply equally to everyone because God will lead one person through one means, and another person through another. *Generally* speaking, it is better not to try to remonstrate with relatives who are not disposed to listen to you. As we become more convinced ourselves, we have greater influence for good. The Holy Spirit leads us by an inward witness or conviction. I Timothy 4:8 points out: "Godliness is profitable for all things."

We must be careful not to nag persons whom we regard as "unsaved." The two most common mistakes that are made toward persons not openly receptive to God's word are requiring that the person become "ultra-spiritual," and secondly, "over-witnessing" to the person. The Bible teaches we must witness, but it should be done prudently. Colossians 4:5-6 (LB) says: "Make the most of your chances to tell others the good news. Be *wise* in all your contacts with them. Let your conversation be *gracious* as well as *sensible*, for then you will have the right answer for everyone."

Our personal life is usually a more powerful witness than our words. The old aphorism that says "What you are thunders so loud I can't hear what you are saying" still has validity. Many people who do a lot of talking and sermonizing of their relatives do not have enough spiritual maturity to back up their witness to give meaning to it. Your own godliness, nurtured by an interior life of prayer, is a most important prerequisite for evangelizing others: "Watch your life and doctrine closely. Persevere in them, because if you do, you will save both yourself and your hearers" (I Tim. 4:16). (When Paul speaks of "saving yourself and your hearers" he means that humans save humans only instrumentally; only God can save anyone, ultimately [Eph. 2:8].)

Of course intercession on behalf of the unsaved relatives is always appropriate, but your intercessory prayer is not going to be successful if you're not grounded in faith and in the Word of God. Converting your relatives may depend on you, but the effect of the prayer is greater if the Word of God is more strongly rooted in you, because then your faith will be stronger. "Faith comes by hearing and hearing by the Word of God" (Rom. 10:17). Your faith is strong in proportion as the Word of God has been assimilated by you, and your evangelizing influence is consequently more persuasive.

John points out in his gospel: "If you abide in me and *my words abide in you*, you shall ask what you will and it shall be done for you" (15:7).

Q Is there any way to know if my prayer for my loved ones is working?

A After a certain time in prayer, you may notice that the burden may be lifted and a spirit of lightness may prevail. This usually means that the answer is assured, even though it may not yet be manifested (cf. Dan. 10:12-13). (Daniel's prayer was heard the first day but was not answered until twenty-one days later.)

The person living in sin is blinded (cf. II Cor. 4:3-4) and unaware of the danger he is in, like a drunken driver careening down the road at high speed. Hence, we need to break the power of the enemy over our unsaved loved ones and to open their eyes from the blindness that he has imposed upon them. The witnessing is the witnessing of Christ's "light in the darkness" (v. 6) "and this light and power must now shine through us, so that others can see that the power within must come from God and not ourselves" (v. 7). Our concern for a spiritually weak loved one may be a "burden for us," but only in praying and fasting for them can we carry their burden (cf. Rom. 15:1 and Gal. 6:2).

Some people unfortunately misinterpret Acts 16:31: "Believe in the Lord Jesus Christ and you shall be saved *and your household.*" The entire passage reveals that the gospel was preached to the whole household, and that they had come to believe (v. 34) — it is not enough for one person, even the head of a household, to believe in order to convert the others. Each one must be brought to that belief. This is accomplished primarily by the good example of the most influential persons in that household, particularly the parents. It is not enough to "claim" your family for the Lord; you must do certain things like "keep on praying and not give up" (Luke 18:1), and remember to hate the sin while loving the sinner (St. Augustine's paraphrase of Jude 23).

Underscoring this family evangelization is the fact that each person has a free will and is personally involved in accepting or rejecting Christ. Claiming someone else's salvation is usually not enough. Once the power of the devil is broken, such "unsaved relatives" will usually make the right choice but while their mind is still blinded (II Cor. 4:3) they can't make the right choice.

These norms provide general guidelines. They do not cover every case. Where there are no guidelines, we must depend on what the Holy Spirit tells us to do (Gal. 5:18).

Q What about "incurable" or almost incurable be-

havior patterns? How does the healing of the family tree program work with deep-seated problems like homosexuality, anorexia, and alcoholism?

A In response to this question, an example of transgenerational patterning comes to mind. Child-battering parents are often persons who themselves were abused as children by their own parents. These strong adverse tendencies are often attributed to a function of the subconscious or unconscious mind. A controversial book, *Brain and Psyche: The Biology of the Unconscious* (Doubleday), authored by Johnathan Winson, maintains that what Freud called the unconscious, in fact represents the function of brain systems that become fixed in early childhood and are highly resistant to change thereafter. They involve an interfacing of the hippocampus, the limbic system, and the prefrontal cortex, which in humans provide an emotional undercurrent to life. If this constellation of negative factors takes control of *conscious* behavior, it may threaten the mental health of the person.

For Freud, the goal of therapy was to move repressed material from the unconscious into the preconscious and then with the help of the analyst, the patient could "work through" the buried conflict so that eventually he could come to understand and eliminate his neuroses. This "unconscious personality," one that is emotionally loaded with deep negative impresses, may leave a very lasting untoward behavior pattern in the adult.

Many of these are mental functions learned once and forever during some critical "time window" in infancy or childhood. In nature we find many parallel examples: lion cubs, for instance, *must* learn to deliver the killing bite to the neck of their prey between the sixth and twentieth weeks of life or they never learn to kill efficiently. Children who do not master a foreign language before puberty will never be able to speak it without an accent.

Perhaps within the similar limited time frame, particularly when parents or other ancestors are influencing us by direct environmental contact, damage may be done, but also good influences can engram favorable behavior patterns on the child. Persons may spend years in therapy and thousands of dollars to obtain an insight into themselves, but still find it very difficult to change. Particularly intractable disorders include alcoholism, homosexuality, various phobias, anorexia, and bulimia. The unconscious predisposition has been engrammed into the neurological system within the three segments of the brain mentioned above and cannot be easily eradicated by psychotherapy alone.

This is where the healing prayer in the healing of the family tree program transcends the capacity of ordinary psychotherapy. Divine intervention steps in to change the unchangeable which is equivalent to "curing the incurable" (or almost incurable). When apparently intractable disorders, not ordinarily amenable to scientific procedures or psychotherapy, become "easily" cured, obviously there is an intervention of a higher power. The utterance of a prayer or devout attendance at a Eucharist for the intention of healing could not be explained as simply a psychological conditioning which produced the effect of the healing, because the most intense psychotherapy could not do the same.

The very success and popularity of the healing of the family tree program may be precisely due to this very fact, that these highly resistant problems are dissolved with ease and simplicity when the client opens himself or herself to divine intervention. The very nature of this process precludes a purely natural explanation, particularly when the cure is immediate and dramatic, although in many cases it may require a repeated prayer or a repeated participation in the Eucharist with this healing intention.

A number of other factors will play a significant part in determining the time that a healing requires, especially the "faith factor" and the "forgiveness factor," in giving and receiving forgiveness — in forgiving our ancestors who may have triggered the problem and receiving forgiveness from God, as engendered by repentance.

Q **We have a family history of suicide. With the amazing increase in the suicide rate among teenagers, I'm concerned about my own youngsters and their future children. Is there any special advice you can give me?**

A Teenage suicide tripled between the mid-1950s and mid-1980s, and it is found to be starting at an earlier age than ever, caused perhaps by social factors, such as separation and family dissolution and reduction in the emotional availability of working parents to youngsters; and perhaps also because of the increase of stress due to school and job competition.

Studies indicate a distinct link within the family genealogy for suicide tendencies. Some family members will keep secret the fact that a relative has been suicidal, so it is hard to gauge the element of continuity. About twelve percent of preadolescents have thought of or attempted suicide, talking about it more than actually attempting to carry it out. Some youngsters seem genetically more vulnerable than others, and these may be the youngsters involved in a "contagion" situation, when there are clusters of teenage suicides in any given community, or a rash of suicides after the suicide of a celebrity.

Those who are particularly vulnerable should be careful of becoming too intensely involved in playing games such as "Dungeons and Dragons," which could lead that type of youngster to possible suicide, as reported in *U.S. News and World Report* (March 31, 1986). Youngsters emulating the parents' possible cavalier attitude about the value of life, could be another spur to suicide. This environmentally and genetically induced tendency could well be the substrate for the transmission of ancestral sin's effects.

Q **Can the family tree healing prayer be used as a "healing of memories" type of healing, for example,**

for hidden feelings of rejection in children put up for adoption, or the insecurities in children of arguing parents or divorced parents, etc.?

A With adopted children, many have feelings of rejection or lack of self-worth that need to be overcome. Even in their most infantile experiences they can register a sense of rejection that can be equivalent to inheriting the effects of ancestral sin. The healing of the family tree program can overlap the healing of memories program for disorders of this type (environmentally, not genetically, induced).

Early childhood traumas often leave psychic scars that become part of the family tree complex; they are not so much spiritually transmitted as observed and registered experientially by the child, but they produce an equivalent effect. Witnessing family fights or frequently being uprooted and being forced to change schools and relate to new acquaintances in early childhood can have a very unsettling effect upon the mind of young children. The divorce of parents or the death of a parent or of a family member may leave a deep scar in the emotional life of a child.

The scars can be healed if the problem is recognized by surfacing it and lifting it to the Lord for his healing. These bondages, directly or indirectly being the bondage of Satan, the enemy that destroys life, may be broken, in Jesus' name. It is the Lord's desire to bring us into wholeness, integrity, in a truly holistic form of human fulfillment, expressed in I Thessalonians 5:23, "May God himself, the God of peace, sanctify you through and through. May your *whole* spirit, soul and body be kept blameless until the coming of our Lord Jesus Christ. The one who calls you is faithful and *he will do* it."

Q Is there any role for angels in the family tree healing program?

A Angels are "ministering spirits" sent by God to serve our needs (Heb. 1:14). There are a number of examples in

Scripture of the bondage between relatives being broken by the power of God either directly or indirectly through the intercession of angels. An example of this type of healing can be found in one of the deuterocanonical books of the Bible, the book of Tobit, Chapter 3. Sarah, the daughter of Raguel, was possessed by the evil spirit Asmodeus, destroyer of family relationships (v. 17) who had caused the death of each of her seven husbands. Tempted to suicide, she decided to pray rather that God would release her from the bondage of earth by a providential death (v. 13). Instead he released her from the bondage of Asmodeus by the power of Raphael, the archangel (v. 17) who was also instrumental in the healing of Tobit (3:17; 6:8).

Q **The whole idea of ancestral sin affecting succeeding generations seems strange to us in this day and age. It all seems too much beyond our control; and controlling our own destiny is something we cherish dearly in our society today.**

A The close identity of a man with his children, and children with their parents, resulting from the tightly bonded unity of the three- or four-generation households of ancient Israelite society, is alien to the modern reader whose sense of self is highly individualistic. But that deep, profoundly human bond accounts for the ancient legal principle of "punishing the children for the sin of fathers to the third and fourth generation."

Where the sin starts and ends is not always clear, in that the sin of the fathers could start at any of several past generations. However, by the same token, it could be made to end at any time, by repentance, and also sin's effects (bondage) could be broken at any time by prayer, especially in its more concerted form, as in this program for healing the family tree.

Q **How will the virtue of good parents affect their children, grandchildren, etc.?**

A Amidst all this negativity regarding punishment for sin, it is good to consider the counterpart of the covenant, namely "showing love to a thousand generations of those who love me and keep my commandments" (Exod. 20:6). "Each generation of the upright will be blessed" (Ps. 112:2). "From everlasting to everlasting, the Lord's love is with those who fear him and his righteousness with their children's children; with those who keep his covenant and remember to obey his precepts" (Ps. 103:17-18; cf. Ezra 9:12). A commitment is needed (Josh. 24:15) to attain this reward.

The offspring of virtuous parents will have a special heritage (Ps. 112:2), including salvation (Ps. 103:17), wisdom (Sir. 4:17), holiness (44:11-14), and prosperity (Ezra 9:12), fertility (Deut. 7:13), and health (v. 15); love-capacity (Deut. 30:6; Rom. 11:28); revelation of God's secrets (29:29), wealth (Sir. 44:10; Ps. 112:3), vigor (Ps. 128:3-6) and the gift of faith (II Tim. 1:5).

The early concepts of immortality emphasized that a man in some way continued living on in his children. "The Lord loves the just and will not forsake his faithful ones; they will be protected *forever*. But the offspring of the wicked will be cut off. The righteous will inherit the land and dwell in it *forever*. But the offspring of the wicked will be cut off. The righteous will inherit the land and dwell in it *forever*" (Ps. 37:28-29).

It must be remembered that part of the life of virtue for parents consists in training the children in virtue: (cf. Deut. 6:6-7; 28:46); "This obligation," said Moses, "is not just idle words for you — they are your life" (Deut. 32:47). You, as a parent, are chosen as Abraham was, to "direct his children and his household after him to keep the way of the Lord" (Gen. 18:19; cf. Deut. 5:10; 28:4-11). Prosperity was promised to Solomon because of the integrity of heart and uprightness of his father, David (I Kings 9:4-5). The promise continued through Jehoshaphat (II Chron. 17:3 and 20:32). A similar reward was shown to Uzziah (II Chron. 26:4-5) and to Jotham (27:2).

While evil *effects* can be transmitted, the moral evil itself is still contingent upon the freedom of the will of each individual descendant; hence, there can be good children from wicked parents (cf. II Kings 12:2; 18:3, 22:2; II Chron. 34:3), with such children *sometimes* left uncontaminated with the effects of the pervasive evils of their parents.

Q **It seems that the inherited punishment comes only from ancestors who hated God according to Exodus 20:6. I don't think that hatred of God is that common among most family trees so as to account for the widespread presence of negative behavior, sickness, etc.**

A The word "hate" that is used in that passage is not found in any of the other of the many passages referring to the transmitted punishment for sin from one's ancestry. When the word is used here, in the quoted passage, it is from the Hebrew word *sane* which corresponds in the New Testament to the Greek word *miseo*. This word is often used in Scripture hyperbolically so that hatred is often translated "lack of love" — "to hate," meaning "not to love" or "to love less." In Deuteronomy 21:15-17 the word "hated" is translated "unloved."

In the New Testament, we find Jesus commanding us to "hate" our father and mother and wife and children and brothers and sisters and even our own life in order to be his disciple (Luke 14:26). This is obviously a "Galilean hyperbole," implying that one must love Jesus even more than the immediate family. (See Matthew 10:37, where the idea is rephrased: "Anyone who loves his father more than me is not worthy of me; anyone who loves his son or daughter more than me is not worthy of me.")

"The Lord says, I have loved Jacob but Esau I have hated" (Mal. 1:2-3). Paul explains God's love for Jacob and hatred for Esau on the basis of preference or "election" (Rom. 9:10-13). God chose Jacob but not Esau. This "hate" was the same as that expressed about Leah in that Jacob loved Rachel more than her (Gen. 29:31 and 33; cf. Deut.

21:16-17). In Scripture very often vivid hyperboles are used to emphasize a point of religious significance. That is the case where the threat of transmitted punishment through the generations is shown to be the result of "hatred" of God — that is, neglect of full allegiance to God.

Q It seems that God threatens punishment on the offspring only where the ancestors have practiced idolatry. I'm sure none of my ancestors have worshipped false gods in recent generations. Why then should I need a healing of ancestral bondage?

A The passage from Exodus 20:5 referring to the punishment as the result of idolatry is only one of many passages in which the hereditary punishment is referred to. In the same book of Exodus 34:7, God told Moses that the guilty will be punished and the children and their children for the sin of the fathers to the third and fourth generation, in reference not simply to idolatry, but to all of the ten commandments and the two tablets of the law that Moses had chiseled out. In the first reference of Exodus (Chapter 20) the "jealousy" of God demands exclusive devotion to himself (cf. 34:14; Deut. 4:24; 32:16 and 21; Josh. 24:19; Ps. 78:58; I Cor. 10:22; James 4:5). (The Hebrew word for jealousy in some of these passages may be translated also as "zeal" as well as "jealousy," depending on the context.) Jealousy in this sense is part of the vocabulary of love. This implies that God will not put up with rivalry or unfaithfulness in this covenant relationship.

When Dathan and Abiram were punished with their wives, children, and little ones (grandchildren) (Num. 16:27 and 31) — a three-generation punishment — it was not for idolatry, but for rejection of the God-appointed leadership of Moses. When Achan and his household were punished, it was for the sin of avarice and plunder (Josh. 7:20-25), not idolatry.

It is an almost ominous warning that God holds up to us that *any* allegiance to any idol (which can be anything that we treasure more than God) can have disastrous effects in our lives (cf. Rom. 2:22; Ezek. 33:31; Baruch 6:7). It prompts us to think of the areas of "idolatry" in our lives and in the lives of our ancestors, and where our eyes have sought "idols" or expediencies other than God. That is why his imperative was such a strong and unequivocal demand: "He who is not with me is against me" (Matt. 12:30). We cannot be lukewarm Christians; we cannot falsify our allegiance to God and Jesus Christ; it is possible to become tainted with sin or wrong thinking and still appear to be Christian. Many "churchy" people practice religion, but not spirituality. Lacking a meaningful relationship with God, they are in reality giving allegiance to the enemy. Even the slightest dilution of faith can have disastrous effects on ourselves and our offspring.

Q **There is much talk of sexual and physical abuse of children these days. Is this an inherited family trait? Is psychotherapy the only way to heal this tendency to abuse? What about the healing of the victims?**

A Some new studies of sexual abuse of children show that it is far more common than had formerly been believed. A national poll of randomly selected adults in 1985 has shown that 22% of adults in the United States have been victims of sexual abuse. Another study noted ever-mounting evidence that sexual abuse can lead to cases of multiple personality where a child escapes into an alternate identity. A survey financed by the Justice Department finds that abuse, particularly sexual abuse, is a key factor contributing to chronic runaway behavior by youngsters.

How much of this is the result of ancestral sin? Obviously, if any of the adult relatives of a youngster have a child who has been physically or sexually abused, it is clear we have environmentally-induced psychological damage that is not therefore in any way engrammed in the genes. There is certainly a "transmission" of a destructive effect, as there would be in any kind of negative behavior directed toward another person; but particularly during the most psychologically vulnerable period of a person's life — in childhood, the damage can be just as deep as if it had been transmitted genetically.

The principle of the transmission of ancestral sin to the "third and fourth generation" seems to be evidenced in this ailment by the fact that an abused child may grow up to be a child abuser or may continue to accept being victimized. For instance, a woman who is sexually abused as a child may marry a wife-beater and tolerate his abuse, or may permit her children to be abused, which effectively brings about the *equivalent* of a genetically transmitted bondage. In prisons and among prostitutes, studies show that as many as 80% of the people in those groups were abused as children.

If this defect in behavior is not strictly speaking genetic or if it is not merely trans-psychogenetic, then there is the possibility that it may be spiritually transmitted as a family bondage; or it may be a form of demonic contamination which lodges in the reconditioned brain of a person who has been psychologically damaged — whose behavior then provides the environment for abuse within the next generation, thereby *externally* transmitting the defect.

Associated with child abuse is the sense of guilt often found in the victims, who may need to be reassured that it wasn't their fault that they were abused. This distortion in the thinking pattern brings with the guilt complex many secondary defects, which in turn could be transmitted in behavioral patterns from parent to child through several generations. Spinoffs of this abuse could be behavioral change, such as regression to thumbsucking and bedwetting, or it may involve altered sleep patterns or inappropriate sexual behavior, among a number of possible behavioral changes. The key to adequate prevention of the side effects of abuse is establishing good communication between parents and children, regardless of the one by whom they were abused — uncle or brother or stranger —

for that matter. The end result of cases that are not treated is a permanently lowered sense of self-esteem; and such people tend to be either ones who decide they deserve being treated badly in life or ones who treat others badly, sometimes becoming child abusers themselves. Studies at Yale University have concluded that 30% of abused children repeat the cycle with their own children, with a lower percentage for those with loving, supportive spouses, or with low-stress lifestyles.

Certainly psychotherapy is encouraged for both the abusers and the victims, as early as possible, but let us not discount the power of Jesus who hates sin but loves sinners like child abusers. And he also loves children in special ways: "Let the little children come to me. . ." (Mark 10:14). I have seen several cases of abused children (and their abusers) marvelously healed by the healing of the family tree program — some through our videotape on this subject.

It may suffice to quote one testimonial letter as an example of how the Lord can reach deep into long-festering areas of the mind to heal such traumas that occur in childhood:

> When I was a young child, a person had molested me who had been into occultism. After that, I found that I was easily attracted to the occult. My body was full of pain and sickness in many forms. During the Mass in the Healing of the Family Tree program, I followed your directions of forgiveness to the person who offended me, in the presence and in the name of Jesus Christ, while repenting of all my involvement in the occult. I was healed in my *whole body* from the crown of my head to the tip of my toes. I had always tried to forgive before this, but this was the first time I asked the Lord to help me forgive and I succeeded in doing it. I praise God, for I feel released from great bondage that had been assailing me for many years.

Q What about dealing with homosexuality? I have heard of a number of ministries to homosexuals, like "Exodus International," "Love in Action," "Desert Stream," and "Homosexuals Anonymous." Do these groups seek to reverse the homosexual tendencies by basically the same method as the healing of the family tree program?

A Only to the extent that they employ spiritual therapy. Genetic causality of homosexuality is a controverted aspect of this very sensitive and complex issue. The Pillard-Weinrich report from the University of Boston (*Archives of General Psychiatry*, 1986) indicates that brothers of gay men are over five times more prone to being gay or bisexual themselves than brothers from totally heterosexual families.

Many Christian groups, ignorant of the complexity of this problem, claim that becoming "born-again" will automatically cure the disorder. Sometimes it does. Other traditional Christian approaches try to cast out the demon of homosexuality. Quite often that works. Most of the new approaches in this ministry, like "Desert Stream" (Santa Monica, California), start with the concept that homosexual behavior is not basically an expression of erotic need, but the outworking of any number of breakdowns and dysfunctions in the early formation of the individual identity. Most often these reach back to the parent-child relationships, which indirectly caused the undeveloped sense of one's own gender — perhaps the most fundamental building block in personality development.

The three biggest difficulties in ministering to homosexuals are: (1) refusing to admit that the practice is *abnormal*, (2) refusing to admit that the act is *immoral*, and (3) *not desiring to change* to the heterosexual lifestyle. Only if these three obstacles are removed (that is part of the healing itself) can one proceed to deal with the root cause of the problem.

In technical terms, the condition is one form of an "ego-dystonic" personality. Such a person is in conflict with himself or herself, unsure of the sexual identity (subconsciously), and seeking that assurance through same-sex "bonding," expressed mainly sexually.

Most ministries to homosexuals are established by former homosexuals and have a roughly 80% success rate in leading people to allow the Spirit to release them into heterosexuality. "Desert Stream," one of the 25 groups listed in the central referral agency of Exodus International, presents a very effective revolving 18-week teaching series, with seminars, conferences, support groups, etc., to bring about "a new identity through Jesus Christ."

In terms of the "family healing" principles, it is interesting to note that these groups strive to plug people into church bodies, where they can develop most fully a "family support," to bring them out of a restricting gay subculture into the family of society at large for their security environment.

In general, sexual problems, whether fornication, pornographic imagination, or anything in our sexually-obsessed culture that leads to sexual addiction, can be compared to drug addiction in their wasting effects. Healing in this context is both *behavioral* and *relational* (intra- and interpersonal), aimed at incubating a new identity. This is inner healing—the only healing that will work in relationships *masked* by erotic needs, such as homosexuality. Healing the family tree program is one such form of inner healing.

In one case that I dealt with through the healing of the family tree program (with the Eucharist celebrated for a homosexual not even present and not aware that he was being prayed for), his mother told me that the three above-mentioned difficulties were dissolved overnight, by his own admission.

After two more celebrations of the Eucharist for his healing — again without his knowing it — he completely changed his lifestyle and gained normal sexual orientation. He is now happily married and expecting a child.

Q I heard of a small town in Spain where almost everyone has some freakish physical defect. How can hereditary defects become so widespread?

A The inhabitants of a small town, Cervera de Buitrago, located in the province of Madrid, Spain, almost all have one thing in common: They have at least six fingers and six toes on their extremities. The abnormality is caused by close relatives' intermarriage. This strange phenomenon was featured in a *Ripley's Believe It or Not* book. Since such multiple intermarriages inevitably involve forms of incest, it would not be too far amiss to conclude again that God "brings punishment for the fathers' sins into the laps of their children" (Jer. 32:18; Is. 65:6). Where intermarriage is permitted or encouraged, it may be equivalent to legalized incest.

This bizarre case exemplifies an obvious overlapping of a genetic defect with the punishment of the offspring due to the sins of the parents; the defect is both spiritually and genetically transmitted. This is a moral issue for humans, but not for animals. Hence the divine sanction. While inbreeding among animals usually leads to refinement of pedigree, inbreeding among humans often leads to multiplication of physical and mental defects. There is a divine imperative against incest, and its effects are manifested in the defects transmitted through the family tree. In general, the more serious sins carry more serious genetic disturbances. Even among the very devout but inbreeding Mennonites in La Crete, Canada, one out of every six has the bizarre twitching and jerking disease, Tourette's Syndrome, while in the general population only one in 3,000 has the disorder. "I will bring charges against you, declares the Lord, and against your children's children" (Jer. 2:9).

Q Can you give some examples of physical healings that have occurred in the program for healing the family tree?

A There are countless examples I could give, but perhaps as one example, I could quote this excerpt from a letter received from a nun in northern California several weeks after the healing of the family tree program:

> Some of my uncles and aunts on my father's side tended to have a hunched back. They have all since gone to the Lord, but my father who is still alive has the same problem. My mother always told me as a little girl to walk straight so I wouldn't have rounded shoulders and a hunched back as was common in my family.
>
> For about the past year I have felt a real tightening up of my back and I seemed to be developing the same defect. So at the Eucharist for Healing the Family Tree, I prayed for my back. I also prayed for a clear memory with regard to the things that I do and can't remember later — a defect that I also apparently have inherited. All during the Mass up until Communion time I felt a sharp pain between my shoulders as if something were being readjusted. I also felt very strong movements going on within my head as if someone were rearranging and moving everything within my head. After Communion, both pains disappeared. From that time on, my back felt remarkably free, the tightness had gone and I could see in the mirror that my shoulders and back were much straighter than they had been (every time I went into my room, I checked in the mirror and was delighted with myself).
>
> Regarding my memory, I began to remember in detail the incidents of my growing-up years that I previously had not been able to recall. I noticed also that in teaching my class, my grasp of the subject was much clearer and I could remember the matter that I needed to present to my class.

In the post-Communion period of the Mass, you mentioned by way of prophetic healing (word of knowledge) — that someone present was having a left ankle healed. For several months my left ankle had been paining me severely, especially so as to disturb my sleep at night seriously. I didn't feel anything during the Mass with regard to my ankle, but as I walked out toward the car, I suddenly knew my ankle was healed. The usual stiffness was gone completely. It was very free so that I could move it in every direction. It has remained flexible all these weeks and hasn't bothered me since. Praise be to God!

Another testimonial to the efficacy of the program for healing the family tree comes from a man in Canada who tells us:

For over a year, I have had a problem focusing my eyes. Things seem to be almost perpetually blurry, even though my eye doctor claimed that my glasses fit perfectly. He wasn't sure whether this was an hereditary eye defect. I had my eyes checked twice within the past year and the cause of the blurriness was a mystery to the eye specialist. After Communion in the Healing of the Family Tree Eucharist, you mentioned that you felt that someone present had a "focusing" problem in the eyes and was being healed. I took out my missalette at that point which has very small letters. I find it almost impossible to read normally, but I was surprised to find that I could read it without any difficulty. The clear eyesight has continued to this very day. I still need to use my glasses, but I can now see things with beautiful clarity, Hallelujah!

Q How important is forgiveness in healing the family tree?

A It is of crucial importance.

The Enemy rebels at the thought of any human, living or dead, receiving forgiveness from God, for the Evil One is irreversibly set against receiving forgiveness himself. Also, he knows that giving and receiving forgiveness is essential to healing. For that reason alone, he would do anything to discourage it.

There is a forgiveness that must be extended to the living and the dead from the Lord; also from the living to the dead and from the dead to living. It cannot be overemphasized that giving and receiving forgiveness is an essential part of the healing process, just as it is for receiving an answer to any prayer, inasmuch as it is an indispensable predisposition for healing. Jesus insisted on this double-direction forgiveness before any petition (Mark 11:25). This forgiveness should be derivative of Christ's forgiveness (II Cor. 2:10), applied to us and others through his blood "poured out for many for the *forgiveness* of sins" (Matt. 26:28). Receiving forgiveness from Christ removes guilt; receiving it from others lubricates the healing love-flow. Giving forgiveness removes resentment.

For those within our family tree with whom we have had some conflict during life, whether they are presently living or dead, we must apply the norm of St. Augustine of "hating the sin while loving the sinner." "Hate every trace of their sin while being merciful to them as sinners," says St. Jude (v. 23 LB).

An often overlooked dimension in the healing process is the need for double forgiveness in and through the person of Jesus Christ; we must *not only forgive the dead but through Christ ask the dead to forgive us* for anything by which we may have offended them. In any family, there is need to give and receive apologies to keep optimum family unity. The total act of personal repentance before the Lord for our own sins is of critical importance, but the Bible tells us we must also repent of or confess the sins of our ancestors (Lev. 26:40, etc.). This is essentially helping them to receive the fullness of the remission of the *effects* of sin, even if their sin has already been removed by the blood of Jesus. Thus, we may be said to help those who have traditionally through the centuries been called "poor souls" among the dead. Where there are sinful habits that seem to be repeated from generation to generation, we may more easily confess the sins of our ancestors in conjunction with our own because of the parallel type of sinfulness.

Q Babies cannot commit sin, and cannot open themselves to demonic contamination by occultism, etc. Why then should we pray for any spiritual healing for them in the family tree healing?

A From the earliest period of church history, we find that infants as well as adults undergoing baptism were prayed over with a prayer of exorcism. Certainly infants had no personal sin, but they were presumed to have been contaminated by the effects of original sin and *in that sense* subject to the devil. Psalm 51:5: "Surely I was sinful at birth, sinful from the time my mother conceived me." Psalm 58:3: "Even from birth the wicked go astray; from the womb they are wayward." Genesis 8:21: "Every inclination of his heart is evil from childhood."

These references could apply equally to original sin and the effects of the personal sin inherited from the child's ancestors. Hence, the early custom of the exorcistic prayer at the time of infant baptism. This was a repudiation of the extrinsic evil of demonic forces that could lodge in either original sin inherited from the protoparents, Adam and Eve, or in effects of ancestral sin inherited from any intervening ancestors. The child was thus better prepared to enter the community of the church, God's family. If a child had not received baptism by the time of its death, later on in the community celebrating the Eucharist, the Christ-presence therein was called upon to produce the same effects posthumously.

Q Most people today are aware that an unborn

child can be damaged by alcohol, drugs, nicotine, etc., through the mother. But can a mother (or father) cause emotional damage to an unborn child? If so, are such "transmitted defects" amenable to the "family tree" type of healing?

A An avalanche of medical studies has shown that a pregnant mother can severely damage her unborn child through nicotine or drugs or alcohol; fetal damage by alcohol has come to be known as FAS (Fetal Alcohol Syndrome).

However, less well known is the fact that the unborn child, like a blotter, can absorb both positive and negative *thoughts* from the parents by a kind of embryonic telepathy, for good or for bad, especially in the last two trimesters of pregnancy. Countless experiments have proven that the personality of a child can be to a great extent formed or malformed by the thoughts of the parents directed toward the child during pregnancy. The same is true of prayer, including the family tree healing prayer in the Eucharistic celebration. The child seems to be "prayer-absorptive." As the parents lay hands upon the mother's abdomen and pray for the child, there is often a detectable response, just as there is in the communication of love.

A simple experiment has shown that if a pregnant woman places her right hand on her right side and her left hand on the left side of her abdomen and alternately communicates love imaginatively through either hand, it will cause the child to move in the womb in the direction of the hand that is mediating the love. After a certain period of conditioning, the child will become restless if the love communication is not practiced. The simple withdrawal of love will affect the fetus; much more of course will the thought of rejection or an impending abortion affect the fetus negatively. The parents, especially the mother in this case, are the ancestors that transmit good or bad to the offspring. In this case the mother is the ancestor only one generation distant from the child. This may account for the fact that the effects for good or bad can be empiriometrically detected in the baby. The effects may be equal but not as dramatically detectable when measured through subsequent (third or fourth) generations.

Unborn babies given a "prayer-bath" daily will fare far better emotionally and physically than their brothers and sisters not blessed with this prenatal routine of prayer.

Q **A friend who had participated in a healing of the family tree program told me that it was announced that all deceased babies (stillborn, aborted, etc.) should be named — even posthumously. Why is that required?**

A It is clear that God knows and sees every aspect of the child within the womb: "Before I formed you in the womb I knew you" (Jer. 1:5; cf. Ps. 139:13). Yet, he desires to have us present to him all our children, whether living or dead: aborted, stillborn, or miscarried. We have a role to play in assuring the union of these children with God in the fullest degree — "*Let* the little children come to me, and do not *hinder* them, for the kingdom of God belongs to such as these" (Luke 18:15-16). Children who have been aborted, miscarried, stillborn, or who live only hours, are usually left unnamed and consequently may feel a kind of alienation from society, because naming has much to do with affinitization to the immediate family and the human family in general. It is important in the family healing program in order "not to hinder them" to give names to such deceased children.

In early miscarriages, abortions, etc., when the sex of the child is unknown, male and female names may be assigned as options to be applied according to the respective sex of the child by God or by their own guardian angels who have been assigned to their special care (Ps. 34:7; 91:11; Luke 4:11; Matt. 4:6).

To neglect to name a child is to disregard its human dignity. In this context, Jesus' words are appropriate: "Beware that you don't look down upon a single one of these little children, for I tell you that in heaven their angels have constant access to my Father; and I the Messiah came to save the lost . . . just so, it is not my Father's will that even one of these little ones should perish" (Matt. 18:10-14). The Lord's love for little children, living or dead, should inspire us to include them in our special prayers as persons within our family tree who may need a healing on this side of the grave or on the other side.

Above all, a mutual parent-child love, or ancestor-descendant love, is the optimum ambience for healing the family tree. "Children's children are a crown to the aged, and parents are the pride of their children" (Prov. 17:6).

Q **Of all ancestral influences on a child, it would seem that the greatest would be from the mother who is closest to the child before birth, and usually for years afterwards. Can she do anything by way of "preventative" healing of her child?**

A Certainly. The prenatal and postnatal effects of the mother and father on the child have been categorized through countless experiments and surveys to show that *ideal* mothers have a high ratio of physically and mentally healthy children. For example, a study by Dr. Gerhard Rottmann of the University of Salzburg, Austria, found that women with negative attitudes during pregnancy had the most devastating medical problems during pregnancy and the highest rate of premature low-weight, emotionally disturbed babies. It was found that the "ambivalent mothers" — those who are outwardly happy but had inner fears or regrets about pregnancy—subconsciously rejected the children, whose spiritual sensor picked up this unconscious ambivalence. The result was a large number of behavioral and gastrointestinal problems in the babies.

A final group called "confused mothers" were ones who had careers or other seemingly legitimate reasons for not wanting to be pregnant but inwardly really desired a baby.

At birth the children of these mothers had an unusually high degree of apathy, and were physically and emotionally lethargic, with bland personalities.

The father too has been shown to have an influence on the unborn child, according to the studies of Dr. Thomas Verny of Toronto, Canada. The quality of a woman's relationship with her husband was shown to have a decisive effect on the unborn child. Confirming this, another study by Dr. Monika Lukesche of Constantine University in Frankfurt, West Germany, involving 2,000 pregnant women, found that the woman's relationship with her spouse was equal or almost equal in importance to the attitude toward her unborn child in determining the emotional and physical health of the child. In a study of 1300 children by Dr. Dennis Scott, it was found — as pointed out earlier — that a woman who regarded her marriage as relatively unhappy had a 237% greater risk of bearing a psychologically or physically damaged child than a woman who felt she was in a secure marriage relationship.

The implications from these reports, in terms of "preventative" healing, are quite obvious.

Q In coping with deep-seated defects that seem to come from the Evil One or are reinforced by him, why does it seem to be such a difficult process?

A We must remember that deliverance is not *necessarily* an instantaneous process. Just as disease is not acquired instantaneously and is not cured instantaneously, so also the forces of evil do not inveigh upon us instantaneously and are not usually evicted instantaneously, although this can happen in very powerful forms of deliverance — particularly when demonic influence has been of only short duration prior to the deliverance prayer. (Mark 1:26 is an example of the immediate eviction of the spirit by the overwhelming power and faith of Jesus.)

We must also keep in mind that deliverance is a

cooperative activity, like marriage; God will not deliver us without our cooperation, and we cannot deliver ourselves without his grace. If it is a matter of being affected through habitual sin, we may compare it to a cancer; if we attack it while it is small where it is relatively hard to see, it is easy to defeat, but if we wait until the cancer has spread and its effects are visible, it is more difficult to cure. Lao Tzu, the ancient Chinese sage, expressed it with his Chinese wisdom: "When a disease is hard to see, it is easy to cure, but when it becomes easy to see, it is hard to cure."

We have to start with the sin in terms of its origin as a thought. There is no sinful act that is not preceded by a sinful thought, or at least a temptation in the form of a thought. If we attack the evil at the very outset while it is still in the thought process, it is much easier to control. This is why Paul said, "Bring every *thought* into captivity to Christ" (II Cor. 10:5). "Resist the devil and he will flee" (James 4:7).

Q **I can see how parents can affect their own children by a powerful influence. But does such influence extend to nieces, nephews, siblings, etc., in non-vertical lineage within the family tree?**

A It is true that effects within a one-step generational relationship can be measured quite accurately, but one wonders to what extent a more distant relationship with similar adverse environments or favorable environments may affect a given person. For instance, to what extent could grandparents influence a grandchild telepathically? Or what inter-influence would a sibling (especially in identical twins) have on a child? Or what influence would an uncle and/or aunt have on a child by their own behavior? Could the emotional effects transmitted in what seems to be a kind of inherited familial telepathy be the basis for ailments for physical sickness, emotional debility such as depressions, and perhaps even spiritual weaknesses such as anger, hostility, and hatred? Could such a relationship have its effect in terms of disintegrating the personality? Would it not be possible for God to permit the failures of anyone within the family lineage to produce a kind of inherited contamination, weakness, or limitation within which demonic forces could lodge — perhaps conditioning, if not the genetic structure, at least the neurological structure by engramming the brain to be preconditioned for behavior patterns manifested through life?

The precise means through which the contamination takes place and the means by which it is transmitted may elude us in the present period of investigation and theological inquiry, but we do know that as a pragmatic point the healing prayer, particularly when Eucharistically oriented, has a powerful effect upon the entire lineage of the family tree detectable as a multi-directional healing within the three- to four-generation span mentioned so often in Scripture.

Q **When we suspect demonic involvement in members of our family, how should we proceed?**

A Cautiously — and with professional help when necessary, especially when analyzing persons who are *suspected* of being under demonic control, to determine whether they are suffering from depressive psychosis or a form of schizophrenia, perhaps even a form of organic psychosis, or some other psychiatric disorder such as an uprising from one's own subconscious that needs to undergo catharsis. Even when such ailments are diagnosed, we should not presume that there is no involvement of the demonic. There may be both a natural and a preternatural activity involved. There could be both a psychological disturbance or, superimposed upon that disorder, a demonic force that may manifest itself sporadically. We must look particularly for involvement either in drugs or in the occult, which most often opens the door to evil spirits; also where there has been activity of a bizarre sexual nature.

Within the occult, some practices are more deleterious,

more dangerous spiritually, physically, and emotionally. For instance, astrology is certainly a dangerous practice but nowhere nearly as dangerous as Satan worship. Within the range of occultic practices, things that should be looked upon as spawning demonic intervention would include astrology, the use of ouija boards, consulting mediums, engaging in séances, practicing fortunetelling or consulting fortunetellers, using tarot cards, holding to reincarnation doctrines, belonging to Eastern religions that accept Christ as a prophet but not as divine (I John 4:1-2), consulting *curanderos* (folk healers), practicing voodoo, palmistry, numerology, "metaphysics," reading tea leaves, *santaria*, cultic practices, Cabala, and being the victim of a hex or curse or employing it against others.

The prayer for relieving such bondage must involve the exercise of consummate faith in Jesus (Mark 9:23), and spiritual maturity reflected in prayer and fasting (v. 29). The power of the blood of Jesus must be called upon to "cover" the victims of such demonic activity, as well as the perpetrators if induced by other persons, living or dead. Protection over the ones who do the praying should be attained by the same means — by calling upon the blood of Jesus — as well as the militant angels, particularly St. Michael the Archangel, the archenemy of Satan (Jude 9; Dan. 10:13; 10:21; 12:1; Rev. 12:7).

Even when there has been no *direct* involvement with the occult or demonic activities, there can be indirect spinoffs that can affect the children or relatives within the family tree of persons who have been involved in this — particularly if they are the victims of a hex or curse from a person involved in the occult. It is helpful to denounce not only the works of the devil but also the occult practices of our forefathers, as we submit ourselves to Jesus Christ.

This particular methodology of deliverance is suggested by Dr. Kurt Koch, who has dealt with over ten thousand cases of occult bondage and has frequently found in these, repeated patterns of inherited disorders moving through successive generations (*Occult Bondage and*

Deliverance, Kurt Koch, Grand Rapids, Michigan, Kregel, 1970). He also has found great power in the Eucharist to effect the deliverance, and in maintaining the clearance, since it provides the strength for spiritual resistance against demonic influences and attacks. He encourages various churches to make the Eucharist more available to persons who have this need.

In confronting the Evil One, it is possible to see at times that the suffering of the living is in fact the direct work of the Enemy who tries to keep us disturbed physically as well as emotionally. The spiritual attacks are the worst, such as despair and thoughts of suicide.

"So be self-controlled and alert; your enemy, the devil, prowls around like a roaring lion looking for someone to devour. Resist him standing firm in the faith because you know that your brothers [members of immediate or extended family tree] in the world are undergoing the same kind of suffering" (I Pet. 5:8-9).

The struggle we are engaging in is fierce, and our strategy is clear: "Be strong in the Lord and in his mighty power. Put on the full armor of God so that you can take your stand against the devil's schemes. For our struggle is not against flesh and blood, but against the powers of this dark world and against the spiritual forces of evil in the heavenly realms. Therefore, put on the full armor of God so that when the day of evil comes, you may be able to stand your ground, and after you have done everything, to stand. Stand firm then, with the belt of truth buckled around your waist, with the breastplate of righteousness in place and with your feet fitted with the readiness that comes from the gospel of peace. In addition to this, take up the shield of faith, with which you can extinguish all the flaming arrows of the evil one. Take the helmet of salvation and the sword of the Spirit, which is the Word of God. Pray in the Spirit on all occasions with all kinds of prayers and requests. With this in mind, be alert and always keep on praying for all the saints [that is, the immediate or extended family tree]" (Eph. 6:10-18).

When we pray the last petition of the Lord's Prayer —
"deliver us from evil," we are praying for deliverance from
every form of evil — bodily, psychological, and spiritual. It
is obviously God's desire to free us, to deliver us completely, or Jesus would not have taught us to pray that prayer
of supplication.

Q **Somewhere I heard of a distinction between
familiar spirits and familial spirits. Is this distinction relevant to healing the family tree?**

A Yes. The term "familiar spirit" is found in the King
James version and seldom found in other versions, but as
it is used in Leviticus, Deuteronomy, I Samuel, II Kings, I
and II Chronicles, and Isaiah, it seems to be a spirit contact or spirit guide, with which a medium or spiritist is
"familiar." This close association with the spirit world as a
means of obtaining arcane knowledge rather than from the
Lord (Deut. 13:3) is forbidden, along with all the other
forms of occultism (18:9-12).

However, the secondary meaning of "familiar spirits"
refers to those evil spirits that are "familiar" with our
weaknesses and deep-seated tendencies. In accordance
with the well-known principle of demonology, such demons
seek out, or are assigned to, the "weakest link in the chain"
of our personality.

For instance, a spirit of anger may become superimposed on a natural tendency toward irritability or impatience; the spirit of envy or jealousy or selfish ambition
may be superimposed on any corresponding behavior pattern (James 3:14-16); a spirit of resentment may be superimposed on our refusal to forgive (Eph. 4:26-27; II Cor.
3:11). The characteristic of weak faith may be overlayed by
"deceiving spirits" (I Tim. 4:1); a spirit of faithlessness may
superimpose itself on one who maintains an unhealthy
skepticism (Luke 22:31).

The *familial* spirits, on the other hand, are those which
are transmitted through the family line — the lineage;

these seem to be the spirits that "hold" us in the bondage inherited from our ancestors' sins, such as a "spirit of infirmity" (Luke 13:11), that frustrate all medical efforts at getting cured. This distinction is important as a basic concept within the science of demonology and has some pastoral implications, especially in the healing ministry.

Q In the deliverance dimension of the healing, is it enough to be delivered from evil thoughts, that is, temptations?

A The kinds of deliverance that are often referred to as forms of "self-deliverance" are simply coming against the powers of evil that may attack us from within or without, either self-engendered thoughts or obsessively imposed thoughts from powers of evil. We must be careful not to submit to "freedom of thought," which is a false freedom through which we could easily surrender our thoughts to the power of evil.

Christ is to be the Lord of all creation "so that in everything he might have the supremacy" (Col. 1:18). We must give him the total supremacy, beginning with the most interior part of our being, namely our will; and after that our thoughts, the fruit of the intellect; and from that all of the relationships within our world, beginning with the most proximate ones within the family tree. "Out of the heart come evil thoughts . . . these are what make a man unclean" (Matt. 15:19-20).

Starting with deliverance of thought, we move to deliverance of word and action. This may take time, depending upon the degree to which the evil has been rooted within us.

Q Does ancestral sin affect only persons, or can it also affect things used by or belonging to the descendants?

A There is even some indication in Scripture that pollution of the environment or of the food and water is the result of ancestral sin (cf. Jer. 9:14-15; cf. Ezek. 20:15-27; Deut. 28:24). There is a hint that even national defense may be impaired because of ancestral sin (Amos 2:4-5). Certainly the cattle of the infected progeny can be affected, as well as one's crops (Deut. 28:18, 30, 39, 42, etc.). Possessions will be stolen (v. 31), etc.

All objects that have been used for occultic or spiritualist activities should be destroyed, for they tend to attract evil spirits to places where they are. I have seen this happen even with astrological symbols. (Astrology itself is regarded by the Bible as an abomination of the Lord.)

If there is poltergeist activity, manifested by furniture moving by itself, various noises, etc., and the identity of the person or persons who may be haunting the place is not known, then the prayer should be offered for whoever may need the prayer, including not only the deceased persons, but those who have been tormented by this activity. It is possible that demons, not disquieted souls of the departed, are causing the disturbance. In any case, all those present at such a prayer or Eucharist should commit themselves to the Lord and put themselves under the protection of his precious blood, asking that they be surrounded with protecting angels, and that the Holy Spirit's presence may dispel the evil spirit's presence through the liberating prayer.

Q Where do we find deliverance?

A Ultimately, in the healing wounds of Christ. The ancient prayer *Anima Christi* is often used exorcistically with the phrase: "In thy wounds hide me." That is where the devil dares not come, for he dreads the precious blood. The Israelites were protected from the angel of death only by the *blood* of the sacrificial lamb on the doorposts. Such households or families were protected by the Blood of the Lamb (Exod. 12:23). Our deliverance is in the Blood of the Lamb (Rev. 7:14). Our immediate contact with that blood is in the presence of that blood shed symbolically in the Eucharist, the ideal milieu for deliverance in healing oneself and/or one's family tree. This is explicitly stated in I Peter 1:19.

Q **Precisely how are negative traits transmitted to subsequent generations such as we might find in criminally inclined families?**

A If negative traits are transmitted even by a kind of spiritual heredity, it would not seem illogical to expect that there would be a "vehicle" for transmitting them. Studies along this line in the field of criminology may give a clue to other negative traits of a non-criminal nature regarding their transmissibility.

A growing number of researchers argue that genetic, biological, chemical, and dietary factors are major contributors to crime. If this is true, it would have a significant effect on the crime rate, because ten percent of lawbreakers may be responsible for half of all serious infractions; consequently, diverting even a small percentage of them from criminal careers would have considerable effect on the crime rate. In the book *Crime and Human Nature*, written by Harvard University professors James Wilson and Richard Herrnstein, it is concluded that biology can predispose a person to criminal behavior. Although this has caused controversy with traditional criminologists who say it is simplistic, it is worth considering for our purposes as representative of transmitted defects in personality. Let's consider some of the possible "vehicles" that *may* be involved in this process:

1. *Brain irregularities may play a role.* Studying violent youths in Connecticut, psychiatrist Dorothy Lewis of New York University concluded that nearly half had suffered "major neurological impairments" such as seizures. Other researchers report that many criminals have abnormal electrical activity in the brain.

2. *Chemical imbalances may be a source of the problem.*

A Chicago chemist, William Walsh, has classified four types of crime-prone persons, based on amounts of certain metals such as cadmium, magnesium, copper, and zinc that are found in hair analysis. He theorizes that either over-supply or shortages of the substances may somehow prompt the brain to cause aggressive behavior. There has been some limited success in applying his theory by eliminating chemical abnormalities.

3. *Other researchers point to diet as a cause of crime.* Delinquents in several institutions were given altered diets to deemphasize sugar and include more nutrients; this resulted in a fifty percent drop in violence in the institutions.

4. *Environment plays an important role in the forming of delinquents.* Dr. Lewis (as in No. 1 above) notes that three-fourths of delinquents that she studied had been abused. "Coupling of neurological or psychiatric disorders with histories of being brutalized can create incredibly violent persons," she says.

5. *Influences of heredity.* Most significantly in one project, psychologist Sarnoff Mednick of the University of Southern California studied *adopted* children in an effort to sort out influences of heredity and environment. He found that youths whose biological parents were chronic offenders were *three times* as likely to be arrested repeatedly as those whose parents had clean records. The increased crime rate was related to the biological parents rather than the adoptive parents. Psychiatrist C. Robert Cloninger of Washington University in St. Louis says that "criminal behavior is essentially a disease."

Almost all of these analysts stress that there is *no proof* that heredity or biology makes crime inevitable. The free will is always a possible contravening factor, except in cases of severely impaired or psychopathic criminals. So, generally speaking, one could not impute criminal activity to biological or genetic factors or even dietary factors *alone*. However, these factors may well be the underlying *predispositions* for transmitted criminal behavior and similar underlying predispositions may account for other negative behavior of a non-criminal nature. These predispositions may well fit into the plan of God's permissive will, by divine providence, to execute the biblical prophecy that "the sins of the parents will be visited upon the children to the third and fourth generation."

Feeling "victimized" by a bad family background, a defective offspring of sinful parents or ancestors may harbor the musings of Jeremiah (12:6): "Your own family . . . have betrayed you," for he had felt betrayed by his own family. It is obvious that the medical and psychiatric professions have an obligation to continue studying and treating the underlying predispositions in order to minimize such negative behavior or, for that matter, to minimize any physical defects that may be transmitted through genetic or any other predisposition. However, just as physical sickness may be treated through natural means such as doctors, surgery, and pharmaceuticals — as well as by supernatural intervention through prayer and the charism of healing — so also these transmitted effects should be approached in the same way using every natural means as well as supernatural means (Sir. 38).

Q **I am embarrassed to say that I'm ashamed of some of my relatives — more than I'm concerned about them. I guess I pray for them, not specifically, but in my general prayer of lifting up to God all for whom I should pray. Do they benefit from my "aloof form of prayer"?**

A A genealogist asked a potential customer whether he had ever had any of his ancestors traced. The man responded, "Well, I had an old uncle who was traced by the FBI all the way to New York before they got him."

Not all of the "skeletons in the family closet" are lovable, but the ones hardest to love are the ones who need it the most. Likewise, the ones who are hardest to pray for are the ones who need prayer the most. God may "bring to mind" a skeleton in your family closet precisely to lead you to pray specifically for that person's needs. Following such promptings can lead to some amazing conversions and healings.

Remember, a "black sheep" is not a "goat." Consider how despicable persons like Nebuchadnezzar turned to the Lord (Dan. 5:21), or the terrorist Saul who became the great St. Paul. God's converting and healing power should never be underestimated.

Q **A friend of mine has a beautiful family that I much admire. I asked her what her secret was, and she pointed to a plaque on her hallway entrance that read: "Jesus is the Head of this Household." How can we make him the head of ours?**

A Start with the realization that "Christ is the head" (Col. 1:18). Then, by an informal prayer, or even a formal "installation" ceremony with the family together, consecrate yourselves to his headship.

The prototype of this ceremony was at the time of the first Passover in Egypt, when instructions were given by the Lord that there be a "lamb for *each household* [family]" (Exod. 12:3). One member of each household was to sprinkle the blood on the doorposts, thus ensuring the safety of all within that house. "When I see the blood I will *pass over you*" (Exod. 12:13) (hence the term "passover"). This blood covenant for our households has never been revoked. The lamb that is used in the new dispensation is the "Lamb of God" — "Christ our Passover" (I Cor. 5:7).

Another family covenant had been made four hundred years previous, between God and Abram: "Between me and you and your descendants after you for the generations to come, to be your God and the God of your descendants after you" (Gen. 17:7). *This covenant includes us today,* since Paul reminds us in Galatians 3:29: "If you belong to Christ, then you are Abraham's seed and heirs according to the promise." God told Abram, "In you *all* the families of the earth will be blessed" (Gen. 12:3). If we can through faith lay hold of that promise, we can have access to incredible expressions of divine mercy and healing not only for close relatives at home, but also for the more distant ones.

"These things [Old Testament events] happened to them as examples and were written down . . . *for us* on whom the fulfillment of the ages has come" (I Cor. 10:11).

Q **At present I am the only one in our family that is interested in healing our family tree. Am I presumptuous to attempt a family healing by myself?**

A Many families and groups have been saved or healed by one faith-filled individual. God offered to save the entire city of Sodom for even ten good representatives (Gen. 18:32).

Noah "when warned about things not yet seen . . . built an ark to save his family by *his* faith . . . *he* became heir of the righteousness that comes by faith" (Heb. 11:7). Noah thus became an instrument, as did Abraham, of the salvation of the members of his family. "Go into the ark *you and your whole family* because I have found *you* righteous *in this generation*" (Gen. 7:1).

The priest Aaron made atonement for "himself and for his whole household" (Lev. 16:6) by his sin offering.

This magnificent truth is not reserved only to Old Testament personages that prefigure the New Testament times. For within our own New Testament age also we find the covenant applied. For instance, the angel promised Cornelius that Peter would provide him with a message "through which *you and all your household* will all be saved" (Acts 11:14). Paul and Silas told the Philippian jailer, "Believe in the Lord Jesus and you will be saved *you and your household*; then they spoke the word of the Lord to him and to all the others *in his house*." Thus, even one member of a family may be the instrument of God in the salvation of all the others in that family tree or household.

Q Can my faith, such as it is, make up for the lack of faith in my relatives, in procuring healings for them?

A The men who brought a paralytic to Jesus for healing (Matthew 9:2) were probably members of his family. It was when Jesus saw *their* faith that he healed the paralytic and forgave his sins.

Thus, we see that we have access to this power of "vicarious faith" in the healing of both the body and the soul. We know that by intercessory prayer we can bring about a spiritual healing to those who have sinned less seriously: "If anyone sees his brother commit a sin that does not lead to death, he should pray and God will give him life. I refer to those whose sin does not lead to death" (I John 5:16).

The ordinance for physical and emotional healing, as well as spiritual healing given us in James 5:14-16, shows that the prayer of faith by the elders obtains an effect, "The prayer offered in faith will make the sick person well . . . if he has sinned, he will be forgiven . . . *pray for each other* so that you may be healed." The next sentence is particularly significant: "The prayer of a righteous man is powerful and effective."

If a member of our family is in a coma, we tend to pray more earnestly for that person than if there were only a minor trauma experienced. By the same reason we should pray more earnestly for a loved one in a "spiritual coma" ("blinded" Paul calls it in II Cor. 4:4).

The readers of this book probably have a deep concern for the spiritual, physical, and emotional welfare of their loved ones. I feel that God will furnish these readers with an opportunity to be "first partakers of the fruits" (II Tim. 2:6) before instrumenting these effects to the members of their family tree. I presume the readers have a very clear understanding of the truth that "God is patient, not wanting anyone to perish, but everyone to come to repentance" (II Pet. 3:9). That states the will of God very clearly, and

143

any request made in accordance with God's will he promises to hear (I John 5:14).

Q I seem to be more concerned for my children and grandchildren than for my parents and ancestors. I feel that my prayers can help my offspring more than my ancestors. Am I right?

A Vis-à-vis our *descendants* as distinguished from our *ancestors*, God's word is full of covenant promises, any one of which would be sufficient for claiming one's children's salvation or healing for; "the man that fears the Lord, God will instruct him in the way chosen for him; he will spend his days in prosperity, and his *descendants* will inherit the land"—(that is, retain their family portion in the promised land as symbolic of their spiritual inheritance) (Ps. 25:12-13; cf. 37:9, 11, 18, 22, 29, 34; 69:36; Is. 60:21). *"His children* will be mighty in the land; the generation of the upright will be blessed. Wealth and riches are in his house and his righteousness endures forever" (Ps. 112:2-3). "For their own good and the good of the *children after them* . . . I will never stop doing good to them and I will inspire them to fear me so that they will never turn away from me. I will rejoice in doing them good and will assuredly plant them in this land with all my heart and soul" (Jer. 3:39-41).

One can even claim the outpouring of the Holy Spirit (the baptism in the Spirit) on one's descendants, "I will pour out my spirit on *your offspring*, and my blessings on *your descendants"* (Is. 44:3). This covenant promise is further explicated in Isaiah 59:21: "This is my covenant. . . . My Spirit who is on you and my words that I have put in your mouth will not depart from your mouth, or from the mouths of *your children, or from the mouths of their descendants* from this time on and forever, says the Lord." Peter even promised in his post-Pentecostal sermon that the baptism in the Spirit could be claimed for one's grandchildren (Acts 2:39): "The promise is for you and *your children*, and for all who are afar off."

Countless other blessings are offered by God's magnanimity, summarized by Moses' prayer found in Psalm 90: "Lord, you have been our refuge from one generation to the next." "They will not . . . bear children doomed to misfortune; for they will be a people blessed by the Lord, they and their *descendants* with them" (Is. 65:23). "All your sons will be taught by the Lord, and great will be your *children's* peace" (Is. 54:13). "For the Lord your God will circumcise your hearts and the hearts of your descendants, so that you may love him with all your heart and with all your soul, and live" (Deut. 30:6).

If you have ever felt the Lord "circumcising your heart to love him more fully," it may give you faith to believe that through your intercession the same could happen for your children and their children.

It is so easy to become a child of the covenant promise. We see parents struggling and making great sacrifices to give their children all the material and educational advantages possible, but they so often neglect to secure for them the best advantage of all. What a beautiful world we would have if everyone, like Timothy, was raised in an atmosphere of great faith, transmitted apparently from his grandmother, Lois, through his mother, Eunice (II Tim. 1:5), and was trained in holy Scripture from his earliest childhood (3:15).

Q **Just how extensive is the "family tree"? Who can be included under the protection and healing umbrella in this program?**

A You may feel that your children are spiritually safe and perhaps also healthy, but you may find that your siblings or parents or uncles or aunts may be lacking something in their own personal fulfillment. A review of the story of Rahab in the second and sixth chapters of Joshua may enlighten you as to how God can reach in those directions also. Rahab put out the scarlet thread which was a prototype of the blood of Christ (Heb. 9:19-20) and saved her father, mother, and brothers and sisters and all of their possessions (Josh. 2:13; 6:22-23). Even though she had been a prostitute up to that time, God inscribed her name in the hall of fame for the heroes of faith in Hebrews 11.

Someone may ask, "How broad is the promise of the 'Blood Covenant' in protecting relatives?" The answer is, "As many persons as you place under it." Rahab quite probably arranged through her intercession to obtain the protection of her in-laws, nieces, nephews, uncles, aunts, etc., in that night of escape. Thus the healing and protective covenant can reach to your "extended family," such as your neighbors, fellow parishioners, or members of your community with whom you associate (cf. Exod. 12:4).

Even flocks and herds were included in the "promise of protection" (Exod. 12:32), so there seems to be no reason why we could not claim similar protection for our pets and our material possessions such as cars and stereos — anything that could be included in that simple, "All that they have" (Josh. 2:13).

Besides the natural relatives which could be placed under the covenant of salvation and healing, one could apply it to one's "spiritual children," which God has promised us (Is. 54:1-3), particularly those who may need prayers in a special way (Ps. 142:4), and even those who get on our nerves or make life miserable for us, for whom we therefore have a *special* obligation to pray (Matt. 5:44).

Q Little is mentioned about "spouses" in the family tree healing sessions. I would like a spiritual healing for my spouse, who does not practice any religion. Is this type of service appropriate for that?

A In I Peter 3:1-2 we are reminded that if a spouse does not obey the word, that person may be saved even without the word if the behavior of the other spouse is used as an intercessory power and as an influence for conversion. In the course of my ministry I have seen a considerable number of wives bring their husbands to the Lord — and vice versa — by employing this principle that Peter states. I have seen marriages on the verge of divorce turned into second honeymoons by virtue of the faith-filled application of that principle.

Recently, I saw an elderly man converted on his deathbed after his wife had prayed for years for his conversion with no sign of success during all the years of her prayer, until only a few hours before the man's death, when he accepted the Lord as his Savior and repented. His death was one of the most beautiful I have ever seen.

Q What if some of my loved ones are lost? Wouldn't a healing prayer be unavailing for them?

A Faithful Christians often express fears that some of their relatives living or dead, are "lost," having repeated the "detestable practices of their fathers" (Ezek. 20:4). The answer to that is in Romans 3:3-4: "What if some did not have faith? Will their lack of faith nullify God's faithfulness? Not at all! Let God be true, and every man a liar. As it is written: 'so that you may be proved right when you speak and prevail when you judge.' "

God's word transcends our limited view of situations. When God showed displeasure with Moses because he failed to put his children under the Israelite covenant by circumcision (Exod. 4:24-26), can we say that he would be pleased with us if, presuming it useless for wayward relatives, we failed to put them under the blood covenant that he has provided?

"God sets the lonely in families" (Ps. 68:6). Perhaps God has chosen you to "set" you into a negligent family to plead for the rest of them. Perhaps he has commissioned you to "stand between the dead and the living" (Num. 16:48), as Aaron did to stop the plague. When you have become strong enough in faith to believe with "no doubts" (Mark 11:23), believing for the healing and salvation of your loved ones, then God will release a torrent of graces from heaven upon them.

Perhaps you have a youngster in your family who resists any Christian influence and never attends church. You might ask yourself if you are looking to God to save him, or to the church services as the essential means of his salvation. It might behoove you to regard what the Lord said to the Israelites when he fulfilled his promise to them and their forefathers, namely, that they were to "give over to the Lord the first offspring of every womb . . . redeem every first-born among your sons" (Exod. 13:12-13). (Humans were to be consecrated to the Lord by their life, not by their death, as animals were in sacrifice [cf. Rom. 12:1].)

God is able to save persons even if they neglect the biblical command "to attend church meetings" (Heb. 10:25). Even if your children are "disobedient to parents, unthankful and unholy" (II Tim. 3:1-2), still grace can match their obstinacy in rebellion: "I will contend with those [the enemy] who contend with you, and *your children I will save*" (Is. 49:25).

Many disappointed parents do not avail themselves of the consolation in the promises of God's word when the faith condition is fulfilled: "The loving kindness of the Lord is from everlasting to everlasting, to those who reverence him; his salvation is to the children's children of those who are faithful to his covenant and remember to obey him!" (Ps. 103:17-18 LB). "He who fears the Lord has a secure fortress, and for his children it will be a refuge" (Prov. 14:26). "Blessed is the man who fears the Lord . . . his children will be mighty in the land. The generation of the upright will be blessed" (Ps. 112:2). "Blessed are all who fear the Lord, who walk in his ways . . . your wife will be like a fruitful vine within your house; your sons will be like olive shoots around your table, thus is the man blessed who fears the Lord" (Ps. 128:1-4). Moses told Pharaoh (a prototype of Satan) that "he [Moses] would go out with young and old, with sons and daughters, with flocks and herds to celebrate" (Exod. 10:9). He even demanded that the livestock be released to go (v. 26). God will likewise back us up in our demand for total release from the power of Satan of all members of our family, even deceased ancestors: "He shows mercy to our ancestors" (Luke 1:72).

Q Are there any conditions required to assure that real healing will take place in my family as I engage in this healing prayer?

A Yes, there are. And the more perfectly you fulfill the conditions, the deeper and more lasting will be the healing itself.

The *first condition* for drawing God's power down in fulfillment of his promise and covenant is to dedicate ourselves totally to the Lord to obtain the full inheritance, as Joshua and Caleb did for the benefit of themselves and their children (Deut. 1:36-38). St. James reminds us (5:16) that "the prayer of a righteous man is powerful and effective." "The eyes of the Lord are on the righteous and his ears are attentive to their prayer" (I Pet. 3:12, quoting Ps. 34). Noah and his family were saved because the Lord said, "I have found you righteous in this generation" (Gen. 7:1). By keeping the Lord's decrees and commands, "It will go well with you and your children after you" (Deut. 4:40).

Contrariwise: "If you ignore the law of your God, I will also ignore your children" (Hosea 4:6). A halfhearted worldly Christian, one who does not really walk closely with the Lord and who is not truly prayerful cannot lay claim to these or any other promises in God's word. But those who yield their will to the Lord in all things will find their faith "growing ever stronger and become better acquainted with the Lord Jesus Christ" (II Pet. 3:18). They will have ever greater reliance on his saving and healing power for themselves and more faith to bring about the fulfillment for the spiritual and physical needs of loved ones.

The Lord gave Moses a command to use part of the dough made from the first of the harvested grain (firstfruits) consecrated to the Lord, and this in turn consecrated the whole batch. This process was to be continued "through the generations to come" (Num. 15:17-21). Paul referred to this in Romans 11:16, "If part of the dough offered as firstfruits is holy, then the whole batch is holy. If the root is holy, so are the branches." By becoming truly holy as the consecrated part of the dough offered as firstfruits, you will leaven the entire family through your own holiness. If you as the root of the family tree are holy, so will be your offspring or branches of your family tree.

As the *second condition*, we must ask God's help to grow in faith as we ask God's help for the members of the family. Make a definite claim for the healing and the salvation of all relatives and acquaintances, naming them specifically, if possible.

Let the spirit lead you as to how you are to pray. Particular Scripture passages may come to mind that seem to fit individual persons in your family, that you may lay claim to, for there is power in the word of God applied prayerfully this way. Some people are led, like Esther (8:3), "with pleading and weeping"; others "with groans that words cannot express" (Rom. 8:26); praying for each person individually that comes to mind; others still are led to exercise a calm, serene but very strong faith that stands on God's word. In whatever form of prayer you use, remember that it is the same Spirit who has pledged to bring about the salvation of these persons who is leading you in the manner in which you claim it.

The *third condition* is to stand firm in faith and believe God, no matter what the circumstances, "walking in the footsteps of the faith that our father Abraham had" (Rom. 4:12). Stand firm, even if your loved ones seem to relapse even more. Don't focus so much on the problem as on the divine problem-solver, Jesus. Believe in him and praise him for their salvation and healing.

The more difficult the test you are put through, the greater the victory. Their present negative behavior or illness has nothing to do with God's keeping his part of the covenant; it is only a call to deeper faith on your part, which God incidentally would use also to sanctify yourself. Keep the blood of the Lamb ever before your eyes in faith, for the Lord has said, "When I see the blood . . . " the promise would be fulfilled. Resolve with Joshua (24:15), "As for me and my household, we will serve the Lord." Lean on God's promise: "I will not violate my covenant or alter what my lips have uttered" (Ps. 89:34). Reaffirm your faith with the words of Paul, Acts 27:25: "I have faith in God that it will happen just as he told me."

The *fourth condition*: in raising young children you must "bring them up in the training and instruction of the Lord" (Eph. 6:4), beginning at an early age. "Train a child in the way he should go, and when he is old, he will not turn from it" (Prov. 22:6; cf. Is. 38:19), "spurring them on toward love and good deeds" (Heb. 10:24; cf. Col. 3:21; Sir. 4:35); in a lighthearted, joyous atmosphere. "You should be like one big happy family, full of sympathy toward each other, loving one another with tender hearts and humble minds" (I Pet. 3:8 LB).

It is important to lay a good foundation for young children by teaching them God's word (cf. II Tim. 3:15). "Let the word of Christ dwell in you richly as you teach and admonish with all wisdom" (Col. 3:16). "Teach God's laws to your children talking about them when you sit at home, when you walk along the road, when you lie down, and when you get up . . . so that your days and the days of your children may be many" (Deut. 11:19-20).

Eli watched his sons become spiritual outcasts because he failed to correct them (I Sam. 3:13), while Abraham on the other hand commanded his children and his household after him to "keep the way of the Lord" (Gen. 18:19). Real love for your children, like God's love for us, will not be over-permissive nor overprotective, and will apply discipline properly, and early enough to be formative (Prov. 19:18; cf. 13:24; 22:13-15).

Perhaps you may respond to all this by saying that in your case it is too late, that the children have grown beyond the point of obediential control at this time. In this event be sure to confess your negligence that may have induced this situation, confessing first to the Lord and then to the youngsters themselves. Then plead the promises of the Lord based upon the covenant mentioned above. It may be that God will have to deal with them more pointedly and more rigorously to compensate for your neglect in training at the proper time.

The *fifth condition* is closely connected with the fourth, and one in which there is frequent failure to implement. You must place your loved ones on the altar of God's will and leave them there, for "it is the altar that sanctifies the gift" (Matt. 23:19). Entrust them to his care, knowing that he will not afflict them unnecessarily. "Though he brings grief, he will show compassion, so great is his unfailing love. For he does not willingly bring affliction or grief to the children of men" (Lam. 3:32-33).

For those who turn to him with all their hearts, especially for such a noble petition, there is great consolation in the words of James 5:19-20, "My brothers, if one of you should wander from the truth, and someone should bring him back, remember this: whoever turns a sinner from the error of his way will save him from death and cover over a multitude of sins" (cf. I Pet. 4:8).

Q **Why not use medical treatment, good nutrition, etc., to circumvent or correct the physical effects of ancestral sin in the descendants, instead of a healing prayer?**

A Your question is more complicated than you might imagine, and it also opens up some interesting theological conjectures. Look, for instance, at the problem of alcoholism, which arises partly from a maladaptive lifestyle, and partly from one's genes, like shyness or coronary heart disease. (One out of three alcoholics has a close relative who is alcoholic, reflecting the genetic feature; yet environmentally, lack of childhood ego-strength and sense of competence are predominant — the "nature-nurture" confluence.) Glimmers of hope from the medical front come from the discovery that *100% of all alcoholics* have a deficiency in a liver enzyme called acetaldehyde dehydrogenase, and most are deficient in adenylate cyclase and monoamine oxidase. Yet some very few people with these deficiencies do not become alcoholics. Is this due to wholesome environment, parental influence motivating one to avoid addiction, in spite of a genetic handicap? Also, do such preventative measures make healing prayer unnecessary or irrelevant? What about the experimental treatments with lithium, or gamma-linolenic acid, or the drug CaAOTA, or zimelidine to cure alcohol addiction, as buprenorphine does for heroin addiction? Will medicine make healing prayer obsolete?

And what about nutritional therapeutics? There are some diseases that modern medicine refers to as "phantom diseases," that is, undiagnosed or misdiagnosed disorders, many of which can be cured by raising the immunity level through good nutrition. Research has shown, for instance, that optimal levels of immune-activating nutrients such as zinc, iron, copper, and vitamin C are needed to protect one from pathogenic bacteria and viruses.

Some people never seem to get sick, while others are quite prone to illness. *One* reason may be that some families have poorer immunity than others from their family genetic code, which in turn may have been affected from poor eating habits *even in past generations,* affecting the present generation.

Dr. Lucille Hurley, a researcher in nutrition at the University of California at Davis, found that zinc deficiency in animals took as long as three generations to correct. Similar factors affect human beings. We are the third generation of people who have eaten overly-processed, overly-refined foods, which are nutritionally inadequate for most people. (For example, a typical American diet has enough vitamin C to prevent scurvy, but not enough to keep our immune systems operating efficiently.) Deficiencies such as this could account for today's record number of allergic reactions and various forms of hypersensitivity.

Significantly, *nutritional deficiency on the part of parents seems to be continued through the offspring.* It is not always easy to determine whether this is basically genetic or environmental, or whether it is simply the deficiency on the part of the mother affecting the unborn child. Yet, over and above these obvious forms of "transmitted deficiencies," there seems to be an environmentally acquired inability to assimilate the proper proportion of nutrients that is transmitted through several generations, usually three to four generations.

This may have some significance if it is interpreted theologically. The question might be asked: Could it be possible that God would allow the "sins of the parents to be visited upon the children to the third and fourth generation" by means of a natural impairment of the genetic structure, perhaps environmentally modified as a vehicle for the divine sanction? Could it also be possible that this induced damage, not just to parents but their offspring through several generations, could be attributed to marginal malnutrition or consuming of allergens that increase susceptibility to infectious agents? This is the implied conclusion of a number of scientific researchers, particularly regarding allergies, premenstrual syndrome, hypoglycemia, and hypothyroidism. Often a change of diet can clear up these problems with an individual, and other times it takes several generations of corrected diet to produce the effect.

There is nothing theologically unacceptable in acknowledging the possibility of a transmitted deficiency being initially a nutritional impairment. It may be permitted by divine providence, through ignorance of one generation regarding nutritional deficiencies, allergies, etc., that subsequent generations may suffer. In other words it would not be inappropriate for God to use *natural vehicles for transmitting disorders as a sanction for the "sins of the parents."*

The theological conjecture would not be incompatible with the generally accepted and highly scientized theory of

Dr. Franz Alexander, a pioneer in the field of psychosomatic medicine. His "psycho-biological parallel theory" holds that there are eleven major categories of human personality types that correspond to eleven categories of diseases which encompass practically all known non-traumatic disorders to the human body. Since ancestral sin can induce *either* psychosomatic or somato-psychic disorders, the Alexander theory offers no contradiction to the theology of the family tree healing.

Q **My co-worker scoffs at the idea of healing the family tree. He says that advances in genetic engineering will make such healing methods irrelevant. How can I answer him?**

A His position smacks of secular humanism, but like most errors, it encompasses some *partial* truth.

The philosophical principle named after the fourteenth-century philosopher William of Ockham — "Ockham's razor" — requires the strictest economy of interpretation of causality. From this we could hold that God would not have to multiply miracles in order to transmit a disorder of a spiritual deficiency of an ancestor when he could simply use modification of the genetic code. This would involve a minimum of divine intromission into the order of nature to accomplish the same effect.

All of the thousands of diseases and disorders (50,000 to 100,000) that could possibly be attributed to genetic malformation come under the control of divine providence, and in that sense, at least, could vehicularize the divine sanction of generational bondage and disease. If this is manifested as a biochemical disorder, it would be in a category of the physical; if it be a crippling effect genetically induced, such as a neurological weakness, this in turn could have an effect on the mind directly or indirectly.

Certain neurological configurations may carry with them a mental disturbance, such as Alzheimer's disease and certain types of dementia. These neurological disturbances have their effects of course in behavior, and therefore are regarded as psychological problems. The malfunction of the brain in itself is a physical malfunction and yet it carries with it such disorders as schizophrenia which ultimately are behavioral or psychological problems. Abnormal sex drives such as homosexuality *may* have at least a partially physical, biochemical component (although this is very debatable).

Many spiritual disorders — including terrorism, kidnapping, sadism, and arson — that are of a psychosocial nature may reflect various outcroppings of hostility which in turn may be physically based. So we find that a physical disorder may indirectly cause an impairment in the psychological structure of man, the spiritual functions of man, or even the social functions. Often these malfunctions may operate on several levels simultaneously.

In spite of this apparent universal causality of disorders based on physical (genetic) disturbances, it would be naïve to presume that genetic engineering will ever be able to solve all of mankind's problems, from emotional immaturity to crime or threat of nuclear war. Human nature will always have its defects, regardless of the remarkable advances of genetics and regardless of the optimism of your secularistic co-worker.

Q **What's the connection between sin and demonic intervention in the transmission of ancestral sin?**

A The contamination within a family tree seems to follow quite consistently the basic principles of demonology, and so it wouldn't be amiss to conjecture that demonic forces may operate on the physical activities of the body, as St. Thomas Aquinas proves (*Summa Theol.*, Part I, 111, Art. 4). What have come to be known as familial spirits seem to watch for weaknesses in the family tree that result from sins some place along the line in the past, and they strive to perpetuate the effects of that sin in the descendants. Many of these descendants themselves have a responsibility for personal sin, and by sinning they carry the bondage even farther in the family lineage.

God's wrath is not limited to the end-time judgment of the world (I Thess. 1:10; Rev. 19:15, 20:11-15). The wrath of God even before the end-times often consists in his abandonment of the wicked to their sins (Rom. 1:24:32) — often referred to in the Old and New Testaments as a "hardening of the heart." The desensitized conscience is itself a punishment from God that carries with it not only the guilt of the perpetrator of each sin but also its effects to that person's descendants.

"For although they knew God, they neither glorified him as God nor gave thanks to him, but their thinking became futile and their foolish hearts were darkened. Although they claim to be wise, they became fools . . . therefore God gave them over in sinful desires of their hearts to sexual impurity for the degrading of their bodies with one another. They exchanged the truth of God for a lie and worshipped and served created things rather than the Creator . . . . Because of this God gave them over to shameful lusts . . . he gave them over to a depraved mind to do what ought not to be done; they have become filled with *every kind of wickedness*, evil, greed and depravity; they are full of envy, murder, strife, deceit and malice; they are gossips, slanderers, God-haters, insolent, arrogant and boastful; they invent ways of doing evil, they disobey their parents; they are senseless, faithless, heartless, ruthless. Although they know God's righteous decree that those who do such things deserve death, they not only continue to do these very things but also approve of those who practice them" (Rom. 1:21-32).

Those who complain of inheriting defects as a result of others' sins very often commit the same sins themselves, "You who pass judgment on someone else . . . *do the same things*" (Rom. 2:1).

Demonic forces cannot intervene except where sin has already intervened, either by the person himself or by his ancestors. Once the avenue is open for demonic intervention, contamination will continue until it is excised. This can be done even generationally by reparation for one's own sins and the sins of one's ancestors (Lev. 26:40), which is an essential part of the program of healing the family tree.

Q **A number of my relatives have been involved in witchcraft. Should I be more concerned about this than other family sins?**

A Involvement in any form of the occult, from Satan worship to astrology, will invariably have serious consequences within the family tree. Demonic forces may superimpose on every dimension of human personality, and thus be "transmitted" hereditarily by reimplanting themselves in succeeding generations. The most tenacious disorders transmitted demonically are those that result from the sins of occultism practiced by the ancestors. Countless case histories attest to this fact.

Dr. Kurt E. Koch mentions many of such testimonies in his book *Occult Bondage and Deliverance*, based on his wide experience of over forty years traveling through more than one hundred countries. One such example was that of a young man who suffered severe attacks of epilepsy, who found no improvement through medications. Along with his strange illness he found extreme difficulty in exercising religious faith and in praying. It was discovered by Dr. Koch that his mother and grandmother had been active charmers, that is, sorcerers, who in South America are called *brujos*. As a young lad this man had been subjected to an occultic type of healing service. He was led in prayer to renounce the occult practices of his ancestors, and following this he was miraculously healed, delivered from his otherwise intractable ailment.

Any single testimony like this may not be too significant in itself, but when the healing (deliverance) process is seen to be repeated in countless cases with the effects always being the same, one must consider the strong probability — if not absolute certainty — that occultic practices can have a bearing on the descendants of those who practice them; but it also shows that there is a way of breaking that bondage within the family tree.

Of course, not every case of epilepsy or similar neurological disorder has a demonic origin. As Dr. Alfred Lechler expresses it, "If a case of epilepsy can be cured medically, the demonic is not involved; if, however, the illness can be cured only by deliverance prayer, then it was not an instance of *purely* neurological epilepsy." One Christian neurologist feels that *sixty percent* of the patients at his psychiatric clinic are not so much suffering from mental illness as from occult subjection or even demonization that induces mental illness.

There are several hundred distinct forms of occultism, and many of these have been practiced for thousands of years.

All of them have two main features: *rules* and *methods* of occultism. Historically neither of these features has undergone any essential change through all the epochs of mankind's history. The very real similarity between the practices in all cultures and times has puzzled ethnologists, anthropologists, and psychologists. (The first attempt to explain this consistency was Professor Carl Gustav Jung of Zurich with his theory of archetypes.)

But another dimension of this consistency is found in the astonishing fact that almost invariably the descendants of those who engage in occultism will have problems of a very serious nature — a strong indication that it follows the pattern of ancestral sin transmission. The sins of occultism on the part of the parents are "visited upon the children" in the form of manic personality types, melancholic dispositions, incurable psychoses, addictions to drugs or alcohol, etc. Dr. Koch explains in his book that "the number of cases in which occultism has had a damaging effect on people is something in the region of 9 out of 10. I could support this fact by means of many thousands of examples, although some scientists persist in saying the problem does not exist."

Q **Are there various levels of occultic contamination?**

A Yes. Both in the person involved and in terms of the effects on the descendants.

Dr. Lechler, during his thirty years as medical superintendent of the largest mental hospital in Germany and in his work as a Christian counselor, has divided occult subjection into *four stages of oppression.*

These stages are: (1) a simple form of occult subjection which may remain unnoticed for years until subsequent events or illness uncovers it; (2) demonization, which manifests a resistive reaction to any form of prayer or Christian counseling; (3) obsession, whereby the person is continually surrounded and controlled by the powers of darkness, especially the mental processes; and (4) possession, a state in which a person is actually indwelt by demons or evil spirits.

These four stages are simply different degrees of intensity of the same basic phenomenon, the effects of which are found in five different areas of human life:

First, the spiritual life as well as the life of faith is affected. It does not seem to affect the Moslem's faith, the Buddhist's or the Hindu's faith. It seems to affect only Christian faith — and to a lesser extent the faith of God-fearing Jews. Many other religious faiths of the world seem to ally themselves to mediumistic phenomena or are indifferent to it. Only the Christian faith stands out in strong opposition, for Jesus said, "the prince of this world has no hold on me" (John 14:30). That is why it is very difficult to turn to Christ totally while involved in fortunetelling, spiritism, or other forms of occultism. If one is already a Christian, he will find that a coldness will descend upon his faith, and he will have very little desire to pray or to read the Bible. If he "meditates," it will be only for self-fulfillment through mental gymnastics, not a seeking of a union with God in prayer. Often the occultic contamination will be hidden in such a way that the devil will not trouble the person as long as he doesn't seek a close union with Christ.

The *second* area in human life that is affected by subjection to the occult is the character of the person concerned. Persons who are involved in forms of sorcery or witchcraft or even lesser forms of occultism often find themselves plagued by fits of temper, argumentativeness, or they acquire a domineering personality. Their social life is often disturbed, and frequently there are addictions to drugs or alcohol and sometimes uncontrollable lusts as well as tendencies toward licentiousness.

The *third* characteristic resulting from occult oppression is seen in the frequent presence of depression or melancholia which often occurs immediately before or after a conversion to Jesus Christ as the person turns from the occultic bondage. This type of depression is neither the endogenous form (arising through disposition or inherited tendency); nor is it a reactive depression (resulting from stress in the person's life); nor is it organically based depression that results from biological disturbance. This type of depression is occultly caused through sorcery, witchcraft, often even involvement in the practice of astrology. It could be called reactive only in the sense that demonic forces react violently to any dislodging of their presence by a conversion process on the part of the person involved.

Fourth, the persons involved in witchcraft or occultism of any kind are far more prone to mental illness, as also are their offspring. Those involved in the healing ministry recognize the very significant statistical difference of typical depression as distinguished from occultic depression found in persons involved in that lifestyle. Families with a "spiritist" background are far more susceptible to mental illness than other families, especially to anxiety, depression, and schizoid forms of illness. Spiritism seems to act as a kind of catalyst for mental deterioration.

The *fifth* area in which disturbance is manifest for those involved in the occult is in the development of mediumistic abilities. A medium is a person who mediates between unseen entities of the invisible spirit world and the world of man. It has been estimated that approximately ninety-five percent of persons in Eastern religions are mediumistically inclined, while in the West the percentage is perhaps in the region of five percent or less. Participating in mediumistic experiences can cause a kind of "spiritist infection" and it is very dangerous to participate in them even for scientific purposes. The psychic abilities develop rapidly after involvement in the occult and usually in any of three different ways: (1) either through inheritance from parents or grandparents who have been involved in that; (2) deliberately experimenting with the forms of spiritism in mediumistic activities such as "channelling" or conducting séances; and (3) through a transference, a person with a strong radiasthetic ability can communicate to another this ability by gripping the hands of the person while teaching him to use a rod or pendulum for "divining" or "water-witching," etc. The apprentice will quite rapidly pick up, through this transference, the mediumistic ability. This may be extended to other powers such as second sight, clairvoyance, clairsentience, trance-like states, astro-travel, faith-healing powers (not divine healing power which is a charismatic gift), and telepathic abilities.

In this book, we are primarily concerned with the mode of transmission by inheritance, that is, through the parents or grandparents, etc., having been involved in the occult. Deliverance from the effects of transmitted occultism is a more serious aspect of the healing of the family tree program, though it is often the most neglected. It is more important to heal one from occultic effects of the ancestral sin of occultism than from the effects of other types of ancestral sin.

We must remember that demonic forces cannot enter into a person or a family except through sin. It does not have to be the sin of the person affected, but it must be sin some place along the line that opens the door to the demonic effect — whether that demonic effect is direct, as in the form of occultic phenomena, or whether it be indirect, such as a spirit of infirmity aggravating or causing a physical weakness or sickness.

Q Is there any one in a family who is more qualified than others to pray for the release of occultic bondage in the family lineage?

A If there is any interruption possible in the transmission of the effects of evil, it must be done by "those who do not live according to the sinful nature but according to the Spirit" (Rom. 8:4) . . . "because those who are led by the Spirit of God are sons of God" (Rom. 8:14). "The Spirit himself testifies with our spirit that we are heirs — heirs of God and co-heirs with Christ" (vv. 16-17). Thus, if you are fully a child of God, you are better disposed for leading your children and your children's children to be more authentically "children of God and heirs of his glory."

Because "in him all things hold together" (Col. 1:17), "since God has put everything under Christ" (I Cor. 15:27), Jesus is "able to bring everything under his control" (Phil. 3:21). Hence, as we submit our lives totally to him, the "everything" placed under his control includes our offspring. Thus, to break the inherited bondage, what is essentially needed is total submission to Christ, the unifying principle in corporate humanity and, *a fortiori*, the family tree.

As a person nearing death sees that his material possessions will soon be useless to him, he writes a will with concern for his children and his children's children. Should there not be an equal or greater concern for the *spiritual* heritage that we leave to our offspring not only by way of good example but also by way of bringing God's blessings upon the offspring rather than communicating the cursed effect of sin?

Just as perfumes kept in drawers perfume the drawer itself and its contents, so also a soul perfumed with grace will perfume all of the persons associated with it, most especially those associated by a blood relationship.

When one realizes that one has been either a cause of transmitted effect of sin or a passive transmitter by not reversing that process, there should arise within one's mind a sense of responsibility to do something to counteract that flow of evil and to transform it into God's promised flow of blessings. A sense of responsibility is a sign of a mature person. If we lack the responsibility of providing spiritually for our offspring then there is basically a spiritual immaturity in that very irresponsibility. Thus, praying for the healing of the family tree should not be motivated only by a desire for one's personal relief but even more emphatically for the prevention of disorders in one's offspring.

Q I can see how I can confess my own sins in a meaningful way, but how could I possibly confess the sins of my ancestors as required by Scripture (Lev. 26:40)?

A One cannot make an act of repentance for an individual's sin vicariously since "imputability" of sin cannot be transferred from one person to another, as from your ancestor to yourself. But there can be expressed to God a kind of regret or shame — something akin to remorse — for the fact that some of your ancestors have offended a living God; a sense of shame before God that your family has been in opposition to God's will. It is a prayerful regret that your family ancestry has been a source of "disappointment" to God.

It is not a matter of merely acknowledging that there are "skeletons in the family closet"—that would be no more than discovering that there were pirates or murderers in the genealogy of your family tree. It is more than a mere irritation on your part that you must suffer the consequences of your ancestors' selfishness and failure. It is a sincere regret that God's dignity and sovereignty has been offended, and particularly a regret that because that offense arose from someone close to you, that is in your family tree. This is the way that Daniel *prayerfully* confessed his sin and the sins of his forefathers (Dan. 9:20), or the prayer of Baruch (3:4-8), or the prayer of Tobit (3:3-5), and the prayer of the holy Judas Maccabeus (II Macc. 12:42-46; cf. Judith 7:19).

Q **Does this approach to healing help to correct poor "bonding," which psychologists have proven to be so critical to good mental health?**

A Yes, it does. This is an area where the Eucharistic-centered healing prayer can be very powerful. A woman who had experienced an ongoing depression and especially back problems wrote in a letter to me: "I have never had any good feelings or memories about my father, nor about my mother; I have never felt any close relationship with either of them and I have difficulty in talking about them. This is also true regarding my grandmother who raised me. Almost all my life I have felt as if I have been in a void with no feelings, as if I were trying to suppress a series of hurts by being emotionally neutral. During the intermission of your service for the Healing of the Family Tree, a woman next to me who had a great deal of discernment told me that something had happened to me when I was two or three years old, and that I needed to go back to that time in the accompaniment of Jesus to review and release the bondage I had from that time. I fought against this and began to cry, uncontrollably sobbing and gasping for breath, as I experienced a deep hurting feeling within me. As I tried to recall these very painful incidents of my past, I experienced a very real pain in my heart and in my back. I also felt physically exhausted. As I lifted my parents and grandmother to the Lord in a prayer for healing of the family tree, I noticed great relief, and during the celebration of the Eucharist, it was more pronounced. After this service, however, I was still crying and my sobs were coming rhythmically as if they were a kind of labor pain experience. A psychologist who was present and praying with me suggested that perhaps I was undergoing a new birth experience or reliving some painful memories of my own birth when I had experienced telepathically some rejection. I felt at this time that I was being bonded to my mother in a way that I had never experienced before. My depression was lifted shortly after that, and I have been full of joy and exultation ever since. The sense of relief is indescribable. I praise God for the healing he has given me, and a new birth and rebonding with my mother, father and grandmother. I feel that the healing process is still going on and my security grows greater each day as I praise God for his goodness!"

Q Much of this healing program is geared to dealing with the past — our own or our ancestors' past. What implications does it have for the future of our families?

A One of the most popular movies of the 1980s, *Back to the Future*, tells the story of a teenager's science-fiction journey back into his parents' past, projected backwards into the far simpler lifestyle of the 1950s. Young Marty suddenly realizes the importance of his parents' first meeting. Through his efforts, Marty's father-to-be is allowed a second chance to create a positive impression by heroically rescuing Marty's future mother. The self-esteem arising out of this past event has far-reaching effects that extend all the way "back to the future." Once he has returned to the present, Marty discovers his subsequent life greatly altered for the better because of a single esteem-building event from the past.

This of course is fantasy. We can't travel back to change the past, but with God's help by means of giving forgiveness, we can transform our *perception* of the past. Christ alone can free us to live decisively in the present while looking confidently to the future (Phil. 3:7, 13).

Release from our *past* record of weakness and sin confronts us with the real possibility of being a positive influence upon the *future* of our family tree. Our attitudes of today can either empower or imprison the children of tomorrow. There is a story of "trans-generational influence" in II Kings 20, where King Hezekiah who ruled Jerusalem around 700 B.C. had visitors from Babylon to whom he showed the treasures of his house. Isaiah then gave him a dire prophecy: "All that your fathers have stored up until this day will be carried off to Babylon . . . and some of your descendants, your own flesh and blood that will be born to you will be taken away and they will become eunuchs in the palace of the king of Babylon" (vv. 17-18). But Hezekiah rejoiced only because there would be peace and security in his own lifetime, selfishly disregarding the future consequences to his family.

This irresponsible attitude toward future generations is despicable, and yet we find that implicitly in the behavior of many people today. When a family has had an illustrious past and is enjoying a happy present, who looks to the future, especially the distant future? How many of us are far-sighted enough, like King David, to lay up spiritual resources for the "temple" that our children will build? Real foresight demands that we make a sacrificial investment today for the sake of generations yet to come.

Q How do we make this "investment" for the future?

A This spiritual investment should include at least several things:

First, while we cannot change the past, we should strive to change the future of our family by avoiding self-centered and shortsighted attitudes today, and by training our immediate children in the same way. For instance, to inculcate in youngsters the importance of not leading a selfish life by seeking the gratification of drugs, alcohol, etc., to the detriment of their own offspring. They should be taught the joys and advantages of good Christian fellowship and the selfless behavior of persons who are concerned about making this a much better world for everyone.

Children should be encouraged to generosity and sharing their allowance, to dedicate some of their time and resources to help the poor, the aged, the blind, or even to give time to broader selfless ventures like the Peace Corps, and they should be encouraged to give at least part of their life for the "building of the Kingdom." Some may even be called to "renounce marriage for the sake of the Kingdom of Heaven" (Matt. 19:12).

Second, parents should keep in mind that their own sins will be visited upon their children and their children's children; and just as they, the parents, have suffered much — perhaps more than they realize — from their own ancestors' failings, they should try to prevent, by a deep and loving concern, the succession of disasters in their own offspring including those not yet born. Parents should thus take a thorough inventory of their spiritual life to see what negative behavior patterns may have lasting effects that will be "visited upon their children," as well as to review the good behavior in their life — prayerfulness and virtue that will bring blessings upon their offspring (Exod. 20:6). Devout parents, as beneficiaries of their virtuous forebears, should express their gratitude to God with the words of Paul, "I thank God whom I serve, as my forefathers did with a clear conscience" (II Tim. 1:3).

Third, they can set specific goals for growth in holiness as already outlined in II Peter 1:5-11, striving to "possess these qualities in increasing measure" (v. 8), without which cne is "nearsighted and blind and has forgotten that he has been cleansed from his own past sins" (v. 9). It is important to be highly motivated to continue to "*grow* in the grace and knowledge of our Lord and Savior Jesus Christ" (II Pet. 3:18). This growth requires that one be saturated with God's word, which is "useful for teaching, rebuking, correcting and training in righteousness so that the man of God may be *thoroughly equipped for every good work*" (Tim. 3:16-17).

John W. Whitehead has written, "Children are the

168

living messages we send to a time we will not see." Although we cannot change the past, we can change the future for our family. To do so, we must transcend the selfishness of Hezekiah who was concerned only about peace and truth in his own days. We must ensure peace and truth as the heritage for our own descendants.

A little more than a century after Hezekiah's death, his descendants were led captive out of Jerusalem in chains. However, Jeremiah wrote them a letter in Babylon with a note of hope that he gives to each succeeding generation: "I know the plans I have for you, declares the Lord, plans to prosper you and not to harm you, plans to give you hope and a future. Then you will call upon me and come and pray to me and I will listen to you. You will seek me and find me *when you seek me with all your heart"* (Jer. 29:11-13). Let us be filled with Jeremiah's optimism and send the Lord's message of freedom and hope "back to the future," by living today with our children's tomorrows in mind.

Q Can an unborn baby be contaminated with evil forces through the mother?

A There are countless examples that could be given of how evil could take control of a family and lead successive generations into deep darkness; this may happen particularly in the very sensitive period of human life, the prenatal existence in the womb, if the mother during pregnancy involved herself in the occult, especially by relating to witches, fortunetellers, *curanderos*, etc. The baby may pick up that contamination and through life may exhibit bizarre behavior or may be the victim of bizarre situations such as repeated business failures, mysteriously missing items beyond average, accident proneness, eccentricity, anxiety states, and frequent nightmares. In the healing of the family tree program, it would be helpful, if one knew the problem began within the womb, to specifically ask Jesus to touch that situation in the past, just as in the healing of memories program. The occultic contamination can be lifted by such prayer. One must remember that the intensity of faith in Jesus is of critical importance, and particularly in Jesus' Eucharist presence in Communion when the healing most effectively takes place.

If there was an environment of occultism events in one's family, it might be presumed that that same environment was present during the person's prenatal period within the womb. A prayer for the healing should focus as specifically as possible on the time or age element in which the influence was present. Such "faith-focusing" techniques enhance the prayer by making it more specific. As helpful as this is, however, it must be reiterated that it is not as important as the intensity of the Jesus-oriented faith.

Where occultism is involved or where there are especially extreme forms of violence, such as torture and murder in the past, the inherited features may continue longer than three or four generations, possibly as many as ten generations (Deut. 23:2). Jesus spoke of many generations of transmitted guilt from Abel to Zechariah where violence had been manifested (Matt. 23:35, Luke 11:51). The Evil One is present in persons committing murder (I John 3:12). Such forces of evil are more tenacious than other forces of evil or of a lesser caliber. Regardless of the type of evil, however, that continues the contamination, it may be eradicated in the presence of deep faith-filled prayer to Jesus, over whom the prince of this world has no power (John 14:30).

Q Does my spiritual life have any bearing on how successful I am in praying for healing of my family members?

A In seeking healing, one must remember that the success of the prayer is closely related to one's personal relationship with God (James 5:16). Repentance from sin (and consequent healing from sin) is closely connected with even physical and emotional healing, for it is the same Lord who "*forgives* all your sins and *heals* all your diseases" (Ps.

170

103.3; cf. Exod. 15:26). For healing, it is necessary to *give* forgiveness to others as well as to *receive* it from God. Colossians 3:13 says: "Forgive whatever grievances you may have against one another. Forgive as the Lord forgave you." Sirach 28:2-3 tells us, "Forgive your neighbor if he has hurt you, and then when you pray, *your* sins will be forgiven you. If a man bears anger for another, how can he seek healing from God?"

Like Paul, we must "serve God as my forefathers did with a clear conscience" (II Tim. 1:3) in order to have our prayers for healing answered. It is important to be totally on God's side when asking for healing or any other need. "If our hearts do not condemn us, we have confidence before God and receive from him anything we ask, because we obey his commands and do what pleases him" (I John 3:21-22). "If I had cherished sin in my heart, the Lord would not have listened" (Ps. 66:18; cf. Deut. 1:43-45; I Sam. 8:18; James 4:3). Those who reject the Lord and expect him to hasten to answer their pleas for healing will feel his rebuff: "They will call to me, but I will not answer. They will look for me, but will not find me" (Prov. 1:28); (cf. Jer. 11:10: "They have returned to the sins of their forefathers who refuse to listen to my words; therefore . . . although they cry out to me, I will not listen to them").

Q I read that biologists, psychologists, and social scientists are coming to see that a wide range of physical and psychological disorders are related to either family environment or family heredity factors. Can prayer change either the environment or the genes?

A With God, all things are possible (Luke 1:37), whether it is changing environment or one's genetic structure. But *neither* of these radical changes necessarily takes place through the family healing prayer. Most often there is simply a suppression of the *symptoms* resulting from these factors.

171

For instance, to mention a physical effect from a genetic cause: Research at the Genetic Engineering Company of California Biotechnology has turned up genetic "markers" or gene patterns within some family groups, associated with high cholesterol levels — a condition linked to heart diseases and heart attacks. (If confirmed, the findings could lead to a screening test to identify people at risk.) After a healing prayer for a family member with hypertension or high serum cholesterol, those symptoms may be clinically absent, with no change whatsoever in the DNA code that disposed the person for those disorders.

At least several of the six types of depression seem to be hereditary as a tendency rather than only "reactive" or environmentally induced. Very often both factors operate simultaneously, so we may consider patterns within the family tree to be affected both by physical heredity and by family environment. Through either means, trans-generational bondage can be manifested. Twenty-five percent of personality traits are genetically influenced as estimated from studies at Texas University in 1988.

The family environment is the only means through which *adopted* persons can pick up contamination from their adoptive parents, while genetic contamination would come from the natural parents or ancestors.

Q How important is it to get other family members involved in this healing program?

A A careful study of how Jesus worked in family situations in his time shows the importance of involving others.

There are numbers of examples of the healing of the family tree, or healing of family members among the living, which are recorded in the New Testament. When anyone showed a concern for a family member or a member of one's household it brought a gentle and powerful response from Jesus. He indicated, however, that he wanted the petitioners to take part in the healing process of their family members. For instance, he did not expect the babies to take the initiative to come to him, but for the parents to bring them for his blessing (Matt. 9:13; Mark 10:13; Luke 18:15). Simon Peter and Andrew, his brother, brought Jesus to the house of Peter's mother-in-law. They were involved in leading Jesus to the healing situation (Matt. 8:14; Mark 1:30; Luke 4:38). It was the father of the possessed son who brought the child to Jesus for the deliverance healing (Mark 9:17; Matt. 17:15; Luke 9:38). It was the Syrophoenician woman who asked for a deliverance cure of her daughter some distance away (Mark 7:25; Matt. 15:21). Both Martha and her sister, Mary, showed a deep concern for their deceased brother, Lazarus, as they turned to Jesus for help (John 11:21 and 32). Jesus expected the bereaved family members and disciples to roll away the stone, removing, as it were, the obstacle to his access to Lazarus. After Lazarus had been called out of the tomb, it was his family that was given the task of unbinding him (v. 43). It was concern for a member of his own household, namely his servant boy, that the devout centurion requested a healing from Jesus (Matt. 8:6; Luke 7:3).

Notice that *in all of these situations*, there is mention of *faith* and there is a notable expression of *loving concern,* selfless charity, and a kind of family love (*storge* in Greek). Yet the loving concern and charity that was present in the request for family healing in these and other situations was not enough to induce healing of the family members. In all of these episodes, there is explicitly a mention of the exercise of faith being present. While Jesus was truly amazed at the presence of faith in the (spiritually) unrelated Gentile centurion (Luke 7:9; Matt. 8:10), he expressed a similar amazement at the *lack* of faith from Jesus' own relatives who were unresponsive to his healing power in his hometown; this lack of faith prevented him from working miracles there for his own family members (Mark 6:6; Matt. 13:58).

These examples show the two major conditions for healing, especially family healing: *faith in Jesus* and *love for our fellow* man. These two virtues are specifically required for anything we ask of him: "We have confidence before God and *receive from him anything we ask* because . . . we do what pleases him . . . *believe* in the name of his Son Jesus Christ and *love one another* as he commanded us" (I John 3:22-23). This provides an attitudinal framework and spiritual precondition for a successful exercise of the healing of the family tree program. As we turn to Christ, the great healer, we must simultaneously disengage ourselves from "the empty way of life handed down to you from your forefathers" (I Pet. 1:18), and give ourselves over totally in faith and love to the spirit of that Healer-Redeemer-Deliverer, Jesus Christ our Lord. As we pray, in his name, against the "curse" of ancestral bondage, he will "turn the curse into a blessing" (Neh. 13:2).

Q Could only one individual in a family bring about widespread damage or contamination to many in the family tree?

A Yes, especially if the person is a patriarch or influential head of the family. Likewise an influential *family* may be the source of poison for a whole nation. For instance, all of the Israelites suffered a three-year famine which the Lord said was "on account of Saul and his blood-stained family" (II Sam. 21:1); because he put the Gibbeonites to death. Such episodes were a solemn object lesson for all of Israel to observe the covenants sworn to in the name of Yahweh. Corporate and generational punishment was designed to teach that sin has a societal effect.

Q What if I feel I have not absorbed any ill effects from my ancestors?

A If you held that position *arrogantly*, a proverb might apply to you: "There is a generation . . . who are pure in their own eyes and yet are not cleansed of their filth." But this attitude of arrogance is not typically present in those who are merely skeptical about generational bondage at least as it applies to them. These persons eventually lose their skepticism when they see the changes in their health, attitude, behavior, etc., after submitting to a family tree healing program.

Q I notice that in my sister's family the children have the same faults that she has. Is this simply imitation or is it generational contamination?

A It could be either or both. But in many cases it is clear that there is a spiritual heredity involved. A "like mother, like daughter" situation (Ezek. 16:44) may be expressed in violent temper or resentment in children, grandchildren, or great-grandchildren. Shimei, a member of Saul's family, hated David (II Sam. 16:7) and reflected Saul's own fury against David (19:1). It was prophesied by the Lord through Nathan that David's family itself would experience a threat to the lives of the subsequent members of his family: "You have *murdered* Uriah and stolen his wife. Therefore, *murder* shall be a constant *threat* in your family from this time on. . . . I will cause your own family members to rebel against you [his son Absalom did]. . . . You won't die from this sin, but your child shall die . . . [on the seventh day the baby died]" (II Sam. 12:9-18).

We find in some families consistent patterns of alcoholism, drug addiction, and abortions down through the generations. In other families we find that the contamination manifests itself in various forms that are not this consistent.

Q I tend to think of my own needs, especially the physical healing I need, which seems to eclipse my concern for the others in my family tree. Will this limit the effectiveness of the healing prayer?

A Concern for your own need is natural, but your concern must be also "for your brothers, your sons and your daughters, your wives and your homes" (Neh. 4:14). Our prayer for healing the effects of ancestral sin is more effective — and more pleasing to God — when we seek not only our own welfare, happiness, and health, but also that of our families with equal concern. "Each of you should look not only to your own interests, but also to the interests of others" (Phil. 2:4; cf. I Cor. 10:24; Rom. 15:1-2). The Bible even reminds us that it is a sin to neglect to pray for others (I Sam. 12:23).

In this context it is strongly urged that a husband should pray for his wife's family tree and the wife for the husband's family tree. It is especially helpful if both spouses would *pray together* for their respective families and ancestors as well as for what they have in common, their own children. Do not underestimate the added prayer power that comes from two praying together: "If two of you on earth agree about anything you ask for, it will be done for you by my Father in heaven" (Matt. 18:19).

Q My brother married a woman deeply involved in witchcraft, although he doesn't believe in it himself. But he is experiencing many serious problems at home and at work. Is this type of problem more resistant to healing than other types?

A Indeed it is. I received a lengthy letter of testimony from a woman whose mother had taken her to a spiritist at the age of five. This spiritist made use of tarot cards, powders, perfumes, etc., as witchcraft paraphernalia. In her letter she says:

I was brought up in the atmosphere of this occultism and witchcraft. Eventually, I left the church for a period of twelve years while practicing the things suggested by this so-called "good witch." During my pregnancy, she gave me a "witch's brew" made of some kind of special tea leaves with the intent of helping my unborn child. When the baby was born, she used to scream almost incessantly, but the screaming habits stopped abruptly from the time of her baptism. Unfortunately, I allowed this witch to babysit my daughter, who is now twenty-two years old and addicted to PCP and other drugs and will have nothing to do with religion. This woman told me that once she had given her husband's soul over to the devil. Upon my return to the church and the practice of my religion — after being given a special gift of God's grace that began with a dream of Jesus — I decided to relinquish my contact with this witch. She was displeased at my decision and there was a hint of an attempt at retaliation. Almost immediately I found myself with a serious back problem from a fall. The back surgery did not help, the pain in my back and left side continues with a protruding disk in the lower back the doctors seem unable to treat successfully.

Both of my daughters are irreligious, have no interest in prayer or spiritual things, have uncontrollable tempers. They both have spoken of possible suicide. In another part of my family tree on my mother's side, an in-law practiced some advanced form of witchcraft with me while I was a child. Her pre-death sickness was a lengthy and terrible agony. One of her sons committed suicide and his son at the age of fifteen was run over by a bus. Another son at the age of fifteen was murdered. Quite a number of my aunts and uncles were afflicted with alcoholism and died from it. There was widespread sexual promiscuity in my family background on both my mother's and father's sides of the family.

After a private prayer for the healing of this woman's family tree, there was a remarkable improvement in the family situation, but at the time of this writing it is clear that more healing prayer is needed because of the high degree of contamination in this family, particularly because of involvement in occultism (witchcraft, astrology, etc.).

The situations in which the contamination seems to be the heaviest are those that involve Satanism, repudiation of religion and the things of God, incest and other sexual perversions, drug and alcohol abuse. There are many other sins that produce contamination, but these seem to produce the heaviest and require the greatest amount of prayer for healing.

Q **How optimistic should we be about getting a healing when our family is seriously contaminated?**

A The words of Ezra may provide an answer to your question: "From the days of our forefathers until now, our guilt has been great. Because of our sins . . . we have been subjected to the sword and captivity and humiliation as it is today. . . . God has not deserted us in our bondage, he has shown us kindness . . . he has granted us a new life" (Ezra 9:7-9).

Thus, we see that there is hope in the goodness of God to break the bondage of the accumulated sins, from our ancestors to our own generation. This Scripture provides the basis for your faith (Rom. 10:17), but it doesn't provide the faith itself. You must provide that, with God's help. Ask him for the gift of faith.

Q **Could you suggest a prayer of acknowledgement of sin for ourselves and our ancestors — a "twofold confession of sin" that Scripture commands?**

A To "make confession to the Lord, the God of your Fathers" (Ezra 10:11), I suggest simply praying such prayers directly from Scripture, but *fervently*. Some examples:

"We have sinned, even as our fathers did" (Ps. 106:6). "Let our disgrace cover us. We have sinned against the Lord our God, both we and our fathers" (Jer. 3:25). "O Lord, we acknowledge our wickedness and the guilt of our fathers" (Jer. 14:20). (This prayer parallels Nehemiah 9:2.) "Do not punish me for my sins, known and unknown, or for the sins of my ancestors. . . . Lord, command that I be freed of this misery so that I can go to my everlasting abode. Lord, do not refuse me" (Tobit 3:3 and 6). "We confess our sins and the sins of our fathers" (Lev. 26:40).

The word "confess" comes from the Hebrew *yadah*. It might better be translated "bemoan" (by wringing the hands). The implication is that we should bemoan the fact that our own family tree has been contaminated by our ancestors or at the same time bemoan the fact that we ourselves contribute to that general contamination by our sins. The wringing of the hands implies not that we can repent for someone else's sins, but that we have remorse, a regret that those sins that were committed offend God and especially because we were associated with those sins, those with that trans-generational connection.

PERSONAL NOTES

PERSONAL NOTES

PERSONAL NOTES

Chapter Three
HEALING
DECEASED MEMBERS
OF YOUR FAMILY TREE
*What Is the Link Between Us
and Our Deceased Relatives?*

Q Isn't it forbidden by God to communicate with
the dead? Yet in this program we seek a "healing" for
them in a possible release of bondage.

A In praying for our deceased relatives, we must be careful not to evoke them, but only invoke God for them and
their spiritual needs. We can pray *with* them and *for* them,
but we are not allowed to talk to them or communicate with
them directly (Deut. 18:11). That could be a form of
necromancy forbidden by the Bible. When Saul used the
witch of Endor as a medium to contact the dead Samuel (I
Sam. 28), it led to dire consequences. But "it is a holy and
wholesome thought to pray *for* the dead, that they might
be loosed from their sin" (II Macc. 12:46).

Q I think of my deceased parents, grandparents,
etc., as mere "memories" I recall in browsing
through the family photo albums. Is there another
way I should regard them?

A We often tend to think that when our relatives pass on
to the next life they have lost all of their influence upon us,
and that we somehow are disengaged from them and they
are only a memory. In reality, they are far more than a
memory.

There is an ongoing effect that they wield upon us. The
seeds they have planted during their life have their lasting

effects upon us for good or for bad. The poet Virgil describes a cruel punishment used by the Romans in which they sometimes compelled a captive in war to be joined face to face with a dead body. The dead body was tied to the captive and he was forced to bear it about until the horrible stench and effluvia destroyed the captive's life.

If we could *see* something like that happening to us in terms of the evil effects of our deceased ancestors, we would be more concerned about disengaging ourselves from the harmful effluvia. We would not regard them as "irrelevant" just because they are out of our life now, having crossed the threshold of death. They are truly in some way attached to us. We must detoxify any bad effects that linger there. We do this mainly through the blood of Jesus, who gives us power to break the bondage of sin's effects from our deceased ancestors.

For those fortunate persons who have had very wholesome ancestors, again they may not recognize what a privilege is theirs and how blessed they are. They often take that so much for granted that they themselves do not strive to become good transmitters of those same blessings as a "goodly heritage" (Ps. 16:6).

Q Some of my deceased ancestors I knew well during their life, and still love deeply. Others are totally unknown to me. Does my attachment to my beloved dead help or hinder them?

A We may still feel a clinging and perhaps a disappointment in the loss of a loved one, and the first thing we have to do is deal with that realistically, whether it be a spouse, or a child, or a parent, or whatever. "Don't cling to me," Jesus told Mary Magdalen on Easter morning, "I have not yet returned to my Father" (John 20:17). Clinging to one in a way that would retard the pilgrimage into eternal life would be morbid grief, which needs to be healed. This can be done in this healing program.

There is a situation often used to provide an atmosphere of healing prayer in dealing with a deceased person — the one that is referred to in Chapter 11 of John's gospel; namely, the death and miraculous resurrection of Lazarus.

There were some who were resentful that Jesus allowed Lazarus even to die, as pointed out in John 11:39: "He opened the eyes of the blind, could he not have prevented this man's death?" Or the petulant remark of Lazarus's sister, Martha: "Lord, if you had been here my brother would never have died" (v. 21). But even that petulant remark was followed by a word of optimism "that even now it's not too late for something to be done." Even after the death of our loved ones, it's not too late for something to be done. There still can be a healing and a release of a bondage both on the part of ourselves and that loved one.

It's very important to make the prayer in this context to be, as it was in the Lazarus incident, a Christ-centered prayer. We have to see the death of our beloved dead by looking at Jesus himself: "See how much he loved him" (John 11:36). It is precisely in this sharing love with Jesus (the love for our beloved dead) that you move into a Christ-centered form of healing prayer. There can be, if you will, a love-filled grief that you must not allow to devolve into a morbid grief of self-pity; keeping it Christ-centered will prevent this. With Jesus you can have a conversation about times in which you shared the moments of happiness with the beloved dead person — perhaps especially spiritual experiences, in which Jesus was very obviously involved. But at least you can recall the happy moments that you shared with the beloved deceased. You can talk with Jesus about how much you missed the person as you faced the loss totally and completely even if it should bring tears, as the death of Lazarus brought tears to the eyes of Jesus himself.

You may find that you have a half-submerged resentment against God, focused on Jesus, as if you have to forgive him for the fact that he "took away" your loved one. Face the fact that Jesus is a loving God, and therefore the death situation was not an act of vengeance or meanness on the part of the Lord, but truly "he loved him."

As you share what is in your heart with Jesus, you might find that he will want to share what's in his heart with you, concerning the beloved deceased person; in doing so, you can become somehow connected with that deceased person in prayer which, theologically speaking, is a function of the doctrine of the "communion of saints" that Paul refers to indirectly in Ephesians 3:15 and again in 2:19: "We all belong to God's household with every other Christian, citizens of God's country and members of God's own family, no longer foreigners to heaven."

Q **Is it too late to heal any unresolved conflicts with deceased family members?**

A Situations may occur to you in which there are friction points in your relationship with the beloved dead, points in which forgiveness is needed, in which you must give forgiveness to the deceased person for having offended you, and you must receive forgiveness from that person for your offending him or her. In doing this, you "unbind" that person who needs — even on the other side of death — to give and receive forgiveness. The unbinding is a parallel experience to that of Jesus' command to the friends of Lazarus, "Unbind him and let him go free." In allowing our deceased persons to be unbound, to go free, there is a great healing that takes place, beyond anything we could possibly understand, in the person of the deceased, perhaps best expressed with the words of John 8:36: "When the Son of Man sets you free, you are free indeed" — since that person "died with Christ to the basic principles of this world" (Col. 2:20).

Q **In forgiving my dead relatives, will it result in their healing, or in mine?**

A In having mutual reconciliation with the beloved dead, you are "unbinding" that person as Lazarus was unbound, but at the same time "unbinding" yourself and experiencing freedom in Christ. This practice will help you to cultivate the habit of not taking others for granted, and not taking for granted opportunities for future reconciliation. You will cultivate the habit of reconciling immediately in a conflict with the living, rather than to wait for a healing after the person's death. Someone has said that a coffin is a poor place to meet your enemy to ask forgiveness. It is not the best place, but it is a "bonus opportunity" for us, as an act of the mercy of God, that may carry with it a "posthumous healing" for the dead, and a bondage release for yourself.

Q Is it true that after a family tree healing, we have a heightened sense of gratitude for our deceased family members?

A There usually arises at some point in this healing a sense of gratitude even for the death of our beloved relatives. The gratitude not so much that they are dead, but that they become another contact-point for us with Christ, and that they have reached their destiny in the presence of God. And, so, as Jesus expressed his gratitude at the occasion of the encounter with the dead Lazarus (John 11:41: "Father, I thank you for having heard me"), we use the death of our beloved as an opportunity to express our thanks to the Father for his care and for his providence in bringing each of us, in our own time, to our own eternal destiny in his presence.

In this situation, it is very easy to have Jesus fill up for us all that we could not give or express to our dead relatives. We perceive the love of Jesus directed toward that person, and we find that love now spreading to us as if Jesus were to embrace our deceased relative and us together — as if Jesus had one arm around you and one arm around your deceased relative, hugging you into a unity with him.

In that union you are aware that in some situations

both you and your beloved dead have been hurt by mutual conflict or been hurt together by a third party. Jesus' hug is now healing that. You also realize that you and your beloved dead have hurt others, and that you are being healed of the guilt of that in Jesus' forgiving embrace.

You are aware that Jesus at this point in the encounter is filling up all the empty spots, all the things that you regretted not having said or done; all the love that you have not expressed properly or tenderly enough or frequently enough to the beloved dead is now being expressed in and through the person of Jesus, and you are hearing a similar response in and through the person of Jesus from the deceased loved one.

Q **I'm afraid to surrender to God's providence regarding the life-span of my loved ones that I depend on now so much. Do I need to be healed of that fear?**

A Death has a way sometimes of making us afraid to get too close to people for fear that we will lose them as we have lost our beloved dead, and it may even make us afraid to approach the Lord with intimacy for fear that God too will abandon us as our loved ones seemed to do in death. This may result in a difficulty in praying, a fear of getting close to God, even in prayer, or it may cause us to have a suppressed or repressed anger against God for the feeling that he may abandon us. We may feel that he abandoned his concern for us in the past in taking our loved ones away.

The way of dealing with this disturbed relationship, which affects so many in their prayer life, is to create within ourselves an awareness that our longing for the deceased relative is also a longing for Jesus himself, our closest friend, our brother, our spiritual relative, our Divine Healer. If our relationship with our beloved dead is Christ-centered then our longing for the deceased friend becomes a longing for Jesus, and the encounter with the deceased friend is not an encounter of necromancy, but an encounter of love with Jesus who embraces our beloved dead, or an encounter with our beloved dead in the embrace of Jesus. This will allow our prayer, including the "image prayer" as a healing prayer, to become a simple conversation with persons we have a closeness to. Jesus becomes part of that prayer-conversation.

Q Are deceased infants (aborted, stillborn, etc.) or deceased children helped in any way by the family tree healing program?

A Some very remarkable things happen as we use the healing of the family tree prayer when applied to *deceased children*. For instance, learning disabilities in other members of the family often miraculously are cleared up, fertility problems in the parents are often healed, and behavioral problems, hyperactivity, and even character disorders are healed in other members of the family, particularly other children when we pray for the release from bondage of deceased babies in the family. This is true whether it be the children of the person who is praying, or the grandchildren or the great-grandchildren, or whether it be deceased babies within the ancestry rather than the descendants.

About two percent of all children are stillborn. Between ten and twenty percent of all pregnancies end in miscarriage (often unknown to the mother). The problem of abortion is so widespread that a million and a half abortions occur in the United States each year; some 3500 children are aborted every day in the United States with four abortions for every ten live births — awesome and horrendous statistics. Consider, by comparison, a city being devastated by an earthquake that killed 3500 people; there would be headlines with subsequent articles for weeks about such a tragedy; yet that happens equivalently *every day* with 3500 aborted — murdered — infants. We haven't begun to understand how really terrible this is, and the wrath of God that will come upon us, unless we as a nation repent of this disruption of the family tree through murder of God's little ones under the euphemistic title of "terminating pregnancy."

A child may be the victim of this atrocity, or may simply die as an act of God intervening to interrupt its life by his divine sovereignty; in the first case it's immoral, and in the second case it is part of the beautiful plan of God. In either case the healing of the parents and other relatives is often connected with how they regard the relationship with their dead child, and how they pray through that relationship with the deceased child.

Babies are the most overlooked group of people when it comes to prayers for the deceased. If there is any kind of incompleteness in a baby attaining his destiny, it would be the fact that it somehow does not fully receive or is not able fully to give the love in its eternal place of repose; the impediments to giving and receiving love would be the unhealed hurts that are experienced very often within the womb, even from the moment of conception.

It has been documented countless times that babies in the womb, particularly during the last two trimesters of pregnancy, have very active senses and imaginations; for they can see, they can hear, they can taste, they can certainly feel pain, particularly when they are aborted—often a very torturous death. They can dream, and they can even cry within the womb. It has been proven that they have a memory that may go back even to the moment of conception, perhaps not even based on neurological activities, but molecular activities within the embryo. We do know that the child's memories are connected with the mother's experiences and the mother's emotional reaction. There is a mother-child telepathy and for that matter a father-child telepathy before the birth of a child. It is very profound, again particularly in the last two trimesters of pregnancy. There is a hormonal and chemical transfer across the placenta that reflects the emotions of the mother, whether that be fear or joy or anger or love or peace; even praying devoutly with the unborn child can have a very lasting effect, as has been proven by many interesting experiments affecting the personality of the child; before-birth relationships are reflected in the life of the child after birth.

Q **Can grieving parents of a deceased infant benefit from the healing program?**

A Yes. Like mothers, fathers also, but to a lesser degree, may suffer grief over the loss of the baby. Because the father and mother very often are unable to share the grief of the child's loss, *ninety percent of bereaved couples* find themselves in marital conflicts within a few months after the loss of the child. This can be reversed by a kind of family healing, particularly through a shared prayer for healing, in which both parents pray and engage in a dialogue to strengthen their marriage relationship, most especially when this is done in the context of the Eucharist. The success of this particular type of healing has been established by a "pastoral-clinical" experience, if we might express it that way. When there is a prayer for the healing of the family tree, particularly for deceased children outside of the context of the Eucharist, it may be done by a confidant or a minister or priest or husband praying with the woman or (correlatively) with the father of the child, encouraging the parents to share with Jesus their grief and their other feelings, such as anger, which is often submerged; and to present the child to Jesus, who is a human who loves children: "Let the little children come to me, for of such is the kingdom of heaven" (Mark 10:13-16).

It is important to name deceased children to prevent family tree "alienation." If it is unknown whether the child is male or female, you should do one of three things: (1) you may provide one male and one female name and allow the Lord to make the choice to fit the sex of the child; (2) you may ask the guardian angel to name the child; (3) you may choose a name which may be either male or female, with variant spellings like Francis with an "i" or an "e."

The following testimony handed to me after a family

tree healing service in Canada speaks for itself:

> Between 1958 and 1963, my wife had five miscar-
> riages. I felt terrible pangs of guilt myself and
> treated my wife rather cruelly because of her in-
> ability to complete pregnancy. During all these
> years I have carried a tremendous sense of guilt.
> Yesterday, at your talk, when you said, "Name
> these children," we both sat down and did. My wife
> named three and I named two of the babies that
> were deceased. I felt the healing start immediately,
> and at Mass, Jesus appeared standing in front of
> me, telling me that I didn't have to worry or feel bad
> any more as our five children were all safe in heaven
> and in his arms. Praise to Jesus Christ for the
> tremendous relief we both have received! Our love
> has grown immensely because of this healing.

This testimony in some way manifests God's desire to "repatriate" those alienated from family unity, whether by namelessness or whatever. "God establishes the lonely [the alienated] in families" (Ps. 68:6; cf. Ps. 25:16). This desire of God for unity in the family (Eph. 4:3) is vitiated in many forms of family disintegration, such as runaway children situations, kidnapping, divorce, separation, in-law feuds, and sibling rivalry. The celebrative joy in the heart of God when disrupted families are restored to unity can be seen in the father's party-planning at the return of the prodigal son (Luke 15:23-24). That is a practice that any "restored" family would do well to imitate.

In relating to the deceased child, always of course in the presence of Jesus, ask forgiveness from the child for any neglect or any evil intent and disrupting of the life of the child in cases of abortion. In the presence of Jesus also for-give any doctors or anyone who may have participated in the death through direct attack or through negligence.

Q What should the healing prayer include, in the

case of bereaved parents mourning the death of their baby or young child?

A The healing prayer should include, in the presence of the Lord, a request that the child be, as it were, one's own "private saint" or "intercessor" with special powers of intercession because of the natural kinship.

Finally, part of the prayer should include a request for inspiration as to how to continue to give and receive love in and through Jesus in relating to the child. After such a prayer, a parent may notice a loosening of the anger, a clearing of the heart and the mind and spirit, and a sense of freedom to give and receive love. With that love that is Spirit-activated, there may come a deep joy and a very deep peace; one may find also that love for any living children is intensified. The healing is not only for the parents but also for the living children in that family.

What might have begun as an interpersonal healing between parent and child becomes now a family healing, embracing the whole constellation of family relationships, with very often miraculous and dramatic results in the physical and emotional healings of the other children of the family. This may extend to parents and grandparents, to other blood relatives, and to in-laws.

In the total consignment of the child to the Lord, to God the Father through Jesus, as if moving toward a more transcendent type of child-parent relationship, the parents should ask the Lord to fill in any needs of that infant, which might include such things as creating within the infant the baptism of desire or some unknown form of grace activity analogous to the sacrament of baptism. With this type of *spiritual* reception, rather than the *physical* reception of the sacrament, it could be ratified by the Eucharist in which at Communion time we join with Jesus in the closest union, praying for the deceased to draw closer to the parent; pray for all persons involved to be magnetized by Jesus and drawn to him; in getting closer to him, we find ourselves growing closer to each other, the union of Communion enhancing the intimacy of that love of kinship.

This Eucharistic healing service is also an ideal time to extend the love of Jesus to others in the family that may have been forgotten, and to others even in the neighborhood or the county, state, country, or the entire world.

As a kind of epilogue to the healing prayer of Jesus, it is helpful to have the child placed in the arms of Mary, our spiritual mother, recalling the words that Jesus said as he expired on the cross, "Mother, behold thy son." Mary is commissioned to be a spiritual mother to all of us and has an intense love for each one of her children, who are parts of her son's mystical body (I Cor. 12:12), and of God's family (Eph. 3:15). She loves each one far more intensely than earthly mothers love their children.

When you reach the point in the prayer in which the Lord enlightens you with the purpose of his providence in this death, or at least his providence in the making good come from the evil (as in the case of abortion), you may find that it's easy to want the child to be eternally happy and to desire that even more than you would desire the child to be restored to earthly life. You will find it easy to rely upon that child as a powerful intercessor for you and your family.

In the Eucharist in which the healing is ratified most completely, in receiving the body of the Lord, ask Jesus to use your body as a channel of his love, your emotions built into the very brain of your body, as channels of his love to all the members of your family, living or deceased. As you consume his precious blood, ask that God will flow through you and the bloodlines of your family all through your descendants, including those who are deceased, for a total healing of your family tree.

Q **You say that deceased children should all be given names, even posthumously. Why?**

A It is *very* important to give a name to a child who has died by abortion or miscarriage or stillbirth, or shortly after birth, because the human being is a social entity; as the child has insights in the presence of God, they are far more mature than the animalistic thought-process of an infant on earth. The child senses an alienation when he or she is nameless, because the way humans relate to each other is by means of identification through names. So in the healing prayer, it is important to give a name to the child so that it may be "written in the book of life" (Rev. 21:27).

Q **I know that there is a Jewish and Christian custom of praying for one's deceased relatives and friends, but did it exist at the time of Christ, or was it started later?**

A Regarding the custom of prayer for the dead among the Jews at the time of Christ (and for at least a century before Christ), there can be no reasonable doubt that it was an accepted practice. The classical passage from II Maccabees 12:42-46 ("It is a holy and wholesome thought to pray for the dead to be loosed from their sins") is but one proof of the prevalence of the custom. Professor E. H. Plumptre, a Protestant scholar, writes: "There is no room to doubt that the Jews looked on the state of the dead as one capable of being influenced for good by the prayers of the living. Prayers for the dead were an established part of the ritual of the synagogue at the time of the Maccabees, and, in that of the temple, sacrifices were added to the prayers" (*Spirits in Prison*, pp. 127-128).

There can scarcely be a shadow of doubt that such prayers for the dead were offered in every synagogue and repeated by mourning kinsmen to whom the duty of rite belonged during the whole period covered by the gospels and the acts of the Apostles. The inscriptions in the Jewish cemeteries in Rome, with their brief supplications for peace, tell the same tale, as also do those from the Jewish cemetery in the Crimea from the first or second centuries after Christ. According to the rules of the rabbis, it was the duty of the *son or next of kin* to say the "Kaddish," or prayer for the soul of the dead. The righteous were to "stand on the dust of the wicked and pray for mercy upon them . . . and bring them to the life of the world to come." This seems to be an interpretation of the words of Malachi 4:3, and it calls to mind the words of the Psalmist: "The upright will rule over them in the morning and their forms will decay in the grave . . . , *but God will redeem my life from the grave* [Sheol, abode of the dead]; he will surely take me to himself" (Ps. 49:14-15).

So, there can be no doubt that prayer for the dead was offered before the time of Christ, and it has continued to be offered from that time to the present day, though not universally, by the Jews. In modern Judaism there is a prayer that is still used: "May God in his mercy remember (*name of person*) for the welfare of whose soul I this day offer (*a sum of money to be vested in works of mercy*). May his soul be united in eternal life with the souls of Abraham, Isaac, Sarah, Rebekah, Leah, and other holy men and women in the Garden of Eden."

Q How old is the belief that the dead can be helped by the prayers of the living?

A When any king of the ancient African country of Dahomey wanted to communicate with his dead relatives, he whispered his message into a captive's ear and then promptly beheaded him. Such primitive attempts to communicate with the dead went beyond the simple belief in the soul's immortality and post-death consciousness. It reflected a belief in a "growth ability" after death, for example, by accumulation of knowledge and other forms of posthumous improvement.

Such prayer for the dead was customary in the early centuries of the Church; the inference is that it would be natural and legitimate that prayers for the dead which we find in Judaism and in Christianity were derived from an earlier source, prior to the time of Christ, but which passed without question and without rejection into the teaching and practice of Christians. We don't know exactly how far these traditions went back, but the story of the Maccabees in the deuterocanonical book of the Bible, II Maccabees, Chapter 12, gives us at least one fixed date of at least one century, possibly a century and a half before Christ. Probably the doctrine was extant from at least the time of Captivity, six centuries before Christ, as E. H. Plumptre writes in his book *Spirits in Prison.*

Socrates and Plato had arrived by a reasoning process at the teaching on post-death purification; others among the Greeks and the Latins reached almost identical conclusions. The Greek "Tartarus" (the punishment section of Hades, the abode of the dead) is the same as the Jewish "Gehenna" (the punishment section of Sheol, the abode of the dead). Both the Greeks and the Jews thought that some souls were eternally punished and others only temporarily, as is indicated even in Virgil's classical *Aeneid.* Hence we have in the Jewish teaching at the time of our Lord the three states, but only two places or locations after death. Two were permanent, Gehenna and Paradise, and the other was a temporary place of purgation connected with Gehenna. This temporary purgation, according to some of the rabbis, ended in annihilation; other rabbis held that it led to a restoration, toward which deceased persons were helped by the prayers of those who were living on earth, especially by prayers of living relatives. For a full discussion of this subject, you might read the Protestant treatises, such as the work by Dr. Pusey, *What Is of Faith as to Eternal Punishment?*, Farrar's *Mercy and Judgment,* and Edersheim's *Life and Times of Jesus.**

---

* This teaching on post-death purification was deepened by the influence of Hellenic Jews, through the deuterocanonical books written mostly during the gap of four centuries between the Old and New Testament writings. The study of the development of doctrine in this intertestamental period will help us to gauge the meaning of much of the teaching that was presented by Jesus, especially some parables, and also the later teaching by the Apostles, as the early Fathers affirmed.The theological teaching in the time of Christ and his Apostles was repre-

Q Why should we consider the Jewish tradition in evaluating Christian theologies regarding praying for deceased family members?

A The teachings prevalent among the Jews at the time of Christ are of the greatest use in determining the framework in which our Lord's teaching would be understood. Only insofar as our Lord and Apostles accepted this tradition, it is to be reckoned as representing the truth by Christians. For this reason we should study that tradition; as a matter of fact, we cannot arrive at the meaning of our Lord's words in some parts of the gospel without it. We also

---

sented generally by two schools of Jewish thought, the school of Shammai and the school of Hillel (the grandfather of Gamaliel, mentioned in Acts 5:34). In both of these schools contemporaneous with Christ, there were taught two kinds of suffering after death — eternal and temporal (purgatorial).

The school of Shammai arranged all mankind into three classes: (1) the perfectly righteous, who were "immediately sealed to eternal life"; (2) the perfectly wicked, who are immediately sealed to Gehenna; and (3) an intermediate class, "who go down to Gehenna and moan and come up again" according to Zechariah 13:9 and a reference in the Song of Hannah in I Samuel 2:6 (cf. Deut. 32:39). The school of Hillel, on the other hand, agreed that some souls had temporal punishment (purgatorial punishment) but that they were annihilated, burned up, and scattered as dust under the feet of the righteous after a temporary period of punishment.

Most of these beliefs about the afterlife were denied by the Sadducees, but the belief of the orthodox Jews and the bulk of the people consistently held to the three categories of souls in the afterlife. Josephus, the historian who wrote approximately A.D. 70, in his book *Antiquities*, Chapter 18, reaffirms the tradition held by the rabbis and the people of that day, and says that even the Sadducees accommodated themselves to the tradition of the people when they were made magistrates. It is abundantly clear that a *post-death purification* was believed at the time of Jesus, by both the learned people of the time and by the man on the street.

A Protestant historian, Dr. Alfred Edersheim, in his book *Life and Times of Jesus the Messiah* says, in describing the beliefs among the Jews at the time of Christ, "there is a kind of purgation, if not purgatory, after death. . . . " In *Sketches of Jewish Social Life in the Days of Christ*, he says (p. 180), "Taking the widest and most generous view of the rabbis, they may thus be summed up: All Israel will have a share in the world to come. The pious among the Gentiles also will have a part in it; *only the perfectly just will enter at once into paradise;* all the rest pass through a period of purification and perfection. . . . Such is the last word which the synagogue has to say to mankind."

find it difficult, without acknowledging this tradition, to understand the later beliefs that prevailed — and to some extent are still held — in various denominations in the Christian religion.

Q **Praying for one's deceased family members for a release of the effects of their sins would seem to imply the existence of purgatory. This doctrine is not accepted by most non-Catholics. Do any Protestants believe in purgatory?**

A Even Luther, the "father of Protestantism," believed in purgatory, while denouncing the abusive use of indulgences.

Outside the historic churches (Catholic, Orthodox, etc.), there are many Protestants who believe in purgatory, especially in Germany, Denmark, and England — both broad-church Anglicans (as they were called in the past) and many British Protestants — some of them outstanding theologians such as R. E. Hutton. These all hold to a doctrine of an intermediate state of progressive purification between death and entrance into heaven. They hold that this state entails a growth in holiness as a kind of divine education and as a work of *healing*, but that it is not to satisfy divine justice, since that was paid for by Christ through his death and resurrection, as held by all Christians, Catholic and non-Catholic alike (Rom. 8:1-4; Heb. 9:28).

A growing number of Protestant theologians acknowledge the existence of this intermediate state of purgation, but an even larger number acknowledge at least the possibility of such a state.

Q **Why should there by any purgation after death to "pay off a debt due to God," since Christ has already paid our debt by suffering on Calvary?**

A The purification that a soul undergoes in the intermediate state of the next life is not a *satisfaction* to the justice of God to pay off a debt that is owed to God, for it is true that our debt for sin has already been paid by him. However, the *application* of that payment can be had only for those sins of which we have repented. Jesus "wrote the check out to us," but we have to endorse it to cash it. Just as there is no cashing of a check without endorsement, there is no forgiveness without repentance. Jesus wrote the check for our forgiveness with his blood on Calvary, but we are not forgiven until we endorse it with our repentance. But even when that is done (as it probably is the moment the soul faces God in death, except in obstinate souls who are damned), still there is a "temporal punishment due to sin," to be undergone for purification from sin's *effects*, and for perfecting the soul's undeveloped capacity before entering heaven.

Consequently, we are dealing first and foremost with sins that a person has committed and that remain unrepented of at the moment of death, and therefore not under the payment made by Christ on Calvary. Secondly, we are dealing also with sins that the person *has* repented of, but for which some temporal punishment is due (temporal being the opposite of eternal).

To understand this, let us consider that some sins bring a visible and temporal punishment with them even in this life. God does not interfere with this punishment from overtaking persons, even those who are truly repentant; the ruined health, for instance, of a drunkard or drug addict is a "temporal punishment," not arbitrarily inflicted nor miraculously hindered by God *even when that person repents.*

Similarly, the impoverishment of a compulsive gambler, the venereal disease of a sexually promiscuous person, etc., are all "temporal punishments." They are allowed by God for many reasons, such as warning of others and for the prevention of a relapse. But these temporal punishments are not, strictly speaking, satisfactions to God; they do not pay any kind of debt due from the sinner to God. The debt has already been paid by our sinless Lord: "... He was wounded for our transgressions and bruised for our iniquities, the chastisement of our peace was upon him and with his stripes we are healed ... on him the Lord has laid the iniquity of us all" (Isaiah 53:5-6).

If there can be "temporal punishment" required of us in this life, regardless of the Redemption, why not a "temporal punishment" in the next life, regardless of the Redemption?

Q In Jesus' parable of Dives in hell and the beggar Lazarus in heaven, he seems to imply that there is no intermediate state like purgatory, just a "wide chasm" between them. In heaven our beloved dead need no help. If they are in hell, no help is possible. So why pray for the dead?

A Jesus in Luke 16 describes the deceased rich man Dives in a place of suffering, which seems to portray our concept of purgatory, experiencing a kind of thirst, but allowed to converse with Abraham in paradise. The dead beggar Lazarus was "at Abraham's side," or "in the bosom of Abraham." This state of paradise is referred to as the "limbo of the patriarchs," the holding-place for those who lived before Christ and hence who were not yet in heaven, because it was prior to the time the gates of heaven were opened — when Jesus died and ascended into heaven. This place of paradise, or "limbo," where the beggar Lazarus was resting was a pre-heaven state of "comfort" (v. 25). Jesus later refers to it as paradise (Luke 23:43) as does the Jewish *Talmud*. Besides this paradise, Jesus mentioned a future *heaven* (for example, Matt. 6:20; Luke 10:20), and he also mentions the punishment of everlasting fire in *Gehenna* in several places.

But in the parable he also appears to accept the contemporary *Jewish* belief in what today we call purgatory. Jesus seems to imply that there existed not just a temporary state of paradise, or "limbo," the place where

Lazarus was before the Redemption — the "bosom of Abraham." He also implies a place of growth through suffering—a "prison" (I Pet. 3:19 and 4:6). This "prison" could well be a "purgatory state" in which Dives was detained. Often mistranslated as "hell" (Hades in Greek), Dives's status could not have been one of damnation, for in that place he grew from selfishness to self-less concern for his five brothers (Luke 16:28) — obviously a place of spiritual growth. This "growth" will be completed for everyone before the second Coming of Christ: "He who began a good work in you will carry it on to completion until the day of Christ Jesus" (Phil. 1:6). This fits the description of purgatory.

Those in paradise, being in a "holding pattern" themselves, could not help those in purgatory, like Dives. They could help only later, when they entered into glory (heaven) with the newly risen Jesus, sharing his intercessory prayer (I John 3:2). In that power of the same risen Jesus, we on earth share in his intercessory power in praying for the dead, as Paul did for Onesiphorus (II Tim. 1:16-18).

A close analysis and exegesis of the parable of Dives and Lazarus in Luke 16 has led a Protestant theologian, R. E. Hutton, to the conclusion of the possibility of a purification and perfecting of a soul after death, as he writes in his book *The Soul in the Unseen World*. (More and more Protestant theologians are moving into the theological position that parallels the Catholic teaching on purgatory in its pristine form without the pietistic exaggerations that have attached themselves to this teaching through the ages.)

These Protestant theologians acknowledge that Jesus' teachings on death and judgment leave open the possibility that at least *some* who die in sin can ultimately attain heaven (Matt. 8:11-12; Luke 12:20; 16:22; John 9:4; 11:9; 12:35). The Jewish *Talmud* mentions both paradise referred to in Luke 23:43, and "Abraham's side," or "bosom" (Luke 16:22), as places of the righteous dead, so this group of Protestant theologians, like the rabbis, do not accept the exclusively heaven-or-hell alternatives.

Q How can our beloved dead (or any deceased person) be in purgatory, since Hebrews 9:27 says, "Man is destined to die once and then face judgment"? This implies a finality of status after death, with no mention of an intermediate state of purgatory.

A In a cemetery in Ohio, there is a tombstone with an epitaph that reads: "Too bad for heaven, too good for hell; where he went I cannot tell."

In a facetious way, that simple epitaph gives a hint at the answer to your question and opens up a vast array of theological problems and something of a mystery as to the immediate state of a soul after death, with the consequent possibility of a need on the part of such a soul for our intercessory prayer for the completion of that individual's destiny.

This question wrongly presupposes that there is *only* an *immediate* personal judgment after each person's death and not also a final judgment: "When the Son of Man comes, and when *all nations* will be gathered before him, he will separate the sheep from the goats" (Matt. 25:31-32). *At that point*, it is true, there will be only heaven and hell — no intermediate stage of purification (Dan. 12:2; John 5:29). This second (universal) judgment "at the great white throne" is detailed in Revelation 20:11-15.

Scripture indicates that there is an intermediate state, at least for some souls, between the two judgments. Jesus fulfilled Isaiah's Messianic prophecy (42:7) to loose the bonds of those in prison (Luke 4:18). His soul entered a "prison after his death, to preach to deceased persons imprisoned there" (I Pet. 3:19). "They had to *give an account to him* who is *ready* to judge the *living and the dead. This is the reason* the gospel was preached even to those who are now dead" (I Pet. 4:5-6). From these quotes, it is clear that after-death evangelization is possible, and that the immediate judgment after death should not be confused with the final judgment at the Second Coming of Christ.

If this after-death evangelization is possible, then

spiritual growth (purification and perfection) is possible. As our prayers and intercessions can accelerate this process before death, why not also after death?

Q **Most Christian doctrines are at least hinted at prophetically in the Old Testament. Is there any such hint about the "release" of the dead — other than those in the deuterocanonical books of the Catholic Bible?**

A Yes. There are many such "hints" in the Old Testament. To quote only a few: "You have delivered [released] my soul from Sheol [the abode of the dead]... that I may walk before God in the light of life." (Ps. 56:13). "The Lord brings the soul down to Sheol the abode of the dead ... and brings it up [releases it]" (I Sam. 2:6)—a quote from Hannah's song. "Our God is a God who saves; from the sovereign Lord comes escape [release] from Sheol — the place of the dead" (Ps. 68:20). Paul later referred to this "escape," describing the man whose works fell short of God's testing: "He will be saved, yet only as one *escaping* through flames" (I Cor. 3:15).

Q **If it is true, as Paul says (II Cor. 5:8), "to be out of the body is to be at home with the Lord," then what need would there be to pray for the dead for purification?**

A The quotation is distorted because it is incomplete and out of context. The full text reads: "We would prefer to be away from the body and at home with the Lord. So we make it our goal to please him, whether we are at home in the body or away from it. For we must all appear before the judgment seat of Christ that each one may receive what is due him for the things done while in the body, whether good or bad" (II Cor. 5:8-10).

The full text of this passage indicates that not all will be equal in their status after death (after the "particular judgment"), and that consequently not only is there reward for the things done that are good, but punishment for things done that are bad. In the case of the latter, the need for purification is needed for "what is due him." The very quotation you give does not refute the teaching on purgation after death, but rather reinforces it.

Q **The Bible speaks of entering into peace after death, Isaiah 57:2: "Those who walk uprightly enter into peace; they find rest as they lie in death." And, Daniel 12:13, "Go your way to the end. You will rest, and then at the end of the days [the end of time] you will rise to receive your allotted inheritance." This indicates no need for purification.**

A It is very true that those who truly are righteous and fully aligned with the Lord in his will in absolute perfection at the time of their death will have no need for purification after death, and consequently no need for prayers. These are the types of persons who are being described in the passages you quote. It is certainly true of Daniel, one of the greatest saints of the Old Testament.

In the second passage quoted, the word "rest" is used to mean "die" (see Job 3:17). In this context the passage loses its relevance. Also, at this "end of time," purgatory will no longer exist, only heaven and hell (cf. Matt. 25:46).

A very few people have attained the degree of righteousness that would make them *totally* prepared for eternal bliss, even though they are made eligible for heaven by the death of Christ, which through faith they have accepted. Such people, like Paul, could say, "For me, to live is Christ and to die is gain" (Phil. 1:21). But if, for instance, on their deathbed they were not *perfectly* resigned to God's will in their pre-death suffering, then they would not be *totally* righteous; there would not be a total alignment of their will with God's will, and consequently, having died in that state with some degree of resistance to God's will, they would be in need of purification after death. They could be helped by the intercessory prayers of others in the "communion of saints" referred to in Ephesians 3:15.

Since all of us are "fellow citizens with God's people and members of God's household," (Eph. 2:19) "we should do good to all people especially those who belong to the family of believers" (Gal. 6:10) whether living or dead. Praying for the dead therefore — even for quite holy persons who need very little purification — is the act of fraternal charity. Such compassionate concern for others with whom we are conjoined in Christ is pleasing to God.

Q **I know that the Catholic Church is the main proponent of the custom of praying for the dead, especially deceased relatives. But it claims its teachings have been often misrepresented. What is the real Catholic teaching?**

A In 1979 the Catholic Sacred Congregation for the Doctrine of the Faith sent a letter to all Catholic bishops about "life after death." Among other things it stated:

> The church believes in the resurrection of the dead . . . and excludes anything that would render meaningless or unintelligible her prayers, her funeral rites and the religious acts offered for the dead. . . . She believes in the possibility of a *purification* for the elect before they see God, a purification altogether different from the *punishment* of the damned. This is what the Church means when speaking of . . . purgatory.

Summarizing the declarations of the Second Council of Nicea in 787 and the Council of Florence in 1439, which agreed with the Greek Church in this matter, the Council of Trent in 1549-63 in the context of the Reformation declared: "There is a purgatory and the souls detained there are helped by the 'suffrages' (i.e., prayers and sacrifices, etc.) of the faithful." These two facts, stated in one sentence, embrace the entire *official* teaching of the Catholic Church on this matter. Praying for the dead must not be an attempt to contact them by necromancy, as in a séance. The Second Vatican Council says that our faith gives us power to be united with our beloved dead *only in and through Christ* ("Gaudium et Spes," art. 18), as parts of his Mystical Body (Eph. 4:1-6).

We have inherited many imaginative excesses that have come down to us from the Middle Ages when poets, writers, orators, and artists took artistic license in portraying purgatory with terrifying imagery. Article 51 of "Gaudium et Spes" urged that the *abusive* presentation of this doctrine should be discontinued and corrected. The Catholic Church does not portray our loving God as a vindictive tyrant demanding his pound of flesh.

At the same time, it is recognized that there is a need for purification experience for many after death. Paul speaks of this purifying and testing experience: "Fire will test the quality of each man's work . . . he himself will be saved, but only as one escaping through the flames" (I Cor. 3:12-14). Catholic theologian William Bausch says that even good persons bring to the death-resurrection complex some unfinished business — that is, "unfinished love." His fellow theologian Conan Regan speaks of purgatory in a kind of mystical description: "Its flames are the intensity of God's love that inflames the soul with yearning for the richness it will soon receive. Purgatory is not therefore so much a punishment as it is a mercy."

This is the gist of the Catholic Church's teaching on this subject.

Q Is purgatorial suffering a torture of some kind? What kind of suffering is it? And how long does it last?

A Imagine two men who have passed away, one after a long life of dedicated service to God and the other after a long life of sin with only a last-minute repentance. For the one who has lived a holy life there should be a more speedy entrance to heaven and for the other a slower entrance to heaven. The ingrained evil habits may perhaps be only slowly eradicated in purgatory and there *may* be some suffering to be borne in the process. The suffering is not an arbitrary thing; it is not a torture inflicted to atone for the offense against God, but probably a kind of a sorrow or grief that would come from the enhanced awareness of how heinous a thing sin is; and from one's recognition of what an outrage it is to offend God by sin. We see the example of the prodigal son who was fully and entirely pardoned (Luke 15). There was no painful punishment inflicted upon him by his father in an attempt to restore justice, but the son must have felt a bitter regret and shame which must have left him "pained" at the thought of his past life. And this sorrow would be all the greater because of the generous and complete forgiveness given him by the father. One cannot say for certain that his long habits of sin were never afterwards a source of trouble or worry or regret and didn't need to be dealt with in that way.

Something of the same order may be true in the hereafter. This kind of sorrow and grief, a sense of unfitness for the presence of God, and regret in having lost that presence during life, and being without it during the time of purgation, may be the real nature of purgatory; it thus would provide both a purification of the soul and the means by which it makes progress. As the old stains of sin are worn away, the divine image is restored in the soul. There is perhaps a *shame* at the thought of having offended him, that would constitute a form of suffering, and a *longing* for him while not seeing him, as a second form of suffering.

Thus, the "suffering" of purgatory is twofold: a *profound remorse* for sin and a *profound longing* for the fullness of God's presence (Beatific Vision). The purpose of this "suffering" is likewise twofold: *first*, a purification from the defilement of remnant sin (and this could be in an instant, at the moment of entering eternity, when the soul separates from the body), and *second*, a perfecting or growth process of disengagement, from long habits of sin and undeveloped love, into exquisite spiritual maturity.

Q I feel that Christ is more concerned about healing and releasing bondage among our living family members than in "releasing" our dead relatives. The dead have had their chance, during life.

A In I Peter 3:19 and 4:6 we see that just after his death on the cross, Jesus went to *preach* to the "confined" spirits of the dead who had been disobedient. He went also to *evangelize,* and therefore expected a change in their state, a kind of conversion and/or growth in perfection. In this we see that Jesus is active in both this world and the next, so we too may rightfully expect and pray for a change in the dead. We must not limit Christ's activity only to this world, for Paul reminds us in Romans 14:9 that Christ is the Lord of *both* the living and dead (cf. Acts 10:42; John 5:21 and 10:36; Phil. 2:10; II Tim. 4:1; I Pet. 4:5).

Q Most of my deceased family members were born-again Christians. Do they really need my prayers?

A The answer to this question may be found on a bumper sticker that I saw recently: "Born-again Christians aren't perfect — just forgiven."

Look at the statement of I John 3:14, "We know that we have passed from death to life because we love our brothers." John is speaking about eternal life, spiritual life; yet a person who has this life-giving love still experiences sickness, troubles, and death. There is some degree of spiritual completeness, and yet the *full* effects of that new life are not manifested on this side of the grave.

Could it not be something similar to that on the other side of the grave, in persons already cleansed of sin by contrition that elicits the forgiveness of Christ? In the born-again Christian there remains some of the *effects* of sin that need to be remitted or dissolved, purified, or purged. Just as in this life when we totally repent and are born again, we still have suffering, so also in the next life, if we enter it even completely free of the contamination of sin there are still the aftereffects of sin and a need for the growth process into the state of virtue, and a need of uprooting of old habits and mental attitudes, as part of the purging, purifying-perfecting process.

Hence, purgatory could have a twofold purpose: (1) to lead us to a deep repentance for sin that had been unforgiven at the moment of death, for those not deserving of eternal punishment (and this remorse or repentance could be a momentary shattering experience as the soul separates from the body and gets a "perspective" of sin), and (2) the purification from the *effects* of sin that has been forgiven before death.

There is a hint of post-death acquisition of perfection in Chapter 11 of Hebrews from verse 32 to the end of the chapter; there are described two categories of persons who were heroes of faith (the first group experienced immediate triumph over those circumstances); as it says in verse 33, "They gained what was promised." But others (vv. 39-40) "did not receive what had been promised. God had planned something better for us so that only *together with us would they be made perfect.*"

The next sentence, introducing Chapter 12, describes something of this "communion of saints" and *exhorts* us to a pre-death cleansing. "Therefore, since we are surrounded by such a great cloud of witnesses, let us throw off everything that hinders, and the sin that so easily entangles, and let us run with perseverance the race marked out for us. Let us fix our eyes on Jesus, the author and *perfecter* of our faith." The concept of being surrounded by a cloud of such witnesses puts us in some kind of a parallel situation with those who are already deceased and have gone before us, and also implies that the perfecting process is not only on earth but also after death, at least in some cases, but in proportion to one's knowledge and gifts, as Jesus teaches (Luke 12:47-48).

Q I have enough sins to repent of and "mourn for." How could I be of help to my deceased ancestors in mourning for their sins too? It's as if God requires a "double repentance."

A There are some Scripture scholars who interpret the second beatitude (Matt. 5:4 — "blessed are those who mourn, for they shall be comforted" paralleling Is. 61:2) as referring to the mourning or repenting of one's own sins *and* the sins of one's ancestors, as required by Leviticus 26:40. The implication is that those who repent of their sins and the sins of their forefathers will not only cause the Lord to remember the covenant with their ancestors (Lev. 26:45), but will make the ones who mourn for those sins to be "blessed." The Israelites fulfilled this command in Nehemiah 9:2: "They stood in their places and confessed their sins *and* the wickedness of their fathers."

In their prayer for their ancestors (vv. 16-18) the Israelites remind the Lord that in the face of their ancestors' sins he was a "forgiving God, gracious and compassionate, slow to anger and abounding in love." There was obviously a feeling among the Israelites that as they confessed the sins of their ancestors along with their own sins, they would avail themselves of the mercy of the gracious and compassionate God, abounding in love. The Israelites even put their confession into writing (v. 38) assigned by the Levites and priests with their seals. The final petition of Nehemiah's healing prayer is for his own sins — the last sentence of the book (13:31): "Remember *me* with favor, O my God."

The command of confessing our sins with those of our ancestors was also fulfilled in the prayer of the Psalmist, Psalm 106:6, and by Daniel (9:20) and Ezra (10:11). Even kings urged their subjects not to follow the pattern of their ancestors in infidelity to the Lord (II Chron. 30:7), with the promise of the breaking of the ancestral bondage (v. 9): "If you *return* to the Lord, then your brothers and your children will be shown compassion . . . for the Lord your

God is gracious and compassionate, he will not turn his face from you if you *return* to him."

The response to this appeal was the fulfillment once again of the mandate from Leviticus, of confessing their sins and the sins of their forefathers (Jer. 3:25): "We have sinned against the Lord our God, both we and our fathers from our youth; 'til this day we have not obeyed the Lord our God." This double confession is repeated again in Jeremiah 14:20. "O Lord, we acknowledge our wickedness and the guilt of our fathers, we have indeed sinned against you." Without this repentance, this *double* repentance, there will be no mercy or compassion exercised by God in his punishment for "fathers and sons alike" (Jer. 13:14).

Our *personal* repentance must be akin to that of the prodigal son: "I will go back to my father and say to him, father, I have sinned against heaven and against you, I am no longer worthy to be called your son" (Luke 15:18). God's response is generous. "If we confess our sins, he is faithful and just and will forgive us our sins and purify us from all unrighteousness" (I John 1:9). The first person plural form ("if *we* confess, he will forgive *us* our sins") could emphasize the corporate nature of sin found in its ancestral transmission. This same corporate nature of sin is expressed in the plural form in the Lord's Prayer ("forgive *us* our trespasses"). Thus, the beatitude "blessed are those who mourn" may very well refer to mourning in sorrow for the sins of the human race, of the nation, of one's family, and of oneself.

Q Some of my own sins seem so remote, I can't even remember them. My ancestors' sins are even more remote. It seems a bit too late to be dealing with them.

A Some of the personal sins that we confess may be recent and some may be in the remote past of our early lives. Time doesn't matter to God. In confessing ancestral sin, the occasion may have been even more remote from the present.

In the miracle of Jesus' raising Lazarus from the dead, Martha reminded Jesus (John 11:39) that already four days had elapsed and putrefaction had set in the body of Lazarus. Jesus speaks about something glorious as the opposite of the putrefied body and said, "Did I not tell you that if you believed you would see the *glory* of God?" *Time*, which had brought about the putrefaction, was not an obstacle to the life-giving presence of Jesus. Long-standing sins or sins of ancestors committed long ago are still subject to the marvelous healing power of Jesus and his loving mercy.

When Jesus told them to take away the obstructing stone from the tomb and to unbind the body, he was showing that the removal of confinement and bondage in spiritually or physically sick persons, even those who are spiritually dead, can be accomplished when he is present. We must unbind those in bondage within the family tree, ourselves included; our ancestors may still be bound, even in death, in a state of unfreedom. We are asked to assume the responsibility of bringing, especially to the Eucharist, all who may be in need of this Christ-presence to unbind them.

As we pray in the Lord's Prayer to forgive those who trespass against us, we should include all of our ancestors who have trespassed against us perhaps by personal acts of effrontery from parents, grandparents, etc.; or perhaps only by our inheriting the effects of their sin have we been victimized by them. Those trespasses of theirs must be included in our prayer of forgiveness.

In the last petition of the Lord's Prayer, "deliver us from the evil one," we call upon the deliverance power of Jesus for all the areas in our family history and our personal history in which the devil or his minions have anchored themselves. To the extent that there is a demonic intervention in the bondage found in our family lineage, our healing prayer must be a deliverance prayer. (The very word "deliverance" originated from that last sentence of the Lord's Prayer.)

Q If any post-death purification is necessary, why can't it be done instantly, at the moment after death, when the soul steps into eternity?

A God does not vindictively inflict suffering upon these souls; yet neither does he suddenly and miraculously eradicate all the effects of long-continued evil habits. Nor does he impart at the instant of death the full glory of holiness for such imperfect souls.

The fruit of the Holy Spirit in the life of an individual is usually the reward of long-continued cultivation in the garden of the soul. Likewise, in the next life, perfection is not attained suddenly. One must bring forth fruit with patience (James 5:7-11).

"If all of this is not done perfectly *before* death (when it's much easier), then it must be accomplished *after* death" (Augustine, *City of God*, 21:13). If never perfected, the soul could never enter heaven (Rev. 21:27), since those who are not *fully* Christ-like could never attain the reward of being with Christ.

We know that God "will not quench the smoking flax" (Is. 42:3), but rather, as Paul says in Philippians 1:6, "He that has begun a good work in you will perform it *until* the day of Jesus Christ," that is, in the time between now (in our lifetime and afterwards) until the day of final judgment.

So a person in purgatory is being perfected, and we on earth can pray — especially for our deceased loved ones who might still be there — for that perfection to be accelerated; we can pray also that there be a purging of any remaining defilement in preparation for entering the kingdom of heaven.

Whether this restoration is accomplished in a moment, or whether it is done as it is usually done here on earth, slowly by degrees, we don't know. Time is gauged differently by God (II Pet. 3:8), and probably also by disembodied souls. Still, the bottom line is: for the imperfect soul, *purgatory is a perfecting in love, and a being made ready for heaven, not a payment of a debt due for sins. That payment has already been made by Christ.*

Q Can you suggest some "systematic" way I can pray for my deceased family members? A "prayer-plan" would help me do this better, I'm sure.

A In offering our assistance to the deceased members of our family tree, we find in Chapter 11 of John's gospel a pattern that could well provide a framework for our prayer. The episode has to do with the resurrection of Lazarus.

1. There is the initiative taken on our part, to reach out to help the dead, expressed in the words of Jesus referring to Lazarus who had already died (John 11:15: "Come, let us go to him").

2. The element of sustained hope is expressed by Martha (John 11:22 LB): "Even now it is not too late."

3. The element of trust elicited from us by Jesus, expressed in verse 23: "Your brother will rise again."

4. The assurance that we can reach to the dead, not directly but through Jesus, expressed in verse 25: "*I* am the resurrection and the life."

5. "Do you believe this?" We are challenged to trust in him; the question is a prod to excite our personalized faith or trust in Jesus (v. 26).

6. The affirmation of this in verse 27: "Yes, Lord, I believe you are the Christ, the Son of God."

7. Next, the step of "locating" the deceased person in time and place, as if positioning him within the family tree (v. 34): "Where have you laid him?"

8. The act of love, or charity, is involved in reaching out to help the dead; a "faith that works through love" (Gal. 5:6) is reflected here in this episode (John 11:36): "See how much he *loved* him."

9. The next direction of Jesus is to remove the obstacles (v. 39): "Take away the stone"; the obstacles must be removed for complete access to the dead, particularly the obstacles of unforgiveness, resentment, and neglect.

10. In verse 42, we find Jesus linking us, the living, to the dead through himself, "Father, I knew that you always hear me, but I said this *for the benefit of the people standing here* that they may believe. . . ."

11. In verse 44, we are reminded that Lazarus "came out with his hands and feet wrapped with strips of linen and a cloth around his face." With his face muffled with the grave cloth, it was as if his pleading to the living couldn't be heard.

12. Part of his bondage was symbolized by his feet being wrapped in the strips of linen, as if he couldn't walk *fully* with the Lord.

13. Seeing his hands swathed in strips of linen, we are shown that he was helpless to help himself and dependent upon the help of others.

14. The upshot of this was the next command of Jesus (v. 44): "Unbind him [that is, break the bondage], take off the grave clothes and let him go." Notice that Jesus worked the miracle of resurrecting Lazarus, but he did not do the unbinding; he requested those around him, especially his family members, to be involved in this process by unbinding the resurrected man. It is as if Jesus says, I have the power over life and death, but I delegate the exercise of the unbinding effect of that power to you, the living. "What you unbind on earth is unbound in the eyes of heaven" (Matt. 16:19). Jesus' own death would be an unbinding of those spiritually dead, extending his healing, life-giving power not only to the limited range of a family tree, but to the larger family of all nations (v. 52): "Not only for that nation, but for all the scattered children of God, to bring them together and make them one." God's ultimate goal is unity in the grandiose "family tree" of God.

Q In family healing services, there is often mention of the "communion of saints." What precisely does that mean?

A Many Christian denominations use the profession of

faith referred to as the Apostles' Creed, which includes the phrase "communion of saints." The word "communion" means spiritual union or interconnection; the word "saints" is used here in the New Testament meaning of persons who are baptized as followers of Christ. The "communion of saints" implies that the Church in its various aspects is really one church, and that there is an interdependence among the members of the church on earth (church militant), the church in heaven (the church triumphant — Eph. 3:15; "the great cloud of witnesses" — Heb. 12:1), conjoined with us in the Spirit (Eph. 2:22), and those in a state of purgation (the church suffering). We are "all members together of one body and sharers together in the promises of Christ Jesus" (Eph. 3:6).

Jesus Christ is the only head of his church, which is his body that is made up of the people who have come to share his divine life. The communion or union among the members is simply the ability to help one another, to relate to one another spiritually in that same head, Jesus Christ, especially through intercessory prayer.

Members of the church on earth may help one another and may also help the faithful departed (who are "saints" in the purifying process) and accelerate their purification. They in turn, though they cannot help themselves in prayer (for which reason they are called "poor souls"), can pray for us and help us by their prayers. This circulation of fraternal help by prayer makes the church a kind of supernatural "mutual aid society." The only way these prayers can be transmitted in their effects is through Jesus Christ, the Head of the mystical body, or communion of saints. He is the communications central switchboard for the church on earth, the church in heaven, and the church in purgatory, as the brain is the neural switchboard for all parts of the body. The implication for helping the living and deceased members of our family is obvious. Without this doctrine, enunciated in the Apostles' Creed, the healing of the family tree would be impossible, in which case we "pray for one another that" we "may be healed" (James 5:16).

Q I heard of some strange customs among primitive tribes who seek the "release" of their deceased ancestors. Is this some kind of attempt to heal their family tree?

A There is a strange cult among the Merina tribe in the highlands of Madagascar, an island off the southeast coast of Africa, where persons dig up their dead relatives and take them home for a gala family reunion. They "visit" with their dead relatives and bring them up to date in the latest family news. They throw parties for them and even take their bodies on tours of places they loved while they were alive. This is a rather primitive attempt to do what healing the family tree attempts to do in a more spiritual way, namely to break the bondage that may exist between dead ancestors and the living.

The living tribesmen don't want their ancestors' ghosts later dropping in unexpectedly, so before they take the remains back to the tomb, they parade the corpses around the house or village for seven times to confuse them and keep their ghosts from finding their way back. In that way, they break the bondage, while still having some vital contact with their beloved dead in these processions, or "visits," of the relatives.

From time to time it is the duty of the dead person's family to exhume the corpse, and the ritual is performed whenever the family has the time and the money to do it, perhaps four times during their own lifetime. A special effort is made to please the ancestors, depending on what made them happy during life. In this primitive way there is some manifestation of deep concern for the dead and a kind of practice of "charity" in relating to them — as bizarre and grotesque as it may seem to us.

When the body has become so badly decomposed that it is unrecognizable, and only shards of bone remain, those remains will be placed with other family remains and wrapped together in a single shroud which symbolizes their concern for the unity within the family tree even after death. They exhume not only the dead members of their immediate family, but as many relatives as they can find, going back in generations as far as they can. A community of a million people practice this ritual; it's viewed as a sense of victory over death and a reestablishing of a family bond, while breaking negative bondage—in a sense a quaint way of "healing their family tree."

Q **A member of my study club would like to attend a family healing service, but refuses to do so because she can't accept the teaching of the need to pray for the dead. What can I tell her?**

A This need of praying for the dead is implied in the almost universally accepted doctrine of the communion of saints; and yet there are some who may not totally believe in the ability to relate to the dead by prayer. Some Christians believe that at the moment of death, the only alternatives for the disembodied soul are immediate advancement to heaven or abandonment in hell. In heaven they don't need our intercessory prayer, and in hell they don't want it, and it can't reach them.

For twenty centuries, the Catholic Church has taught that some of the dead can be helped by our prayers and sacrifices—those souls still in some way spiritually incomplete. Also a considerable number of other Christian denominations (Anglicans, some Episcopalians, early Lutherans, Orthodox, etc.) accept the doctrine with slight variations in the understanding of it. The acceptance or rejection of the doctrine or variations in its understanding should not be allowed to cause any disunity within the Body of Christ, since *much* of what happens after death is beyond our clear understanding.

It is only through much arduous theological investigation (outlined elsewhere in this book) that we can come to any kind of conclusions about this delicate issue, but it is of great significance in the second dimension of the program of healing the family tree — namely, the dimension of releasing deceased persons (usually ancestors) from bondage that they have accrued to themselves. If members of the family tree who are deceased are in need of some kind of completeness or maturity that they have not attained prior to death, then neglecting this doctrine would be to neglect those deceased family members' need for healing.

Q Why should the dead be in need of purification?

A There is a purification process in purgatory, according to this teaching, for those who have leftover temporal (non-eternal) punishment due to either forgiven or unforgiven sins. Punishment for sins already forgiven may be a difficult teaching for many non-Catholics to accept. If the sin is forgiven, it is gone completely, according to the many passages of Scripture that emphasize the mercy of God, such as Hebrews 8:12: "I will forgive their wickedness and will remember their sins no more" (there are more than five hundred other passages referring to the mercy of God).

But the doctrine of temporal punishment due to sin that has already been forgiven *does not deny* that the guilt is totally taken away, for God dissolves all guilt of repented sin. The teaching on purgatory speaks only of the *restorative process* that is needed to clear up the *effects* of that sin. The repentant soul has already been "purified" of sin by the blood of Jesus that it has availed itself of in that very act of repentance; but it has not necessarily been purified of the remnant effects of that sin — such as the uprooting of the tendency or habit of sin, "cancelling the acquired propensity to evil," as St. Gregory of Nyssa wrote in the fourth century.

Q When I studied classical literature in college, I was appalled by the descriptions of purgatory by Dante, who was a Catholic. Did he reflect the Catholic Church's teaching on purgatory?

A Dante Alighieri's "Purgatorio" in his *Divine Comedy*

perhaps did much to give rise to some distorted views of the nature of purgatory. Apparently, he was influenced by certain conjectures and theories of both Christians and pagans—St. Anselm, St. Bonaventure, and St. Augustine, as well as Boethius, Lucan, Statius, Ovid, Horace, and Virgil (according to translator John Ciardi). Dante's complex political concept led to misconceptions after his time, due to the prestige given to such classical literature. Vatican II specifically urged that such misconceptions be rectified.

Q Is there physical pain in purgatory?

A If there is pain in purgatory, it is certainly not neurological pain as we understand it here, for there are no bodies with nerves to feel pain. The suffering that may be experienced would be the deprivation or temporary delay of the vision of the Triune God in heaven, who is so clearly understood at the moment of death as the be-all and end-all of our existence. The "pain of loss," as it is called, which is eternal for those damned in hell, is recognized as only temporary in purgatory, and the pain is simply the unfulfilled yearning to be in the presence of God who is the center of the soul's entire being. Hence, Camus (seventeeth century) conjectured that "purgatory is like hell in its suffering, but like heaven in its love."

The pain is an expression of love. It is love of the soul yearning for the encounter with the beloved in the way that a woman waiting for the return of her beloved from war has a deep yearning as she stands on the wharf waiting for a ship on the horizon bringing her beloved back home. There is a void — an unfulfillment because the beloved is not yet present; and yet there is a happy expectancy within that unfulfillment, that yearning, that emotional "reaching out" for the beloved. Until she is in the arms of her beloved, there may be said to be some "pain," even in the midst of that happy anticipation.

Obviously, this kind of suffering is not the kind of suffering that would be induced in a torture chamber, which is one of the distorted views of purgatory. It is a purifying "fire," as Pope Paul VI described it in his 1968 "Creed of the People of God"; it is a kind of fire of which we have little or no knowledge. We know that our prayers and sacrifices (sacrificial suffering) have an intercessory power (II Cor. 4:15; Col. 1:24, etc.). Particularly the celebration of the Eucharist offered in behalf of souls who are in this purifying yearning experience can be of great help to them. When they have been helped by this form of fraternal charity through our intercessory prayer and sacrifices, we can be sure they in turn will pray for us.

Q **Is purification of the soul the only purpose of purgatory?**

A No. There may also be a need for an after-death *growth process* to come to a full understanding of the heinousness of sin, for one thing — coming to appreciate the degree to which God's awesome majesty has been derogated. Purgatorial *suffering*, says St. Thomas Aquinas, does not remove guilt, but purgatorial *love* with its implicit repentance does remove the guilt of venial sin. This immediate *cleansing* by repentance leaves only the need for *growth* in love, patience, humility, and other virtues.

The purging is not totally a negative act of erasing sin, which is immediately forgiven. It is a process of growing in deep appreciation of God, while being enveloped in the "fire" of his love, his burning love, a non-consuming love, but a refining love such as that refining fire mentioned in Revelation 3:18 and many other places in Scripture (cf. Job 23:10: "When he has tested me, I will come forth as gold"). Job's refining was *in spite of* his basic righteousness described in the next sentence: "My feet have closely followed his steps, I have kept to his way without turning aside" (v. 11).

Origen (third century) asked, "Would you enter into heaven with your wood, hay, and stubble unburned (I Cor 3:13) and thus defile the kingdom of God? This fire consumes not the creature, but the 'wood' of bad works and presents us for the reward of our good works" (cf. Rev. 22:12; Is. 40:10; Matt. 16:27).

There are may righteous souls in purgatory perhaps, who are undergoing a growth and learning process that they neglected to attain during life. While yearning for heaven, they are perfectly conformed to the will of God in enduring the delay, as St. Catherine of Genoa's visions of purgatory revealed.

Praying for the dead, as in the family tree healing program, is a means that God uses to accelerate this learning and maturing process in our beloved dead. To assure us that this happens, God allows the living who pray for the release of their ancestors to experience remarkable healings and deliverances from bondages that have resulted from the sins of those same ancestors.

Q Recent research in OBE (out-of-body experience) or NDE (near-death experience) tells us something about the next life. What bearing does this have upon our relationship with our loved ones in our family tree who are deceased?

A This experience is quite common, according to Dr. Glenn Gabbard, a psychoanalyst at the Menninger Foundation, who says that there is good, solid, and scientific methodology showing it to be a pervasive experience that occurs in roughly half of the people who experience cardiac arrest (heart attack). There is most frequently the experience of going through a tunnel, perceiving a light, the body "outside of itself" hovering over the physical body, etc. Many cultures over the centuries have described similar experiences in the aftermath of a disease, seizure, or injury that brought persons to the brink of death. Of course there is much skepticism in the medical community, so not all psychiatrists and psychologists are looking at these experiences seriously enough to consider them worthy of research. They do not agree about the meaning of these experiences; some say the cause is biochemical, others relate it to a higher state of consciousness or admit that it simply constitutes an evidence of life after death. But the consensus, with a few notable exceptions, is that there is indeed something very significant happening in the OBE.

In the *American Journal of Psychiatry*, an article by Dr. Bruce Greyson, a University of Connecticut psychiatrist, classified the experiences that people have in the OBE into four groups:

1. *Cognitive:* The thinking becomes faster and clearer; the patient may undergo a review of his entire life.

2. *Affective:* Intense feelings of peace, joy, and an experience of brilliant light.

3. *Transcendental:* Other-worldly perceptions, feelings of being in another realm; communication with other worldly beings or deceased relatives or friends. (In this type of experience there is particular interest for those engaging in the program of healing the family tree.)

4. *Paranormal:* Enhanced vision or hearing, apparently extrasensory perception; out-of-body experience, precognition, ability to foresee the future.

"All of the hard evidence that is available," says Dr. Greyson, "points to the fact that this is not fantasy. People's experience in this seems to be different than what they had fantasized before." A Gallup poll published in 1982 found that as many as eight million Americans have had a near-death experience at some level, and, as University of Connecticut psychologist Kenneth Ring expressed it, "They can't all be making it up."

Q **Many people claim to have seen "ghosts," and sometimes they recognize them as deceased loved ones. If these are real are they an indication of our deceased relatives asking for some kind of help or release?**

A Many "ghost-hunters," who explore the parapsychological phenomena of haunted houses and such, have assembled a massive amount of proof of the existence of entities commonly called "ghosts." Prestigious organizations such as the British Psychic Association employ elaborate means to record the presence of these ghosts by tape recordings, videotapes, photographs, etc. Some people ("ghostbusters") are psychics, while others are religious exorcists who attempt to dispel the ghosts from the place that is "haunted." This may be a limited place, such as a room or building, or a stretch of road or a bridge; or it may encompass an area of the open sky or an area of the open ocean such as the so-called "Bermuda Triangle."

Various forms of eerie phenomena (including voices, appearance of signs, persons, aerial phenomena, or the mysterious disappearance of things such as hundreds of ships and aircraft in the Bermuda Triangle) seem to indicate that those phenomena are caused either by evil spirits, such as devils or demons, or by disembodied "earth-bound" souls who have not yet reached a point of total commitment in their destiny, many of whom appear to be confused and not even aware that they have crossed the line of death into another life.

A closer investigation of *recognized* ghosts indicates that they resisted the will of God by not accepting death, clinging to this world, and as a consequence became "earth-bound" spirits.

Countless dead or dying slaves thrown into the sea in the area of what is called the Bermuda Triangle were considered unsaleable in the West Indies or America; the slave merchants often collected more money through insurance for dying or dead slaves than by selling them in America. The Eucharist was celebrated in the Bermuda Triangle itself on board ship in 1977, specifically for the release from bondage of those slaves who met their untimely deaths with hatred for their murderous slave traders. The curse seemed to be lifted at that time, and all the mysterious phenomena of the Bermuda Triangle simply ceased. (Evil forces may build up again in that area, but if they ever do, the power of the Eucharist may again be invoked.)

In so-called haunted houses, the disquieted spirits that roam there are often the victims or perpetrators of vicious crimes of violence. When the Eucharist is celebrated within a haunted house, offered for the release of such disquieted spirits, or for the casting out of the forces of evil in the event of demonic infestation in the form of poltergeists, the phenomenon almost always disappears. ("Poltergeist" is a German word that means "noisy ghost," such as observed in table-rapping.) For reasons no one knows, poltergeist activity seems to be prevalent mainly where disturbed or hostile teenagers or young persons live or have lived. I have had personal experience with a number of cases of poltergeists myself and I have seen the power of prayer — and especially the Holy Eucharist — dissolve these disturbing forces.

It is hard to know whether the bondage resides in the place or in the witnesses or in the deceased relatives of persons who are associated with the place. Where there is demonic activity, it sometimes follows the persons if they move elsewhere. In that case some form of deliverance needs to be administered to that person rather than to the location alone.

Just as we must use every precaution to use conventional means of therapy for hallucinations, etc., for those in schizophrenic states before we attempt an exorcistic form of cure, so also in investigating ghosts we must make sure that there is not a subjective cause, such as simply an overactive imagination on the part of the witness. Normally, hallucinations must first be ruled out before one should attempt to use anything as drastic as exorcism.

Particularly important in understanding the phenomenon of apparitions of deceased relatives is the understanding of the relationship between the observer and the apparition observed. If it is a disembodied spirit that is recognizable as a relative within the person's ancestry, perhaps there is a need to give forgiveness and to pray for that person's release, and to bring that person under the authority of Jesus Christ, who is the ruler of all creation with "authority over every other power" (Col. 2:10).

Q Can places as well as persons be contaminated? Is it possible that the healing could be extended beyond the family to the home of the family — the house and property?

A It seems beyond a doubt that places can become contaminated as well as people. (St. Alphonsus labeled this as "infestation.") Before binding any evil spirits that may be present or before seeking the release of any disembodied spirits (deceased humans) that may need release, we should commit ourselves to Jesus, who is Lord over all powers of the universe (Rom. 8:38-39). Ideally, the Eucharist should be celebrated in the place and for the persons who may stand in need of this release. We must be careful not to allow the process of healing of places (especially where there has been the ghost-type of disturbance caused by a demon rather than an "earth-bound" human soul) to be limited to simply a negative act of casting out that which is unwanted. Jesus reminds us of the danger of "seven devils worse than the first" entering a house clean (of evil spirits) but *empty* (Luke 11:25), rather than clean and *filled* with the fullness of Christ (Eph. 3:19). Demons seek "dry places," especially where love and prayer have "dried up" (Luke 11:24).

Hauntings often occur in places where there have been occult practices, or the use of drugs, or where murder or sins of lust or criminal acts or torture have been committed. These areas particularly may need a special prayer for the release of persons, particularly deceased persons who have been involved in the occult in those places, or in the criminal activity, or in the use of drugs or sexual sin in the location itself. Even when we don't know who those persons are, the double approach may be needed — the exorcism of the *place* as well as a prayer of release for any *persons* who may have been involved there in some malevolent work contrary to God's will.

If you are dealing directly with persons who have been involved in the occult, it is not enough to have them simply withdraw from occult practices; they must positively *renounce* and *reject* in the name of Jesus (Mark 16:17) all commitment to them, and *expressly* repudiate any covenant or involvement with the forces of evil, as well as curses, hexes, or any other imprecation.

Q Do our deceased relatives want to apologize to us for hurting us during life?

A Your question might best be answered by a testimony. In the course of one of my talks in Canada, I suggested that we should "listen" for possible requests for forgiveness (release of bondage) of deceased family members. One young woman present had been the victim of incest — attacked repeatedly by her father when she was small. That evening after I suggested "listening" for the request for forgiveness, she had a kind of an apparition in a half-dream state, in which her deceased father spoke to her asking her forgiveness with deepest sincerity for having abused her sexually. She forgave him through Jesus, applying the principle of II Corinthians 2:10-11: "What I have forgiven — if there was anything to forgive — I have forgiven *in the sight of Christ* for your sake, in order that Satan might not outwit us, for we are not unaware of his schemes." From that moment, the young woman experienced a tremendous release from her bondage of resentment against her deceased father that had plagued her for most of her life. She sought me out to tell me, with the greatest sense of exultation, of how delighted she was to be freed of this almost lifelong bondage, and to know that her deceased father was also freed from his bondage, through forgiveness that she was privileged to channel from Christ to him. Thus, in a few moments, an "infected" part of her family tree was healed.

Q My neighbor told me that her dead husband has

appeared to her several times. I didn't know what to say, except to tell her to pray for him. Could he have been seeking some kind of release?

A A study conducted at the University of Arizona in Tucson, with five hundred widows, came up with an astonishing conclusion: *more than half* claim to have been contacted by their deceased husbands, some as long as twenty years after the husband's death. Most of the dead husbands communicated in subtle ways, according to the findings. In many cases they seem to have wanted to rid themselves of some guilt; perhaps they had not expressed enough love for their wives during their lifetime; or perhaps they had even been unfaithful during their lifetime.

Communication in these cases seems to take many forms, but often without any words. The communication in most cases seemed to imply there was some unfulfillment on the part of these deceased husbands. This particular parapsychological phenomenon, if it is ever proved to have any validity, would not be in any way contrary to the theological implications of what is believed among Christians with regard to the belief in afterlife intermediate stages of growth and purification or purging.

Q Can ancestral sin be reversed? That is, can our sins affect our deceased ancestors?

A There is no indication of such a thing. However, the rather common understanding that a defect can be transmitted *from* one's ancestors has led to a practice in some areas and among some tribes of reversing that trend so that the sickness or evil oppression is transmitted backwards from the living to the dead. As a form of occultism in some places, it is a common practice to write down the illness that one has on a piece of paper together with a magic charm or spell and throw it into the grave as a deceased person is buried, or to put it in the coffin.

A symbolic magic ritual is often connected with this; for

instance, a person who is ill may want a piece of his or her clothing or other article to be placed in the coffin as a vehicle of the individual's illness to be transmitted to the dead person and carried into the next life. A man with arthritis in his hand, for instance, may throw a glove as a symbol of his hand into the coffin or grave of the deceased person with the hope that he might be relieved of the arthritis that would be carried into the next life by the deceased person. Occasionally, it happens that in these customs a person who is dying actually wants to take with him an illness of a relative. There is no way of knowing whether or not such practice has any effect upon the dead, but it certainly cannot be regarded as an acceptable practice.

Q **Is it better to undergo a purging in this life rather than the next? If so, is that demonstrated in the Bible?**

A The purging is more easily done in this life than in the next. The words of Jesus in Matthew 5:25-26 are appropriate: "Settle matters quickly with your adversary who is taking you to court; do it *while you are still with him* on the way, or he may hand you over to the judge, and the judge may hand you over to the officer, and you may be thrown into prison. *I tell you the truth, you will not get out until you have paid the last penny*." This specifies and reaffirms what Jesus spoke of elsewhere (Matt. 18:34), in terms of debt payment for moral failure of the unjust steward whose "master turned him over to the jailers . . . *until he should pay back* all he owed."

Jesus refers to several types of judgment and accountability, and hence sanction, in Matthew 5:22: "[a] Subject to judgment . . . [b] answerable to the Sanhedrin . . . [c] in danger of the fire of hell." In this, he implies that hell is not the only way that justice is administered for sin, and that there is a way of "making payment" that is completed at some time, unlike the endless "payment" of souls damned to hell. The payment "to the last penny" (or farthing), says Tertullian (second century), implies that even the smallest offenses are to be paid for. St. Augustine wrote in *The City of God* (21:13), "What is not remitted in this world is remitted in the next."

Q How much will the prayer for deceased relatives affect what happens at the last judgment?

A Probably not much at that time, but much *before* that time. The prayer, if needed by the deceased, will hasten the purgation of your deceased relatives, and break any remnant bondage that you have derived from them. God's mercy will be manifest in them, as elicited by your intercessory prayer.

The concept of corporate guilt, which underscores the healing of the family tree program, is found implicitly in the commonly accepted teaching among all Christians that there is a time for a last judgment. This last judgment, by its very nature being public, implies that all of humanity *is in some way* as one person — that their evil is connected in the "realm of sin" in a way that is unrecognizable in the individual. Humans often sin with one another — for example, by conspiracy, adultery, and bad example. Each person is in some way responsible for the other and is guilty with the other. The judgment upon each person therefore in some way concerns all. The judgment upon the individual is at the same time a judgment upon the whole, while the praise and the reward accorded an individual reflects also upon the commonweal (common welfare).

By way of analogy, poison injected into one part of the body affects the entire body through the bloodstream, and nutrients or vitamins ingested affect the whole body.

The corporate dimension of sin (not just Adamic sin), and also the corporate dimension of righteousness, underlie the need for the general, or last, judgment in which "all mankind stands before the Judge" (II Cor. 5:10; Rom. 14:10; cf. I Cor. 3:10-15). But there is also a non-corporate dimension of sin and righteousness that requires an individual or *particular* judgment, which takes place at the moment of death. The sanctions of this are effective immediately at death (Heb. 9:27).

Almost all Protestant denominations agree with the Catholic apostolic constitution *Benedictus Deus*, in which it was solemnly defined that persons dying in a state of great holiness receive, without delay, the eternal Beatific Vision of God, and that the wicked dying in mortal sin likewise without delay begin their punishment in hell. The part of that constitution that is debatable among Christians is the parenthetical section about the soul passing through purgatory *if necessary*, prior to heaven. The *immediacy* of the reward or punishment, temporal or eternal, is evident from the parable of the "Rich Man and Lazarus" (Luke 16:19-31) and in St. Paul's expressed desire to die and be with Christ (Phil. 1:22-23; II Cor. 5:6-9). This is reinforced with the testimony of the early Church Fathers in their discussion of the *particular judgment* immediately after death, as distinguished from the *final judgment* at the second coming of Christ. "He will come again to judge the living and the dead," says the Apostles' Creed (cf. I Thess. 5:10; Rev. 20:12-13; Eccl. 12:14; Jer. 25:31; Matt. 12:36; John 5:22; Acts 24:25; Rom. 14:10; II Cor. 5:10; Rev. 14:7).

Q Do non-Christian religions believe in after-death purification?

A Through the ages, various beliefs have flourished regarding purification or sanctification after death, even in the ancient pagan religions. Zoroastrianism, for instance, speaks of the twelve states of purification that a soul must pass through before entering heaven; the Stoics too conceived a middle place of enlightenment called *Empyrosis*.

From the period of Romanticism and Idealism, the ideas of transmigration of souls and reincarnation, taken over from Hinduism and Buddhism, have gained a foothold among some who call themselves Christians. There has developed a kind of unscriptural "Christian theosophy" which holds that the human personality has a post-death development on a succession of other planets as a kind of extraterrestrial "health spa" for the soul. This tenet is alien to traditional Christianity.

Q How divergent are the views of life after death among Christian denominations?

A Among various denominations there are three basic positions regarding the state of a deceased person in the period between death and the resurrection (rapture).

The *first* view is that an individual judgment takes place immediately after death that brings the soul either to bliss or perdition. This leaves no room for the improvement of a person's mistakes of his life or to expiate his life's guilt.

The *second* position is that a soul enters a sleep that continues until the *last judgment*, which will occur after the general resurrection. A few denominations hold this position but have difficulty explaining their abandonment of the fundamental idea of the continuity of personal conscious life. It is simply a state of "suspended" punishment or reward and is hard to vindicate by Scripture.

The *third* position admits that at least some persons who are unprepared for heaven enter an interim state in which the correction of the person's moral weakness and spiritual limitations is still possible. This third position of purgation for imperfect souls holds logically that such a situation would cease with the last judgment. This is explicitly held by the Catholic Church; the Eastern Orthodox Church practices intercession for the dead, without holding to a formal doctrine of purgatory as such.

Purgatory, according to Roman Catholic teaching (and some non-Catholic denominations) is a state of purification after death in which the souls of those who die in venial sin and of those who still owe some debt for temporal "punishment" for repented mortal sin are rendered fit to enter heaven. Such souls continue to be members of Christ's Church and can be helped by the "suffrages" of the living — that is, by prayers, alms, and other good works, and most especially by the celebration of the Eucharist (Sacrifice of the Mass). Their salvation is assured, but its "completeness" (Eph. 1:14; I Pet. 1:5) is delayed until "the last penny is paid" (Matt. 5:26; 18:34).

The doctrine is a continuance of the ancient Jewish belief in the efficacy of prayer for the dead (II Macc. 12:42-46). Daniel (9:20) prayed for his deceased ancestors. The authority of the church has supported this teaching through its twenty centuries of existence based upon the tradition of the early Christians who (according to some Fathers of the Church) were taught this by the Apostles themselves.

The Eastern Church affirms belief in an intermediate state after death, but their belief is somewhat vague, as it is in the expressions of the ante-Nicene Fathers on the subject. The longer catechism of the Orthodox Church states: "Such souls as have departed with faith but without having had time to bring forth fruits, may be aided towards the attainment of a blessed resurrection by prayers offered in their behalf, especially such as are offered in union with the oblation of the bloodless sacrifice of the body and blood of Christ and by the works of mercy done in faith for their memory."

Some Anglicans accept the doctrine of purgatory, but most Protestants believe that at death the souls of believers are made perfect in holiness and pass immediately into glory. The rejection of an intermediate state after death is a corollary and perhaps an overextension of the doctrine of justification by faith and a misunderstanding of Catholic teaching on "justification by works." Actually, recent ecumenical discussions (for example, Lutheran-Catholic dialogues) have shown that there is little or no discrepancy between the Protestant teaching of "justification by faith," ratified and proven by good works, and that of the

Catholic teaching on the same issue. Both Catholics and Protestants hold that *salvation* comes by faith in the blood of Jesus (Rom. 3:22), while *sanctification* that proves the validity of that faith comes from works (works of virtue: prayer, almsgiving, mortification, etc.). "Faith without works is dead" (James 2:17).*

Since there is no essential diversity between Catholic and Protestant teaching on "justification by faith" and "sanctification by works," it could not logically be the basis for discrepancy in the teaching of an intermediate stage after death, since we are not dealing with salvation or justification as such. In the present context, we are dealing only with the use of prayer and good works to hasten the purification and perfecting of our spiritual state here on earth, and, when used as intercession, to accomplish the same thing for any deceased persons who need it. In other words, there is agreement on the "justification [salvation]

---

* What precisely does this mean — "faith without works is dead"?

The Bible clearly teaches that we become saved by the instrumentality of faith in Christ. Paul says, "To the man who does not work but trusts God, . . . his faith is counted as righteousness" (Rom. 4:5). This saving faith, however, issues in, and is seen in the works of charity, obedience, etc. In this sense, faith without works is dead.

Catholics agree with Protestants in the bannerlike statement headlined by the Reformation: "*Faith alone justifies, but not the faith that is alone.*" Saved by grace, we are led by God to do good works (Eph. 2:8-10).

Notice the *apparent* contradiction between Paul and James. Paul in Romans 4:2 says that Abraham was *not* justified by works; but James says (2:21-23) that he was. The problem is solved when we realize that Paul is speaking of the means of salvation, while James is speaking of the evidence of it. These two are speaking about different kinds of "works," and also about different kinds of faith. James speaks about the *works of mercy*, while Paul speaks about the *works of the law*. (Both Jesus and the prophets chastised Israel for minding the works of the law without the works of mercy.) "Faith" for James was belief in God (Deut. 6:4). For Paul, it meant the response of the whole person to the revelation of God's love — a loving trust in God. Dr. J. Jeremias states it succinctly: "Paul is speaking of *Christian faith* and *Jewish works*; James speaks of *Jewish faith* and *Christian works*." The bottom line of all this — when the mutual misunderstandings are removed — is: The test of our faith's genuineness is the *kind of life* produced by it (Titus 3:8). As an old Puritan pointed out, "Judas heard all of Christ's sermons!"

235

by faith" principle. And there is also agreement on the "sanctification by works" principle. In this healing prayer, we are simply taking that "sanctification by works" principle and applying it to deceased persons by way of intercession.

Q I was raised to believe that purgatory is a torture chamber in the vestibule of heaven. Tell me it isn't so.

A It isn't so.

Think of purification or purging when you think of purgatory — words used consistently in Catholic documents on this — not punishment, and certainly not torture! Any "punishment" due to sin is *negative* (deprivation of God's unveiled presence), not positive punishment like burning, scourging, etc.

However, even the concept of purging has many connotations, the most frequent one in Scripture being to rid a person of his sins (Ps. 65:3; Heb. 1:3, 10:2; II Tim. 2:21). That type of purging has only *negative* connotations. But to "purge" a fruit tree was to *prune* it. This has the *positive* connotation of causing it "to bring forth more fruit" (John 15:2).

The Greek for pruning has also a third connotation (also positive), namely cleansing; consequently, in the next sentence Jesus says, "You are already *clean* because of the word I have spoken to you." Jesus' overlapping of the meanings of "pruning" and "cleansing" points up the fact that there is a cleansing through the pruning-deprivation experience in the "cutting away." The soul's deepest desire — unobstructed union with its Creator — is being temporarily "cut off" from the vision of that Creator, that is, the Beatific Vision.

The distorted notion of horrible physical afflictions, including those caused by fire in post-death purification, has wrongly emphasized the idea of positive punishment rather than purification. We cannot overlook the unfortunate influence of certain great Christian classics that have led to this general misconception, such as Milton's *Paradise Lost* and Dante's *Divine Comedy*, or the influence of great paintings like Michelangelo's *Last Judgment*, or the great hymns such as *Dies Irae,* not to mention over-dramatized, threatening eschatological sermons.

However, the fantasizing of poets, artists, and writers should not cause us to reject the truth of post-death purification, even though the pictorialization of it may be distorted. The use of fire, for example, is clearly metaphorical and, as a means of purification, it is an appropriate symbol (cf. I Cor. 3:12; I Pet. 1:6-9; a "refiner's fire" in Mal. 3:2-3, etc.). Unlike hellfire, says Aquinas, it is purifying (purging) rather than afflicting.

Any purging of the soul after death would seem to have more of a positive connotation than negative. The sin would have been repented of at the moment of death when the soul perceives God as the be-all and end-all of its existence. And the disembodied soul, unencumbered with the limitations of brain-dependent cognition, perceives the horror of offending the Creator. Immediate repentance would cause any possible guilt to be dissolved instantly — except for hell-bound souls who died in obstinacy to grace.

The positive effect of being purged to become fruitful, and of developing the undeveloped love capacity, is the main purpose of the purging experience of the disembodied soul after death, in those cases where it would be needed.

Q Are there any liturgical passages that suggest after-death purging of the soul is a perfecting rather than a punishment?

A In the ancient formula of the canon (Eucharistic prayer) after the consecration, there is a prayer for the living, followed by the prayer for the dead and summarized with the words *"make us* [the living and the dead] *worthy* to share eternal life." This emphasizes the ongoing belief of a perfecting rather than punishment that is needed in the next life as well as in this life. The prayer for improving our *worthiness* is closely connected with the consecration of the bread and wine into the "Lamb of God, who alone is *worthy*" (Rev. 5:12).

Q How much of the notion about purification of the dead is mere theological conjecture, and have Church authorities done anything to separate fact from fiction in this matter? I would like a solid theological footing as I pray for our deceased family members.

A The Council of Trent (1549) commanded all bishops to "teach only the *sound* doctrine of purgatory handed down by the venerable Fathers and sacred Councils," and bids them to exclude from their teachings "the more difficult and subtle questions relating to the subject which do not tend to edification." This caution was reaffirmed by the Second Vatican Council (where the word "purgatory" is not even mentioned, nor is the word "suffering" or punishment connected with post-death purification); there is a warning for all to "work hard to prevent or correct any abuses, excesses, or defects which may have crept in here and there in this teaching about post-death purification, and to restore all things to a more ample praise of Christ and of God." It urges us to "accept with great devotion the venerable faith of our ancestors regarding the vital fellowship with our brethren who are in heavenly glory or who are *still being purified after death*." It proposes again the decrees of the Second Council of Nicea, the Second Council of Lyons, the Council of Florence, and the Council of Trent ("Gaudium et Spes," Vat. II, art. 51). The Councils of Nicea II (787) and Florence (1439) are ecumenically important because they express the points of agreement between the Greek and Latin churches regarding such things as to *how* souls on earth could help souls in purgatory. The Council of Trent (1549-63) treated these questions again in the context of the Protestant Reformation. The Decree on

Purgatory (1820) consolidated the accumulation of theological insights up to that point.

Vatican II focuses our attention on the fact that our greatest union with the members of Christ's mystical body, both living and dead, is within the Eucharistic sacrifice as we are joined with the worshipping Church members here and beyond the grave ("Lumen Gentium," Vat. II, art. 50). This has very significant implications for the program of healing the family tree; it explains why the greatest success in breaking the effects of ancestral bondage is found in the Eucharistic celebration.

Q It is interesting to learn about all the theological conclusions about afterlife purification, the scriptural basis for it, etc. But can you strip all this information down to the very core of the doctrine, at least as the Catholic Church teaches it?

A The *official* teaching on purgatory by the Catholic Church states only two points, namely: (1) that it exists, and (2) that persons there can be helped by our prayers, good works, alms, etc.

There is *no official* teaching about its location, about duration, about punishment, about the nature of the fire, etc. Nor is there any teaching that claims that every person must go through purgatory. It is recognized that it is possible to enter heaven immediately after death if the repentance and fervor are such that the soul is able to avail itself of the fullness of God's mercy, like the good thief on the cross who was blessed by Jesus' deathbed promise: "Today you will be with me in paradise" (Luke 23:43).

Q I know that Scripture says in several places that there are different degrees of reward in heaven for each person (for example, Rom. 2:6 and Rev. 22:12). But do these correspond to varying degrees of purging that persons may undergo before entering heaven?

A Variations in purification as required for each individual may be by various limits of duration, or various degrees of intensity, or possibly by various kinds. (It *may* be that an adulterer would undergo a different kind of purging than a glutton.) At any rate, in general, the purification process of a greater or lesser degree has nothing to do with a greater or lesser degree of glory had by those in heaven, which correspond to their holiness attained in life. "The sun has one kind of splendor, the moon another and the stars another; and star differs from star. So it will be with the resurrection of the dead" (I Cor. 15:41-42).

Q Where is purgatory located? How long must one be there? How does the purification take place? The more I know about such things, the closer I can feel (emotionally) to my deceased loved ones.

A Our knowledge of these matters is severely limited. Notions of time and space in the post-death experience of a soul are probably vastly different from our experience of them here. Also, the concept of joy in suffering while in *perfect* accord with the sovereign will of God, is beyond our present experience.

The spatial location of purgatory, as distinct from heaven and hell, was often fancifully imagined, as by Dante, with an exact latitude and longitude. St. Thomas Aquinas and St. Bonaventure have imagined that purgatorial fire was material fire without producing a material "burning" effect — a position rejected by the Greek Church. Regarding the duration, it was often misconstrued that there were definite days or months or years in purgatory because of numbers given to indulgences — a false understanding of the very nature of indulgences.

Q When living with a person, you become familiar with that person's attitudes, feelings, emotional reactions, etc. When a person dies, do all these men-

tal processes change? What does a deceased person think about while awaiting entrance into heaven?

A We can only guess, unless we rely on the many private revelations and visions about purgatory given to saints like St. Catherine of Genoa. With remarkable consistency these communications reveal that within this purifying judgment, the soul experiences the immensity of God's love — "the flame of Yahweh" (Song of Songs 8:6). The fundamental approval that God has extended to this person draws him or her to undergo the purification in peace and perfect willingness; the soul is happy to see itself stripped of all selfishness in preparation for everlasting bliss. But the yearning, a kind of "painful love" seeking complete fulfillment, is the predominant activity of the person's mind.

Twenty centuries of Church tradition have reaffirmed the teaching that those on earth can by their "suffrages" expedite this purifying process of "painful love" for those who are deceased; this is a function of the "communion of believers," or "communion of saints," in Christ's mystical body. It is done only in and through Christ, the head of that body, and only because that body constitutes a family of God by which all humans are related.

When prayers are offered for deceased persons who, we suspect, might be undergoing this purifying process, it often happens that there is an astonishing healing that takes place among the living as an indication of a total or partial release of the soul being purged, and/or the breaking of the residual interpersonal bondage (transmitted disorder) that we have inherited. (This is especially true if the prayer is in the context of the celebration of the Eucharist.)

Hence, the second aspect of the healing of the family tree program relates to the breaking of the bondage derived from deceased persons; the resultant release not only has an effect on them, but also on us the living, who are related to them by ancestry or consanguinity.

This phenomenon indicates that the "dead" are conscious and in some way "living, " since they react to God-focused healing prayers; for God "is not the God of the dead but of the living" (Matt. 22:32; Mark 12:27; Luke 20:38). Because of the soul's immortality, no one is ever really "dead," only a body can die.

In Hebrews 9:27-28 we read, "Christ *will appear a second* time, not to bear sin, but to bring salvation to those who are waiting for him." Could this mean "waiting" during life, or also in the afterlife? This leaves open the *possibility* that a deceased soul may not have reached its ultimate destiny but perhaps be in an intermediate state of purification "waiting for him."

Q The Bible forbids communication with the dead. Isn't prayer for the dead a communication with the dead?

A Let it be made very clear that the Bible forbids us to evoke the dead (Deut. 18:11), which would be the sin of necromancy. While *it does forbid evoking the dead, it does not forbid invoking God for the dead* and their needs. We know that not even death can separate us from God's love (Rom. 8:38-39), for his love and mercy for us will endure forever (I Cor. 13:13). We know that both the living and the dead are members of God's family (Eph. 3:15). And from the earliest Christian experience, as shown among the Corinthians, there was an awareness of the ability of those on earth to relate to and help those who are deceased (I Cor. 15:29). Thus, there is nothing that forbids us to ask Christ to help the dead to receive his love and forgiveness more perfectly in an ongoing way, especially if we ask this as Christ offers himself to the Father for all in the Eucharist.

Q Was belief in after-death purgation held in the early ages of Christianity, or is it only a recent teaching?

A It has been a tradition from the earliest ages of Chris-

242

tianity, recorded in the catacombs and other archaeological sites, and taught as a doctrine by many of the early Fathers of the Church, such as Tertullian, Origen, Ephraem, Ambrose, Cyprian, Augustine, Basil the Great, Gregory of Nyssa, Gregory the Great, and Gregory of Nazianzus.

Even the great Protestant reformer, Martin Luther, stressed the advisability of praying for the dead to receive the fullness of forgiveness in the risen life so as to be admitted to the Beatific Vision.

Q Many of the Old Testament Scripture "proofs" of purgatory are found only in the "Catholic" Bible, which includes more books than the "Protestant" Bible. Please explain.

A This teaching on prayer for the dead dates among the Jews from more than a century before Christ. The Bible extols the heroic Judas Maccabeus for praying for his dead soldiers to be "loosed from their sin" as they looked forward to "the resurrection of the body" (II Macc. 12:42-46). This scriptural passage and several others that have to do with the purification of deceased persons from the effects of sin are found in the deuterocanonical books of the Bible, which are regarded by all Christians as *inspiring* but only by some Christians as *inspired*. In spite of controversy about the inspiration of deuterocanonical books accepted by Roman Catholics, Orthodox Christians, and some Anglicans and Episcopalians, there is no controversy over the fact that they serve as historically reliable sources.

It is an historical fact that the pre-Christian Jews prayed for their dead that they may be "loosed from their sins." *This was an early form of healing of the family tree* as it related to deceased members of that family. This is recorded in the Septuagint version of the Bible translated in Alexandria (Greek version) of the Old Testament that contained seven and one half books not found in the Hebrew Bible of the Palestinian Jews. (It is significant that a number of quotations in the New Testament from the Old Testament shows that the Septuagint version was used by the sacred writers of the New Testament.) It is in that Septuagint version that we find passages referring to post-death purification and customs of praying for the dead.

Q Did St. Paul say anything about prayer for the dead?

A Paul does not approve or condemn the custom of baptism for the dead (I Cor. 15:29). He thus at least does not disapprove of the practice in the early Church in Corinth of extending spiritual help to the dead, striving to bring them to the fullness of Christ's grace. Paul himself prayed for the deceased Onesiphorus to find mercy, as well as for his bereaved family (II Tim. 1:18).

Q Were there any Old Testament examples of praying for the dead?

A Yes. Several (mentioned elsewhere in this book). Daniel prayed for both the living and the dead as a form of a healing of the family tree prayer, fulfilling the command of Leviticus 26:40 to confess the sins of one's ancestors (Dan. 9:20). We see this same custom practiced in Baruch 3:1-8. Another example is found in Numbers 14:19.

There is less difficulty in accepting an *apparent* injustice on God's part in punishing us for the sins of the ancestors, when we see that fact as encouraging us, the living, to help our sinful ancestors through prayer.

Q Did the Apostles teach anything about prayer for the dead?

A At least two of the early Fathers of the Church, St. John Chrysostom in the East and St. Cyprian in the West, claimed that *this practice of praying for the dead was derived from the teaching of the Apostles themselves.* St.

Polycarp, who was a disciple of St. John the Evangelist, had an annual memorial celebration of the Eucharist offered for the repose of his soul (A.D. 155).

Q How did the Eucharist come to be connected with prayer for the dead?

A It started in the first century, and by the sixth century, Masses were being said in series for deceased persons. Unfortunately, within a few centuries after that, abuses arose in which the celebration of the Eucharist came to be regarded as an almost mechanical means of releasing persons from any post-death bondage, and often these Eucharists were celebrated in a slovenly and non-devotional manner, in which there was more concern for quantity than quality of the Eucharistic prayer.

In rebelling against these abuses, the Protestant reformers unfortunately "threw out the baby with the bath" by rejecting a venerable tradition from the Apostolic Age.

From the eighth century, there has been incorporated into the Eucharistic prayer in the Roman rite a special formulary prayer for the dead; and a special day is still celebrated on November 2 — "All Souls Day," in which there are special prayers and Eucharists offered for deceased persons.

Q Have there been any private revelations or visions about the state of the dead, sharing need for prayer, etc.?

A There have been many private revelations from reliable sources, especially great saints, such as Teresa of Ávila, Catherine of Bologna, and the saintly Curé of Ars who attest to the urgent desire of "uncompleted" deceased persons to be prayed for. Those saints had great devotion in praying for the souls in purgatory. Great mystics like St. Catherine of Genoa had extended revelations of the experience of purgation after death. Nothing in any of these private revelations contravenes the teaching of Scripture.

Q Does the science of parapsychology tell us anything about purgatory?

A Hundreds of persons were interviewed by Dr. Raymond Moody in researching his book *Life After Life*; these were persons who had experienced near-death experiences (NDE's), that is, who underwent clinical death and were resuscitated. A number of these patients reported having seen *persons in the other life who were undergoing a learning and adjustment process.* Some of these patients reported seeing a "realm of bewildered spirits" where the dead seemed to be trapped and attempted to communicate with living relatives (as did Dives in Jesus' parable) hoping for some kind of help to move on to the complete union with God. This school of learning on the other side of the grave seems somehow to be a place in which there is a making up for a lack of love exercised during life toward God and one's fellow man. The result of this scientific research does not contravene theological teaching that has been traditionally held in Christianity for twenty centuries and even before.

Q Do any non-Catholics, other than some Orthodox Christians, believe in prayer for the dead?

A An increasing number of Anglicans and other non-Catholic groups are coming to accept the belief of an intermediate stage of purification for "uncompleted" souls, between death and the resurrection of the body. The word purgatory evokes some untoward feelings and prejudices, and yet there is the acceptance of the possible need for purification and the awareness of a terrible injustice we would be inflicting upon our beloved dead if they were indeed in some need of our help and we refused to provide it because of a theological prejudice.

Q When Jesus said he was called to release captives who were in "prison" (Luke 4:18), could he have been referring to purgatory?

A That is one *possible* interpretation. This intermediate stage might well be called in some way a "prison" because of the confinement or unfulfillment experienced there. This is perhaps the place referred to as the "prison" that Jesus visited, where he preached to the spirits there who formerly were disobedient (I Pet. 3:19-20)—the souls in this spirit world that Jesus visited after his death but before his resurrection ("he descended into hell," Hades, abode of the dead). It is also referred to in I Peter 4:6 where he says that Jesus went to evangelize the dead. This indicates that there was some place in which progress, improvement, increased knowledge, or purification could take place.

Q Do our prayers somehow help the dead to grow in maturity?

A Since both the living and the dead are part of the family of God (Eph. 3:15), and we are all meant eventually to be *mature* citizens of heaven with God's people and members of his family (Eph. 2:19), we have the privilege and perhaps the obligation to help those deceased members of our immediate family, and of the larger family of God, to attain that maturity, the fullness of their destiny. "He who overcomes will inherit all this" (Rev. 21:7).

A group of Anglican theologians reporting to the Archbishops' Commission of Christian Doctrine stated that the living may usefully pray for the dead through Jesus Christ, that during the state of purification they may develop "a deepening of character and greater *maturity* of personality, when they are ready to give and receive total love and can grow into the image of Christ so that they will be able to proceed to the everlasting Beatific Vision."

Q Should we pray to the dead, or only for them?

A Although we may not pray to the dead, except to address them prayerfully *in Christ*, asking also their prayers for us, we do this in and through Jesus who stands "between" the living and the dead, as prototyped by Aaron (Num. 16:48). Mutual prayers of the living and the dead for each other are appropriate, since "all who belong to Christ, having his Spirit, form one Church and cleave together in him" (Eph 4:16).

Invoking the dead (the sin of necromancy) is forbidden by Deuteronomy 18:11, and four times condemned by the Holy See in the Catholic Church. But invoking God *for* the dead and their welfare is commendable (II Macc. 12:46).

Q Is purgatory a joyless place?

A The souls in the period of purgation have three sources of joy. *First*, they know they will never be damned, for "no torment will ever touch them" (Wis. 3:1); *second*, they know they will never offend God again by sin; and *third*, they know they will someday see the face of God . . . "their hope is full of immortality" (Wis. 3:4).

Q Did Jesus ever say anything about forgiveness after death?

A In Matthew 12:32, Jesus speaks of a sin against the Holy Spirit that is not forgiven in this life nor in the next, implying that there is some forgiveness in the next life — that is, purifying of the soul in a period after death.

Q How do we know that the purgation is only temporary?

A In the parable of the unjust steward, Matthew 18:36, Jesus says, "He sent the servant to be punished *until* he should pay the whole amount" — the implication of a limited payment for delinquency, not eternal punishment. (There is a parallel passage to this in Luke 12:59.) It is limited "payment" that Jesus refers to.

The words of Jesus in another parable (Matt. 5:26) reaffirm this: "You will stay until you pay the last farthing." Tertullian, a second-century Father of the Church, says this implies a temporary posthumous detainment and that the "prison" that Jesus refers to is Hades, the abode of the dead.

In Revelation 3:2-3, it says: "I find that what you have done is *not yet* perfect in the sight of my God." Imperfect but not damnable souls must be spoken of here, since the good in them "has not died completely" (v. 2); they are not worthy of damnation, yet unlike the others who have kept clean (purified), these would need to be purified at death, when the Lord "comes upon you like a thief" (v. 3). This passage speaks of an after-death limited time of perfecting.

Q What is the so-called "theological conclusion" argument for purgation after death?

A Perhaps some examples will answer this question better than a lengthy explanation. Revelation 21:27 says: "Nothing defiled shall enter heaven" and Hebrews 12:14 tells us, "Without holiness no one will see the Lord" (cf. I Pet. 1:15; I John 3:2-3). A question arises: What will happen to those who have not repented of small sins like impatience and arguments? They can't be sent to hell for such failings (since they are not mortal sins — "sins unto death" [I John 5:17]). "All wrongdoing is sin — but there is sin which does not lead to death." Yet neither can these souls get to heaven, for they are in some way defiled. So there must be a way by which the non-mortal (venial) sin can be removed or purged; that is called purgatory.

This form of "proof" is called a "theological conclusion," but it is based on Scripture and derived from its implications.

Another example of this form of conclusion can be found in Hebrews 12:23, which says: "You have come to God, who is judge of all mankind, and to the *spirits of good people* who have been made perfect." This arrival at the "heavenly Jerusalem" (v. 22) must have been preceded by a purification by which good persons are "made perfect" or purified. Hebrews 11:39-40 points out to us: "None of these [Old Testament heroes] received all that God had promised them; for God wanted them to wait and share the even better rewards that were prepared for us." There was not perfect fulfillment, even after death, for Old Testament faith champions. They had to wait for something better (Heb. 9:28), when Christ opened heaven by his redemptive act on Calvary.

This waiting must have involved the perfecting process of learning, being evangelized, as stated above in I Peter 3:19 and 4:6. This growth or purifying process was prior to heaven. The teaching, for example, Esdras 4:35 (a quote from a deuterocanonical book that was in the Latin Vulgate Bible only prior to the Council of Trent and accepted by some Anglican theologians today), says: "The righteous dead are in places where God is keeping them waiting."

Q **Do Protestant theologians make use of the "theological conclusion" in analyzing the questions of afterlife purgation?**

A Yes. For example: Looking at the incident of God's taking the life of the illegitimate baby of David and Bathsheba (II Sam. 12:15-23), a Protestant Scripture scholar, Gleason L. Archer, Jr., in *Encyclopedia of Biblical Difficulties,* says, "They needed this rebuke as a reminder that God's children, *even though forgiven*, must bear *temporal consequences* of their sin and patiently endure them as an *important part of repentance*." If this principle applies to the consequences of sin in this life, there is no theological reason why it would not be equally applicable in the next life through a purging process. If this much is acknowledged, then healing one's family tree can be seen to include possible healing of that family's deceased members of "temporal consequences of their sins." This is one example of the line of reasoning used by Catholic as well as some non-Catholic theologians.

Q Why should non-Catholics look into the Catholic teaching on this subject?

A Regardless of the religious persuasion of the reader, it behooves him to give special consideration to the teaching of post-death purification as presented by the Roman Catholic Church, especially since that denomination has done the most extensive theological and scriptural evaluation of this issue, and secondly, because the Catholic Church has held this teaching and practiced it in its liturgy for twenty centuries, back to the Apostolic times.

A careful consideration of the Catholic teaching on this issue will show that it in no way contravenes the basic Protestant teaching regarding justification through faith in Christ held by all Christian denominations. The Catholic teaching on purgatory is one of the most misunderstood teachings in its whole theology, misunderstood by *both* Protestants and Catholics.

The Second Vatican Council specifically avoids even the word "purgatory," which prejudices so many people, and it does not refer to suffering or pain, or flames of purgatory, but simply refers to our need to cultivate "friendship with those who are still being purified after death" and urges all "to work hard to prevent or correct any abuses, excesses or defects which have crept into this teaching, and to restore all things to a more ample praise of Christ and of God." Yet the basic doctrine of the nine councils and pronouncements in the history of the Church that have dealt with this teaching stand intact. Such a wealth of research behind such a balanced theology deserves at least a respectful consideration by persons of any denomination.

Q My non-Catholic friends tell me that our Catholic belief in purgatory is an insult to Christ, whose blood washes away all sin. How should I respond?

A Many persons die in grace and in the friendship of God, but are burdened with venial sins and imperfections of which they have not repented *"with godly sorrow"* (II Cor. 7:10). *Any sin or fault that is not repented of,* even an act of impatience or lack of resignation to God's will in suffering or neglect of prayer, etc., *would not come under the cleansing blood of Christ* (Acts 20:21; 26;20). Absolute repentance for a failure to do God's will is a condition for the application of his mercy: "Produce fruit in keeping with repentance" (Matt. 3:8; Luke 3:8), and yet part of God's mercy according to Catholic teaching is a post-death cleansing experience to clear away these last hindrances (II Pet. 3:9) before entry into the direct vision of God (I Cor. 13:12), face to face (cf. I John 3:2).

Q How is the question of praying for the dead connected with the healing of the family tree?

A This has twofold significance for the healing of the family tree program. Our deceased family members and ancestors may need to be released from the confinement of bondage as an aftereffect of their own sin, and that release may have an indirect bearing on *our* release from the inherited effects of *their* sin, whether it be physical, emotional, or spiritual problems that we ourselves are experiencing. More important than the release of ourselves from the trans-generational bondage initiated by deceased ancestors is the fact that those ancestors themselves may be helped, encouraged, supported, and relieved by our intercession by prayers and good works.

Q Since the word purgatory is not found in the Bible, the only basis for the doctrine is tradition. Doesn't that make it a "weak" teaching?

A The actual word purgatory is not found in the Bible, just as many other doctrinal words are not found there, such as "baptism in the spirit" (only "baptized in the spirit"). The teaching on purification of the dead from the effects of sin is not explicitly in Scripture, but it is *implicitly in Scripture in at least fifteen places* (quoted throughout this book) — over and above the twenty centuries of tradition in the Church's teaching, as well as the ancient inscriptions in the catacombs attesting to that tradition from the very early ages of Christianity.

Vatican II reminds us that *sacred tradition is not above Scripture but serves it* by explaining it, confirming it, and explicating it. Tradition unfolds the meaning of Scripture the way a sermon does, in no way contravening the basic sufficiency of Scripture but putting light on it. That is why Paul tells us to *hold fast to traditions* learned either by word of mouth or by writings (II Thess. 2:15). St. Jude tells us to fight for the faith "handed down" (the meaning of the word tradition — v. 3). This includes anything pertaining to holiness, faith, worship, etc. It even includes the criterion by which we know which books are truly inspired and are part of the Bible (including those books that make more directly a reference to purification after death, as well as authenticating the teaching itself about after-death purification). The Bible itself encourages the use of tradition not only in the classical passages, II Thessalonians 2:15 and Jude 3, but also in II Timothy 1:3 and 3:4 and in the many oral teachings referred to in II Thessalonians 3:6 and Hebrews 2:1, and even "insights" as in I John 3:24.

This tradition is found quite consistently in the early Fathers of the Church like St. Clement of Alexandria who spoke of some deathbed conversions requiring further "sanctification by purification" in the next life. St. Augustine in his commentary on Psalm 38 asks God to purify him here in order to avoid a cleansing after death.

Ancient catacomb inscriptions corroborate the custom of praying for the dead, and especially the celebration of the Eucharist for the deceased. This tradition is supported by such early Fathers of the Church as Ephraem, Cyril of Jerusalem, John Chrysostom, Cyprian, Tertullian, Origen, Ambrose Caesarius of Arles, and Gregory the Great.

The loving concern that the early Christians had for the release of their beloved dead from bondage gave rise to the custom of requiem Masses, not only funeral Masses. There are countless examples of private revelations in the lives of many of the Church's greatest saints regarding the beneficial effects of prayers and especially the Eucharist offered for the deceased undergoing their purification. (However, tradition, as a formal source of truth that serves and explains Scripture without contravening it, as Vatican II says, is the consistent age-old teaching of the Church; it does not include private revelation, no matter how reliable.)

Q What are the "pains" or "punishments" endured during purgation?

A We know very little about the "pains — if any — in purgatory," but certainly there is a kind of "pain" and "yearning" for the fullness of God's presence like the unfulfillment of an ardent lover who can contact the beloved only by letter. Also, the "poor souls" can be said to "suffer" from knowing that they are impeded temporarily from the Beatific Vision by their own fault; yet in such "suffering," as in the purifying spiritual "dark night" of the mystics, there is great joy and peace.

The very extensive private revelations on purgatory given to St. Catherine of Genoa in the fifteenth century led her to state that *the desire of the soul for God was nothing else but God's own love inflaming that soul as a purifying fire*, cleansing it from all "dross" left by love-weak or love-deprived acts or thoughts in the individual's life on earth. It is simply God's magnificent design for completing the unfulfilled capacity of the soul to love.

If this may be called a punishment, it is a *negative* punishment of "deprivation" of the complete presence of God. *We do not have any doctrinal assurance of any "positive" punishment in purgatory*, as Suarez, the great theologian, pointed out.

Without doubt, the temporary deprivation of the Beatific Vision, for which the soul would otherwise be prepared, is the keenest form of "suffering" in purgatory. Some theologians call this the "temporary pain of loss," with the soul's awareness of the Creator being so near and yet so far.

This intense longing for God, rooted in the very nature of the human soul, is heightened by the knowledge that the effects of earthly failure *could have been expiated so easily on earth* by deep repentance, heartfelt prayer, and good works.

It is quite possible, but not a matter of doctrine, that besides the pain of loss, there is a "pain of sense" that could consist of spiritual sorrows, of real soul affliction, deep remorse, chagrin, shame of conscience, etc., capable of inflicting a kind of pain on the soul cognate to a humiliation experience (cf. Sir. 2:4). Both St. Bonaventure and the theologian Suarez hold that the pain of loss — that is, the yearning for God's presence—far exceeds any pain of sense that *might* be experienced in the purgation process. "My soul thirsts for the living God; when can I go to meet with God?" (Ps. 42:2; cf. 63:1; 143:6). St. Thomas Aquinas conjectures that this pain of loss accompanies the pain of sense.

Q The word "fire" often associated with purgatory frightens me.

A It is not appropriate to compare the pain of earthly fire with the purgatorial fire of divine love, since they are on two entirely different entitative levels. "They shall be saved, yet so as by fire" (I Cor. 3:15). Since this "fire" is the flame of God's love, it destroys only evil, not the beloved contaminated with the evil, as St. Ambrose writes in his commentary on Psalm 118. It burns only dross, not the gold that is purified in the fire. Isaiah 13:11-12: "I will punish the wicked for their iniquity and ... I will make a man more precious than purified gold" (cf. Num. 31:22-23; Job 23:10:

"He knows the way that I take; when he has tested me, I will come forth as gold"). Proverbs 17:3: "The crucible for silver and the furnace for gold . . . the Lord tests the heart" (cf. 27:21). Wisdom 3:7: "Their hope is full of immortality afflicted in few things; in many they will be well rewarded, for God has tried them and found them worthy of himself. As gold in the furnace, he has proved them, and as a burnt sacrifice he has received them and *in time, honor will be given them.* The just will shine and will run like fire through stubble." Sirach 2:3-5: "Wait on God with patience; join yourself to God and be faithful that you may be honored in the end . . . accept whatever comes your way and be patient . . . when you are humbled, for gold and silver are tried in the fire, but acceptable men in the furnace of humiliation."

It would not be a *total* fulfillment of God's will if the love were not kindled to the *fullest.* "I have come to bring fire on the earth and how I wish it were already kindled," says our Lord (Luke 12:49). If this fire is not kindled *to the fullest in this life* (on the earth), then after this life, the fire of divine love, the "flame of Yahweh" (Song of Songs 8:6; cf. Ps. 29:7) will penetrate the soul as fire penetrates the iron in the furnace and fills up what is lacking. That beautiful presence of God's love that makes the soul yearn for him with an intensity that is beyond description is the purifying process of purgation — a kind of "baptism at the entrance of paradise," as St. Ambrose describes it.

Q Are there any beautiful, uplifting descriptions of purgatory? So much is morose and depressive.

A In his masterful book *Catholicism*, Father Richard Mc-Brien states that we do not know whether purgatory is even a place, or whether it contains real fire as we know it, or whether there is suffering parallel to that of the souls in hell. These descriptions may or may not be true, but they definitely are not part of Catholic doctrine as defined. His description of purgatory is more in line with the authentic teaching of the Church: "Purgatory is best understood as a process by which we are purged of our residual selfishness so that we can really become one with the God who is totally oriented to others. . . . The kind of suffering associated with purgatory therefore is not suffering inflicted upon us from outside as a punishment for sin, but the intrinsic 'pain' that we feel when we are asked to surrender our ego-centered self so that the God-centered loving self may take its place. It is part of the process by which we are called to die and rise with Christ in the paschal mystery (John 12:24)."

Q How does this bittersweet suffering change the soul?

A Its *first* function would be to remove the guilt of sin by inducing repentance in a very deep degree. The classical passage from II Maccabees 12:46 says that the souls there need to be "loosed from their sins." *Second*, it would remove the inclination toward sin, the inordinate desires and habitual inclinations towards sin experienced on earth, and *third*, it would act as "temporal punishment" due to sin, dissolving lifelong habits of sin that induced a weakness in the soul (though acquired through the body).

From the sixteenth century, the view has been prevalent that the *guilt* of sin was removed *at entry* into purgatory, but not the above-mentioned *effects* of guilt (the liturgy seems to follow this theological view).

Persistent habits of sin or uncontrolled desires may have left deep spiritual scars on the faculties of the soul, scars that penetrate below the level of consciousness into the very fibers of the personality. Before entering heaven in the unspeakable holiness and majesty of God, all of these must be removed. The whole person, in other words, must be made over and formed more completely into the image of God to which it was made, which sin has to some degree effaced.

Modern authors hold that the "remains of sin in the

soul" are more deeply embedded than the person is aware. Therefore, there is probably an ongoing process that lays bare, so to speak, successive layers of the infected personality and exposes to view the faults there that are deeply buried. In this purification process, the *full personality* emerges for the first time. On earth, the lusts and habits of avarice, etc., even embedding themselves in the subconscious mind, have prevented a person from acting to the fullest extent as a child of God. Now, he is enabled to live to the utmost, for the first time revealing the richness of his personality and is thus prepared for entrance into the direct vision of God in his inscrutable majesty, glory, and splendor.

Thus, purgatory is not a place of negative suffering designed to punish the soul, but a state of positive progress where the person is enabled to possess God by first truly possessing himself. This "suffering" is not something of the nature of torture as we understand it on earth; it is the suffering that is accepted readily and even joyfully and eagerly, as one would eagerly strive to make an early appointment with a dentist or doctor to correct a dental or medical problem, seeking the cure in spite of discomfort in the treatment. In the healing of the family tree program, our task is to help our beloved dead within our family tree to be "loosed from their sins" so that the effects of those sins will no longer burden them, and also will no longer have their deleterious effect upon us as an inherited bondage.

Q Why is the guilt or sin removed by repentance but not the punishment due to sin?

A Washing can remove a clothing stain, but before the clothing can be worn, it must be dried and more than likely ironed. In this laundromat called purgatory, there is a follow-up of the repentance washing, namely atoning. As Isaiah acknowledged, he was a "man of unclean lips"; a *seraph* applied a live coal to his mouth saying, "Your guilt is taken away *and* your sins atoned for" (Is. 6:6-7) (note the distinction between guilt and its atonement—between sin and punishment due to sin). Both the guilt *and* the atonement for guilt are removed through the applied fire of divine love in the bittersweet experience of purgation. However, the basic guilt is removed at the first moment of repentance, *by its very nature*, while the resultant temporal punishment may be extended.

We know that sin by its very nature has consequences in physical, psychological, and spiritual orders, and even though we have experienced the grace of forgiveness for this or that sin, that does not guarantee that we have been totally healed of the wounds of sin or that we have totally eradicated the attraction or inclination or habit of sin. By analogy, you may repent of adultery and be forgiven by God, but still have to support a child that was the result of that act of adultery.

God wants us to be *completely whole* (I Thess. 5:23) and holy, with a "holiness without which no one can ever see the Lord" (Heb. 12:14; Rev. 21:27). In purgatory we become fully who we are as God created us to be. It is a healing process that involves "holistic healing." In purgatory *we* receive not just redemption, but the *"fullness of redemption"* referred to in Ephesians 4:30 and I Peter 1:5. In this state of purgation, "We rejoice in the *hope* of the glory of God" (Rom. 5:2). It is in this "spiritual laundromat" that the side effects of evil are washed away.

We can almost hear the command of Jesus to "loose the bonds" of the dead, as he commanded the family of Lazarus to loose the binding swaths of his burial clothes (John 11:44).

Jesus "learned to obey through suffering" (Heb. 5:8). There is a similar process for those in purgatory who in a special way thus become Christ-like as they too learn to obey through suffering. Purgatory is a state of relearning, to be fully trained in the ways of God, for "suffering is part of training" (Heb. 12:7).

The purging may be said to be *destructive* to the negative elements of sin and its remnants, but *constructive* in

259

the sense that it leads the soul from imperfection to perfection, to an ever higher degree of perfection. After one of her revelations on purgatory, St. Catherine of Genoa wrote, "The souls in purgatory having their wills perfectly conformed to the will of God and hence partaking of his goodness, remain satisfied with their condition, which is one of entire freedom. . . . " In purgatory we give the final and perfect fiat—a yes to God's will in the accomplishment of perfect obedience; in the blaze of divine love, we are profoundly enlightened.

Growth in holiness is not an instantaneous spurt but a gradual process of progress (cf. Col. 3:9-10). It is the same in post-death purgation, where we come to reflect the perfect humanity which is the image of Christ (Eph. 4:13-16), "sharing in the divine nature and escaping corruption" (II Pet. 1:4). As we "come to God . . . having been placed with the spirits of the saints *who have been made perfect*" (Heb. 12:23), we will join them, fully ablaze with divinity: "Then the virtuous shall shine like the sun in the kingdom of their Father" (Matt. 13:43). Perhaps St. John had a mystical vision of purgatory when he wrote, "I then saw something like a sea of glass mingled with fire. On the sea of glass were standing those who had won the victory . . . " (Rev. 15:2).

Q **When our prayers help release a soul in purgation, how do they relate to us after that?**

A As those persons who are materially helped by us on earth will pray for us (II Cor. 9:14), so also those who are spiritually helped in their state of purgation will become our special prayer partners in all of our needs in life, and our special friends through all eternity.

Q **A good Christian friend of mine says that once you're saved, you're always saved, and that means you're always "heaven-ready," with no need for purgation.**

A Those who hold the "once saved, always saved" position in its *most literal form* (a position condemned by the Bible in Jude 4) are persons who assume that salvation by grace gives them the right to sin without restraint because God in his grace will freely forgive all their sins even without *subsequent* repentance (a similar heresy is condemned by Paul in Rom. 6:1). The more moderate believers would maintain that the "once saved, always saved" position does not entitle you to sin, but simply affirms that the person is locked into a position of perpetual preparedness for heaven.

It is true that Jesus said that no one can snatch his sheep out of his Father's hand (John 10:28 and 29; cf. 6:39), yet it is possible for them to reject him. They can break away from the handclasp of God, though God will not break away from their handclasp. There is a great security in the "born-again" experience (I John 3:9): "No one who is born of God will continue to sin . . . he cannot go on sinning because he has been born of God." Obviously, many born-again persons have human failings, but they will not have a life that is *characterized by sin*.

Yet, a born-again, Spirit-filled person can still sin, as Saul did (I Sam. 18:10). The Lord says, "When a righteous man turns from his righteousness and does evil, I will put a stumbling block before him" (Ezek. 3:20; I Pet. 2:8). "Therefore, son of man, say to your kinsmen, the righteousness of the righteous man will not save him when he disobeys . . . the righteous man if he sins will not be allowed to live because of his former righteousness. . . . If he trusts in his righteousness and does evil, none of the righteous things he has done will be remembered" (Ezek. 33:12-13; 17-18; cf. Council of Trent, Sess. 6, Canon 23).

Hence, the command of Peter, "Obey God *because* you are his children [born into his family]; *don't slip back* into your old ways — doing evil because you knew no better, but be holy now in everything you do." There would be no need to urge a born-again Christian to avoid backsliding and to continue to seek holiness if it were automatically assured without any effort on his part; hence Peter's exhortation.

He goes so far as to say, "It would have been better for them not to have known the way of righteousness, than to have known it and then to have turned their backs on it" (II Pet. 2:21).

The same is true for those who are baptized in the Spirit and are familiar with the word of God (Heb. 6:4-5). Saul was Spirit-filled (I Sam. 10:6), but "the Spirit left him" (16:14). Of course for those who totally apostatize, they prove that their faith was not genuine from the start (cf. I John 2:19). A state of being confirmed in sin after having a knowledge of the truth is a "dreadful thing" (cf. Heb. 10:26-31).

Hence, born-again Christians need to continue to grow and to continue to repent. A neglect of either form of spiritual improvement would keep them from removing former habits of sin or from attaining enough repentance or from fully exercising their love capacity, and hence leave them in need of post-death purification.

Realistically, we must presume that no one is perfect. There is still deep theological meaning in the bumper sticker that says: "Born-again Christians are not perfect, just forgiven." Repentance doesn't imply perfection.

If the repentance is not total at the moment of death, then the sin erasure is not total at that time, and further purification is needed. There will always be the need "to abstain from the sinful desires which war against your soul" (I Pet. 2:11). While it is true that "if the Son sets you free, you will be free indeed" (John 8:36), yet we should "live as free men, but do not use your freedom as a cover-up for evil" (I Pet. 2:16).

It is all too easy to cover up the evil or sin or faults committed after we feel that we have been made righteous by the blood of Christ (cf. Heb. 1:3). To be always "heaven-ready" our repentance must be frequently "updated." And *besides* this sin erasure, a high degree of virtue cultivation is needed. A weed-free plot is not a garden. "Repeated sickness requires repeated medicine," wrote Tertullian in his treatise *On Repentance* (third century).

Q When is it impossible to have improvement in the afterlife? Is this only in the hell of the damned?

A If at the moment of death the likeness of the soul to God is not merely imperfect but totally obliterated beyond all possible restoration, then and only then can we say the soul is damned, or "lost." Only God can know to whom this happens or how often or how seldom it happens. Hence, it would be rash to say that any living person has no longer any hope of salvation. The most probable opinion is that if a soul departs out of this life without even a spark of the divine life in it, it is damned, or "lost." "Withersoever the tree falls, there it shall lie." Paul says, "Their destiny is destruction [because] their god is their stomach . . . their mind is on earthly things" (Phil. 3:19).

If the spiritual life is *not* totally extinct, there is hope for progress and restoration. "Smoking flax he shall not quench" (Matt. 12:20; Is. 42:3). A sick person may have some hope of being healed, but when life is extinct in death, the hope for healing vanishes. It is the same with the soul. The spiritually dead soul in hell is in a state of irreversible malice.

Just as malice in hell is irreversible, so heavenly fulfillment is irreversible. Even the pagan Plato writes in the *Phaedrus* that "there is a law that the paths of darkness beneath the earth shall never be trodden by those who have set foot on the heavenly road."

PERSONAL NOTES

PERSONAL NOTES

PERSONAL NOTES

Chapter Four
HEALING POWER
OF THE EUCHARIST
FOR YOUR FAMILY TREE
Why Is It the Most Powerful Means of Healing Known to Man?

Q Is the Eucharist the only framework for the healing of the family tree program?

A It is not the *only* method, just the *best* method of healing, because we are dealing not just with grace but with the very Author of Grace, Christ himself, in the Eucharist. There are several Eucharistic passages in Scripture that refer to healing power, including the ultimate healing by rapture, "He who eats my flesh . . . I will raise him up at the last day" (John 6:54).

Q Does the Liturgy of the Word within the celebration of the Eucharist play any role in the program for healing the family tree?

A The Word of God ensures that the bonds of love in the Christ-centered family will be established. "My mother and brothers are those who *hear God's Word* and put it into practice" (Luke 8:21).

The hearing of God's Word — that is, the liturgy of the Word in the Eucharistic assembly — thus provides the basis for a unifying bond to displace the bondage of disunity (conflict, hatred, etc.) that is often part of ancestral infection (Job 4:11).

Q How does the Eucharist help deceased family members?

A Since the Eucharist is a reenactment of Calvary by which we "show forth the *death* of the Lord until he comes" (I Cor. 11:26), the total forgiveness that Christ expressed at the time of that death on Calvary — "Father, forgive them" — is reexpressed in this reenacted Calvary experience. The deceased for whom we pray at this time — as well as the living — are cleansed with that forgiveness; the pouring out of his blood is the cleansing element that removes the sin and its effects. By receiving Christ's forgiveness for ourselves and for our family members, and extending that forgiveness to all who have hurt us, the living and deceased are enabled to be eligible for heaven, where that *total* love, *total* freedom from resentment and bitterness, is enjoyed by the citizens forever as "spirits of good people *who have been made perfect*" (Heb. 12:23).

Q What are some non-Eucharistic forms of the family tree healing program?

A Many persons do not have the opportunity to use the Eucharist in the healing program because it involves the clergy, and that may not fit in with their convenience or even with their own denominational beliefs. But there are other ways besides the Eucharist. The one I would especially like to suggest to break untoward behavior patterns is a deliverance prayer, invoking the power and authority of the name of Jesus by his precious blood against the evil of sin, the forces of evil that enter with sin, and the residual effects of sin. God wants to break the curse in a family or break any bondage through the name of Jesus. You should not curse the enemy, but only the works of the enemy (Christians don't curse *people*). Michael, the Archangel, said to Satan, "The *Lord* rebuke you" (Jude 9).

Plead the blood of Jesus over your home and over the room where the person sleeps who might have any kind of defect or bondage; over the pillow, the clothing, the possessions of the person. You can invoke the name of Jesus and the blood of Jesus over all those things.

But, added to that deliverance prayer, there must be the intention to *resist* whatever the enemy tries to activate (James 4:7). For instance, for anyone with compulsive temper tantrums, the prayer should be accompanied with the grace-spawned intent to resist those urges. Often a prayer against a spirit of infirmity when sickness is involved (Luke 13:11) will break the ancestral bondage. The phrase in the Lord's Prayer, "deliver us from the evil one," when said with *faith*, is powerful. The plural form (us) makes it fitting as a prayer for family problems.

The main point to keep in mind here in the prayer of deliverance is that every evil spirit is subject to us, if we are *thoroughly* permeated with the Spirit of Jesus, "because the one who is in you is greater than the one who is in the world" (I John 4:4). (The word "world" here means the community, system, or family of those not born of God [cf. 4:2-3].)

In breaking the bondage, it is good to use an "image prayer." When you think of the sequence of one generation to the next, the parent to the child, to the grandchild, and so on, visualize each generation as a stratum or layer. In each stratum include the brothers and sisters, uncles, aunts, etc., in each generation horizontally. Try to see all those in each level: for instance, in your own generational level, all your siblings — brothers and sisters, step-brothers and step-sisters, etc. Between each layer or stratum mentally place the cross of Jesus or ask Jesus to pour his precious blood with its healing power. Continue this between each level, between great-grandparents and grandparents and parents, between parents and children, between children and their offspring down through the generations even to unborn generations. Include in the prayer all those who are above in the generational lineage, and those who are below — that is, our ancestors and our descendants. In each layer, place the blood of Jesus or the cross of Jesus. This could be done whether you do it in conjunction with the Eucharistic celebration or not. If this is done under some form of pastoral leadership, it could be a "guided" prayer, directed by the pastoral leader.

Q **Does the "born again" kind of commitment have any bearing on the healing itself? Is it part of the Eucharistic celebration in the healing program?**

A It's very important in the Eucharist service that the commitment is made to Jesus as the Lord of our lives, really *receiving him as Lord* (John 1:12), at the same time we receive him *as a Redeemer or Savior*. This appropriation, or receiving, is part of the act of becoming born again, receiving the full effects of redemption, called salvation (in its initial sense). "Receiving" Jesus can become a more profoundly meaningful act when it is ratified by *receiving* him in Communion devoutly.

This born-again commitment, like receiving Communion, can be repeated endlessly and frequently (articulated as the so-called "sinner's prayer"), and it can be deepened in terms of the intensity of the commitment, in the same way that renewing the marriage vows can deepen the commitment in marriage. In this receiving of the Lord and surrendering to his control, there is a loving release. As Jesus accepts us when we let go, submitting ourselves and our family to his care, the forgiveness and fullness of life come into us, a peace and serenity pervade our soul, mind, and body — peace that the world cannot give (John 14:27). That is a sign that deep healing is taking place.

The repetition of this commitment and the repetition of the family healing prayer within the context of the Eucharist is very helpful. To do this more than once would assure a deeper level of healing. That is why Jesus commands us to *keep on asking*, seeking, and knocking (Luke 11:5-10; Matt. 7:8). He further tells us to: *"Keep praying until the answer comes"* (Luke 18:1 LB). Healing may come step by step as one repeats the prayer for the healing of the family tree.

In most cases there will be a dramatic healing of one or several members of the family, on the first occasion that the healing prayer is exercised; when there is an upbuilding of faith with each partial success of healing, the next healing will be even deeper and more far-reaching.

Q How can I be assured that my sins and those of my ancestors are actually forgiven? This seems to be such an important part of the overall healing process.

A Most Eucharistic services have an initial period of time for repentance (penitential rite) as implicitly required by Scripture (I Cor. 11:28). After this required examination of conscience, an act of repentance is the most obvious step, a "confiteor" prayer or confession to the Lord. "If we confess *our* sins" (this plural form could imply that we should confess both our sins and those of our ancestors [Lev. 26:40]) "he is faithful and just and will forgive us our sin and *purify us* [purge us from all unrighteousness]" (John 1:9).

Hence, the faith involved is not just a belief that a healing of illness and other effects of sin will take place, but prior to that, a faith in the great mercy of God to provide a spiritual healing from sin itself, in ourselves and our relatives, living and dead.

All of this is especially emphasized in the "penitential rite" of the celebration of the Eucharist and is also reaffirmed within the liturgy of the Lord's Prayer. The very fact that the plural form is used is to emphasize the familial content "forgive *us* our trespasses." We ask forgiveness through the blood of Jesus, "which is poured out for many for the *forgiveness* of sins" (Matt. 26:28).

Q Will the Eucharistic-centered healing break this bondage of my family members involved in the occult?

A Paul answers that question by showing the mutual exclusion of the force of evil and the force of good in the context of receiving Communion (I Cor. 10:21): "You cannot drink the cup of the Lord and the cup of demons too; you cannot have a part in both the Lord's table and the table of demons." In this statement of Paul, we see a spiritual justification for the Holy Eucharist as a bondage-breaking power for those who have within their family lines or in themselves any connection with the occult or the demonic.

Among the living as well as the dead, many are in what might be called "partial bondage," that is, a *limited* degree to which demonic forces can inhibit the fullness of life, health, and the flow of God's life of grace. These should not be forgotten either in our prayers or at the Eucharistic healing service.

Q My niece has anorexia and is getting medical and professional care for it, but nothing seems to help. Can I help her through this family tree healing program?

A An example of the remarkable effects of the Eucharist may be seen in persons healed of anorexia and/or bulimia —both rather intractable disorders. There are indications that in some cases a spirit of self-starvation may superimpose on the physical or psychological conditions that engender this disorder. For these cases the words of Christ have special meaning. "I am the Bread of life, he who comes to me will never go hungry and he who believes in me will never be thirsty" (John 6:35). I suggest that you have a Eucharist offered for your niece, at which she should be encouraged to feed on this "true bread from heaven" (John 6:32). It is the most powerful means of dispelling the spirit of anorexia nervosa, or self-starvation, as well as bulimia and other eating disorders.

Self-destructive eating disorders are often prompted by the same deceiver who tried to entice Jesus to turn stones into ordinary bread (Matt. 4:3). Ideally, the ratification of the healing process within the Eucharist will be found to be effective in proportion to the *devotion* with which the

"Bread from heaven" is received, and in proportion to the *frequency* with which it is received "therapeutically."

Q In what way can the Eucharist be of help to our deceased family members?

A In "showing forth the *death* of the Lord" in this Eucharist (I Cor. 11:26), we emphasize the truth also that Jesus became available to the departed by his own entrance into the abode of the dead (Hades in Greek) (Acts 2:27-31), where his power to heal the incompleteness of any departed soul is available to them. "He was put to death in the body but made alive in the Spirit, through whom he also went and preached to the spirits in prison who disobeyed long ago when God waited patiently in the days of Noah while the ark was being built" (I Pet. 3:18-20). In the Apostles' Creed we say, "He descended into hell" (that is, Hades — abode of the dead). "He is ready to judge the living *and the dead.* For this is the reason the gospel was preached even to those who are dead so that they might be judged according to men in regard to the body, but alive according to God in regard to the Spirit" (I Pet. 4:6).

At the time of uplifting the sacred species in some liturgies at the close of the Eucharistic prayer, there is symbolized not only the resurrection of Christ but also his Ascension — the "total rapture." Our prayer at this time should be that all of those who are waiting to go to heaven, whether on this side of the grave or beyond, will be "lifted up" by Jesus to be reunited with him in his celestial family. That is the ultimate in the healing process.

Countless examples and clinical case histories of persons who have been "treated" by the program of healing the family tree attest to marvelous signs, showing that we do have access to the whole range of members within our family tree, both living and dead. Many of these cases are detailed in the pioneer study of this subject, *Healing the Family Tree*, by Kenneth McAll (Sheldon Press, London). Other less publicized studies and the private experience of those who have engaged in this program attest to the same power that is accessible to us, particularly through the devout participation in the Eucharist in healing effects of ancestral sin, with signs that even the dead can be in some way "healed."

Q You speak of "healing" the dead family members. How can one "heal" the dead? If healing comes mainly through the Eucharist, how can a dead person receive Communion in order to be healed?

A In celebrating the Eucharist, we follow the command of Christ to "do this in *memory*" of him (Luke 22:19), and the way in which we *memorialize* this experience is by "proclaiming the *death* of the Lord until he comes" (I Cor. 11:26).

It is precisely in this memorialization of Christ's *death* that we acknowledge that he has entered into the abode of the dead: "He descended into hell" (Hades — abode of the dead). By his own death he has a special access to the dead to draw them to himself and to lead them to the fullness of the *life* of grace and holiness (I Pet. 3:19 and 4:6).

In participating in the Eucharist we should pray that Jesus who said he has come to give us life more abundantly (John 10:10) may come to the dead, especially our dead family members to give them the *abundance* of eternal life.

In receiving Communion it is helpful sometimes to mention particular names of deceased persons that come to mind so as to receive communion on behalf of that person who does not have access to the abundant life of grace in the Eucharist as we do. In particular there may be a need to pray for this "abundance of life" for aborted babies whose lives have been cut short and who have been rejected from the human race by the aggressive crime of abortion and thus prevented from growing up within the family and participating in the societal benefits of the family tree.

Healing means giving a fuller, richer degree of life. That is precisely what the healing of the family tree is designed to do, for each family member, whether living or dead.

Q **What if I pray for my deceased relatives and have a Eucharist offered for them, and they are not in need of any prayers?**

A "No prayer is wasted," as the ancient dictum has it. If deceased persons are prayed for within the context of the Eucharist or by any prayer and have no further need for purification, the prayers are not unavailing, for the deceased in heaven may be drawn more deeply into the intimacy of God's love by means of these prayers (St. Thomas Aquinas called this "accidental glory"). They themselves may thereby increase in their own intercessory power as they "watch over us, the living" (Heb. 12:1).

When Jesus referred to the "many rooms in my Father's house" (John 14:2), perhaps he was implying not only that there were different degrees of reward for good works performed, as mentioned many times in Scripture (for example, Rom. 2:6; II Cor. 5:10; and Rev. 22:12), but also that through our prayers, persons in the Father's house might be advanced to other "rooms" of greater splendor. This of course is conjecture, since much of what we question about the next life is clouded in mystery.

Q **I never heard of the Eucharist used as a sacrament of healing. Is this something new?**

A The anointing of the sick is the main "sacrament of healing" (James 5:14-15), but the sacraments of baptism (I Pet. 3:21) and reconciliation (penance) (John 20:23) are also healing sacraments, and just as good nutrition can heal undernourished persons, so the Eucharistic banquet can heal by nourishing a sickly soul.

The healing power of the Eucharist has been attested to by many of the great champions of Christianity, great saints such as St. Elizabeth of Hungary, St. Malachy, St. Thomas Aquinas, St. Bernard, and St. Teresa of Ávila. The hagiographies are replete with stories of healings within the context of the Eucharist, most especially prior to the fourth century, when devotion to the Eucharist as a healing sacrament was at a very high peak. Many of the terminal illnesses that were instantly cured through the intercession of St. Augustine of Hippo occurred in the post-Communion period of the Mass he was celebrating. There were not only obvious signs of healing among the living, during the Eucharist, but also countless revelations that affirm that the dead had been "healed" in some way; and the living released from a transmitted bondage within their family tree by this sacrament.

The following note handed to me during a family healing retreat is typical of countless cases of healing during the Eucharist, especially at the Consecration and after Communion:

> During the healing Mass last night, you spoke a prophetic word that someone in the audience was being healed of a hearing defect in the left ear. At that moment my left ear opened and I could hear clearly even when I kept my hand over the right ear that was not defective. I am delighted with this healing and I praise God for all he has done through this marvelous method of healing.

Q Can we enhance the healing power of the Eucharist by participating in it more actively?

A Yes, by virtue of the "priesthood of the laity" (I Pet. 2:5). By our associating with Christ in the reenactment (not repetition) of the Calvary experience in the Eucharist, we actively participate in the work of redemption (extrinsically, not essentially), just as we do through our sufferings (I Pet. 4:13; Col. 1:24, etc.). Our Eucharistic participation involves, among other things, an intercessory power along with that of Jesus himself because we "belong to him"

(Mark 9:41). As we intercede for all those who are, or are to become, beneficiaries of his redemptive act, we are no longer regarded as servants but as friends (John 15:15) — in some way on a par with Christ (I Cor. 3:23) — as he entrusts to each of us a precious dimension of his relationship to the Father and to the brethren. In this capacity as intercessors within the Eucharist, we are empowered to "clean up" the defects that have invaded our family tree.

Q Is there any particular time in the Eucharistic liturgy that the healing power flows in a more pronounced way?

A Speaking only from experience rather than theology, I would say that the two most pronounced periods of healing in the liturgy are during the time of the consecration of the bread and wine into the body and blood of Christ and the post-Communion period. However, quite frequently remarkable healings take place also at the time of the lifting up of the Sacred Species, when the great "Amen" is sung, closing the Eucharistic prayer within the Mass, symbolizing Christ's resurrecton. In this we show that in Christ's rising he defeated Satan and his minions, for he said, "If I be lifted up, I will draw all men to myself" (that is, out of the dominion of Satan). When we allow the uplifted Eucharistic Christ to become a cynosure to draw our entire family constellation, living and dead, to him, his healing presence manifests itself often with breathtaking healings.

Q What is the "paschal mystery" referred to in the Eucharist, and how does it relate to this healing program?

A The "paschal mystery" is a Christic process of moving from death to life (not life to death), and then into glory. It is a "Good Friday to Easter Sunday to Ascension Thursday" cycle that Jesus asks us to reenact (John 12:24) to effectively produce fruit (such as healing family problems).

In the Eucharist, the "paschal mystery" of our faith is celebrated, reflecting Christ's dying, rising, and returning in glory: "Christ has died, Christ is risen, Christ will come again." Our gathering as a family of God is to celebrate these three aspects of Christ's mission: (1) his dying, that is, his laying down his life for love of us; (2) his rising, that is, the presenting of himself as a source of new life for us; and (3) his coming or returning, that is, the completion of the cycle of redemption to join us with himself.

From the perspective of the participants in the congregation at the Eucharist, there is the same triple function symbolized: (1) as we die to our sins; (2) as we rise to a new level of life in spiritual vitality and health; and (3) as we return to the Lord in a deep and profound union with him, greater than we had experienced before that Eucharistic encounter.

By our intercessory prayer, we reach out to embrace all of our family members, living and dead, to be caught up in this same threefold movement in response to Christ's threefold exercise of redemption. In doing so, we request for them the fruit of redemption in its fullest degree — that is, *complete* salvation, which includes healing of the family tree. Peter reminds us that we are "redeemed from the empty way of life handed down from our forefathers, by the precious blood of Christ" (symbolically shed in the Eucharistic celebration) (I Pet. 1:18-19).

Q **In seeking a healing in the celebration of the Eucharist, should we look forward to a future exercise of Christ's healing power, or should we claim some healing from what he has done for us already in the past by his death for us?**

A We have a "windshield view" and a "rear-view mirror view" of the redemption of the present Eucharist — a future anticipation of the perfect healing it will bring at the rapture (John 6:54), and a "past review" of the restorative power of the redemption as we memorialize it (Luke 22:19).

We anticipate sacramentally here on earth now what will be further enhanced at the time of our total incorporation into Christ, the rapture referred to in reference to the Eucharist: "He who eats my flesh and drinks my blood abides in me, and I will *raise him up* at the last day" (John 6:54; cf. vv. 39-40, 44, 57). It is only in this Eucharist-related rapture that the Christian is ultimately incorporated into the mystery of redemption. Communion is a sacramental anticipation of that. As such it carries within itself its own therapeutic and purging and deliverance power. The bread and wine transformed into the Christ-presence is reflective of our own transformation, when our glorified bodies (I Cor. 15:44) will reflect the glorified body of Jesus that we now receive in Communion (15:49).

In celebrating the Eucharist in fulfillment of Christ's command as a memorial, "Do this in memory of me," we remember because we cannot afford to let the mystery of redemption become something of the past as if distanced from us today.

We must be *reminded* that Christ has *died* for us, therefore we are free; that he has *risen* for us, therefore we are risen to a level of membership in his family; and he will *come again and again* memorially in the Eucharist, therefore there will be no end to his concern for us in matters of health or any other need, as he shows his patience toward us "for a thousand generations" (Exod. 20:6; 34:7).

Q Why is Eucharistic prayer to be preferred over other prayers for healing ancestral bondage?

A For several reasons. In I Corinthians 11:26, Paul says, "Whenever you eat this bread and drink this cup, you proclaim the Lord's death until he comes" (cf. Matt. 26:29). In this proclamation, or "showing forth," of the Lord's death, we show forth all that is connected with his death, the fullness of redemption, the effect of which is salvation; and the fullness of that salvation involves the fullness of life in abundance, which includes complete health in body, mind, and spirit.

The word "salvation," from the Latin word *salus*, means health, fullness of health. Hence, the salvation-reflecting sacrament is meant to be not only *salutary*, but *salubrious*. There seems to be built within the Eucharist an element of health-giving power. This is reflected also in the fact that only persons who eat healthful foods with proper nutritional values are healthy. By consuming this most spiritually healthful food, we are assured of being spiritually healthy, dissolving the ailments and defects in mind, body, and spirit that we suffer, often as a result of the transmitted effects of ancestral sin.

Hence, the Eucharist is the most appropriate means of dealing with the suffering that comes to us because of our forebears' sins. This is particularly true, since the "Lord's Supper" is a meal and is communitarian; participating in it points up the intended unity in the family constellation. "Because there is one loaf, we, who are many, are one body, for we all partake of the one loaf" (I Cor. 10:16).

The *one* loaf that was used in the early Eucharist was broken in many pieces to symbolize unity in plurality (cf. the motto "*e pluribus unum*" on U.S. coins) in the corporate body of believers. There should be a love-linked unity in a family tree, as there is in any societal unit, and yet a diversity. The unifying power of the Eucharist itself that Paul refers to here is the basis for the unifying and healing power it brings to the family tree.

In receiving this Body of Christ (now in the appearance of bread and wine) ravaged by the scourging and crucifixion, there is a healing for our bodies, ravaged by trauma, disease, and sickness. There is a "showing forth" of a healthy spiritual and an emotional vitality enjoyed in the freedom from disease and sickness. We "show forth" the death of the Lord (I Cor. 11:26), who in his body was "crushed for our iniquities" (Is. 53:3). The same body present in the Eucharist is the one that bore our sins and heals us: "He himself bore our sins *in his body* on the tree so that we might die to sin and live for righteousness. By his wounds *you have been healed*" (I Pet. 2:24). But family healing also comes through Jesus' *blood* (I Pet. 1:18). These two references from Peter's first epistle reflect the healing and saving power of the two Eucharistic species—the body and blood of Jesus. Hence the preference for the Eucharist as a family tree healing vehicle.

Q Why is the healing of the family tree accomplished more effectively in the Eucharist than in a simple private prayer?

A There are several reasons:

1. The Eucharistic celebration is experienced as a corporate expression of faith — a *shared* faith (cf. Mark 2:5, where Jesus worked his miracle in response to the *shared* faith of the four persons — probably family members, who lowered the paralytic through the roof into his presence).

Whenever any group, especially a natural family or spiritual family (congregation), prays together as a corporate unit, it is more effective for healing than an individual praying alone: "If two of you on earth agree about anything you ask, it will be done to you by my Father in heaven. For where two or three are gathered in my name, there am I with them" (Matt. 18:19-20). One might say in prayer, one plus one doesn't equal two, but equals perhaps many more, by God's sovereign design.

2. In the Eucharist, this shared, or corporate, prayer is not a simple informal gathering; it is under a formal spiritual headship which adds a new "ecclesial" dimension of power.

3. Another dimension of this special power of the Eucharist is derived from the fact that the Eucharist is referred to by Jesus in several places as able to induce the *ultimate healing* called the rapture (for example, John 6:54, 40, 44).

4. And, finally, the healing power from the Eucharist comes especially through Communion, which involves a

mutual indwelling with Christ: "Whoever eats my flesh and drinks my blood remains in me and I in him . . . so the one who feeds on me will live because of me" (John 6:56-57). In that Communion there is a direct encounter with the Divine Physician himself, and in several places the Scripture reminds us that everyone Jesus touched he healed. He touches us in his Eucharistic presence in Communion. That fact optimizes the chance of a healing taking place. But as he touches us, we touch him (John 6:56). "All who touched *him* were healed" (Matt. 14:36; cf. Matt. 9:20; Mark 3:10). Even the faith expectancy of a remote touch could bring about a healing, as happened to the woman with a hemorrhage (Matt. 9:21), "If I only touch his cloak, I will be healed." A far deeper encounter is the union of Communion — the closest touch of God in his healing presence.

For these reasons, the Eucharist is the best framework for the healing of the family tree. Experience has proven this to be true, as measurable by the number and impressiveness of testimonies about healings during the Eucharist, as compared to those from private prayer.

Q To obtain the healing effect of the Eucharist, is it enough simply to attend the service, or must it be done with special fervor or devotion?

A The success of the healing service depends greatly on the faith-filled love or devotion — far more than most people realize.

In receiving any sacrament such as the Eucharist, especially when concerned for its release of healing power, it is good to keep in mind the theological distinction between the two sources of efficacy: first, the intrinsic power of the sacrament (*ex opere operato*), to use the theological term, and second, the subjective element of devotion or fervor, that is, the faith-filled love response (*ex opere operantis).* The first source of efficacy is *quantitative*, the number or frequency of acts of participation in the Eucharist; the second is a *qualitative* factor of devotion or fervor that animates the recipient at the time of receiving the sacrament.

The scriptural basis for the first mode of efficacy may be found in the words of Jesus in John 6:56: "Whoever eats my flesh and drinks my blood remains in me and I in him" (that is, union with Christ, independent of devotion). The second mode of efficacy may find its scriptural support in the words of Jesus where he tells us to *hunger* more for this food that brings eternal life than for ordinary food (John 6:27). The hunger or yearning is an aspiration of love which increases the power of the Eucharist in proportion to the intensity of that love.

Thus, one should not regard the healing power of the Eucharist as merely an automatic thing, without regard for the subjective element of faith-filled love in its reception. This factor is so important that it can make the difference between a successful healing or disappointment in the healing of the family tree program. Hence, it is highly recommended that a prayer for one's family members, living or dead, should be as much as possible an ongoing prayer, reinforced with *frequent* participation in the Eucharistic banquet, by devoutly receiving Communion.

Q **There is so much controversy about the Eucharist among different religions. How can this be a vehicle for healing?**

A The *main* vehicle of the healing power released in the family tree healing program is connected with participation in the Eucharist. In light of this, it seems incongruous that the doctrine regarding the Eucharist is one of the most controverted points in the history of Christian theology. Cardinal Merry Del Val listed more than 150 interpretations of the four-word sentence, "This is my body." Out of those many interpretations, 90 are currently used today, and these are scattered among the more than 20,000 Christian denominations throughout the world.

On these doctrinal issues of the Eucharist, we find that

75% of the world's Christians (not 75% of Christian denominations) accept the belief in the "Real Presence" of Christ in the Eucharist.

"This *is* my body which is to be given for you . . . this *is* the cup of my blood which is to be poured out for you" (Luke 22:19-20; cf. Matt. 26:27, Mark 14:22-24, and many passages in John 6 that refer to the Eucharist). "Anyone who eats and drinks without recognizing the body of the Lord, eats and drinks judgment on himself. That is why many among you are weak and sick and a number of you have died" (I Cor. 11:24-25). "If anyone eats this bread, he will live forever; this bread is my very flesh which I will give for the life of the world" (John 6:51). "My flesh is real food, my blood is real drink. Whoever eats my flesh and drinks my blood remains in me and I in him" (vv. 55-56; cf. also I Cor. 10:16).

These and other passages are taken literally by many who are "*non*-fundamentalists" (basing their theology on eight cross-referential contexts), yet are not taken literally but only symbolically by many who *are* "fundamentalists." Thus, the two camps reverse their theological stance when the doctrine of the Eucharist is involved. Jesus lost *many* of his disciples because of this teaching on the "Real Presence" (John 6:66).

It is, I think, further significant that the success of the healing of the family tree program has been found to be far more widespread when used by those who believe in the "Real Presence" of Christ in the Eucharist: the Anglicans, Episcopalians, Orthodox, Lutherans, Catholics, etc. (also, these denominations celebrate the Eucharist far more frequently than others).

However, many Protestant theologians today are either privately or publicly reassessing their theology regarding the acceptance of the doctrine of the "Real Presence." Others still ask the question the Jews asked: "How can this man give us his flesh to eat?" (John 6:52), and the question many of his disciples asked, "This is a hard teaching; who can accept it?" (John 6:60).

Q I heard a priest say that there are four dimensions to the Eucharist. What are they? And are they somehow part of this healing program?

A In participating in the Eucharist as part of the family tree healing program, it is good to recall the four dimensions of the Eucharistic celebration and their relationship to the healing process: thanksgiving, meal, memorial, and sacrifice.

First, it is a *thanksgiving* as illustrated by the fact that Jesus "gave thanks" (said grace) within the actual words of consecration (Matt. 26:26; Mark 14:22; Luke 22:19; I Cor. 11:24). "The cup of *thanksgiving* for which we give *thanks* . . . is the blood of Christ" (I Cor. 10:16). (The very word Eucharist in its later derivative meaning signifies thanksgiving for a "good gift.") God's best Gift is Jesus (II Cor. 9:15), and Jesus' many gifts to us include our healing.

Second, it is a *meal*. The Eucharist is spoken of as the Lord's Supper, since the first celebration was the *Last Supper*. Today a Communion meal is had in response to Christ's command: "Take ye and eat, take ye and drink." A meal is an act of fellowship, and normally it is among those with whom we are familiar, or with family members. Hence, it is an appropriate context for healing the family tree. The Eucharistic assembly itself is a representation of the larger family of God, and its communitarian dimension reflects the aphorism "Humans are the only animals that don't like to eat alone." Thanksgiving, Christmas, and family reunions are centered around a meal. In the Eucharistic banquet, we celebrate, among other things, the healing love of God.

Third, the Eucharist is a *memorial* indicated by the words of Jesus "Do this in memory of me" immediately after the words of consecration. Hence, in the celebration of the Eucharist, the *anamnesis* (or memorial) prayer follows the sacred words of consecration and continues the theme, "In *memory* of his death and resurrection, we offer . . . his body and blood."

In memorializing the redemptive act, we recall it as including the warranty for the healing we seek; the reason for that is the fact that Jesus didn't die to save souls; he died to save persons. That means that our body, mind, and spirit come under that saving influence. Thus, divine healing of the body, mind, or spirit is part of the fruit of redemption that is memorialized here (I Pet. 2:24; Is. 53:4-5, 11).

Fourth, the Eucharist is a *sacrifice*. This is indicated again within the words of consecration, "my body given for you . . . my blood *shed* for you and for many." It is also explicitly stated by Paul: "Whenever you eat this bread and drink this cup, you proclaim [show forth] the Lord's *death* until he comes" (I Cor. 11:26). The sacrificial element is intimately associated with the Eucharist, and it is in this symbolic shedding of blood, "unbloody sacrifice," that the Eucharist derives its healing power, for healing is included as an effect of Christ's sacrifice (Matt. 8:16-17).

Q Since Christ doesn't "die" on the altar, how can his "death" in the Eucharist be said to bring about any healing effect?

A There is an important theological distinction to be made here. First, though most Christians believe in the reality of the *presence* of Christ, they do not believe in the reality of the *death* of Christ on the altar. The *person* of Christ is held to be real, though seen only as bread and wine, but the death is not real; it is only a symbolic or "mystical" death, seen only in the symbolic shedding of the blood. (The blood-shedding symbolism, according to most theologians, is the fact that the wine is *separately* consecrated from the bread as Jesus did at the Last Supper.)

It is also important to understand that the death of Christ is *not repeated* on the altar, for Scripture tells us very clearly, "Christ died *only once* as an offering for the sins of many people" (Heb. 9:28 LB). "Christ died for us *once and for all*" (Heb. 10:10). "By that *one* offering, he made forever perfect in the sight of God all those whom he is making holy" (Heb. 10:14). So the sacrifice of the Mass does not "cause Christ's death again" but merely proclaims it as Paul says (I Cor. 11:26).

Thus, the Eucharist is *not a repetition* of the Calvary experience of redemption but *merely a reenactment* of the Calvary experience of redemption — just as Shakespeare's play "Julius Caesar" does not repeat the death of Caesar but merely reenacts it.

Therefore, the Eucharistic sacrifice is not real; instead it is a mystical, bloodless, unbloody sacrifice. But the *Person* being sacrificed in that symbolic way is *real* on the altar. It is because the Person is really present physically, that divine healings take place most frequently and most dramatically in the context of the Eucharist, where Jesus' blood breaks ancestral bondage (I Pet. 1:18).

Q Besides praying for an increase in faith, is there anything else I should do to make the Eucharist healing service more effective?

A Seeking a "faith-lift" is important, but it should be incorporated with a "love-lift" also, to produce optimum answer to prayer, as St. John tells us (I John 3:23).

It was at the occasion of the first Eucharist — the Last Supper — that Jesus spoke so eloquently of his love for us and gave the command for us to love one another. This also makes this "Sacrament of Love" an appropriate vehicle for the healing program, since the healing of the family tree breaks the generational *bondage* and replaces it with a golden *bond* of love, as successive parts of Christ's mystical body are healed in subsequent generations. Thus, Christ's love becomes the matrix for our familial love and is the vehicle for healing.

Q I am afraid of "failing" in my prayer for family healing, since I experience a kind of "spiritual emptiness." I envy those who seem to be bursting with spiritual life.

A No one is on a constant spiritual "high." And many devout souls are seldom "high." God often serves the cake without the "frosting." But feeling isn't as important as filling — filling yourself with *God's* goodness, not yours.

At Communion time we are in the closest union with Jesus. "He who eats my flesh and drinks my blood abides in me and I in him," the mutual union of "Communion" (John 6:56). In this *infilling* with the presence of Christ, we have an occasion to fulfill the pleading of Paul in Ephesians 3:19, "that we may be *filled* to the measure of all *fullness* of God." It is only with this *total infilling* with Christ that we have security against contamination or recontamination with the forces of evil. Jesus tells us that after evicting the enemy, the house is "clean but empty" (Luke 11:25) — rather than "clean and full" with the fullness of Christ. This emptiness leaves it open to "seven devils worse than the first."

Pray to appreciate more fully the truth that "you have been given *fullness* in Christ, who is the head over every power and authority" (Phil. 2:10), so as to experience "the *fullness* of him who *fills* everything in every way" (Eph. 1:23). This is the antidote to your "spiritual emptiness."

Q I know we can't have heaven on earth, but I would like a little taste of it here. If my family with all its problems were healed, I would regard that as "a little bit of heaven."

A You have touched on the best stimulus for the virtue of Christian hope, which, along with faith and charity, plays a strong role in this healing program.

In receiving Communion, we show forth, or "proclaim the Lord's death . . . until he *comes*" (I Cor. 11:26). His future coming—the parousia—is sacramentally anticipated in the Eucharist: "I will not drink with you of the fruit of the vine until I *come* in glory" (Luke 22:18). That is when the fellowship of the Last Supper will be ultimately consummated in the great Messianic "wedding supper" to come (Rev. 19:9). The import of this theology is clearly eschatological and hope-oriented. The Eucharist therefore is a kind of sacramental anticipation of the banquet of heaven, in which we enjoy a state of total, complete, and irreversible healing (Rev. 21:4). The bondage of sin (ancestral and otherwise), as well as the effects of sin, will no longer exist at that time.

Q I can see why the Eucharist would be sanctifying, but how can it be healing?

A The death of Christ that is "proclaimed" in the Eucharist was the source of our salvation and purification (Heb. 1:3). Since salvation even etymologically speaks of a state of perfect health, it is on that score also that Communion is designed for a therapeutic effect as well as a sanctifying effect (Matt. 8:16-17).

Q Is the anointing with oil used during the healing service?

A In the healing of the family tree program, it is customary among some to have an anointing service, using olive oil as a symbol of healing as Jesus commanded in Mark 6:13, and as is stipulated in James 5:14. The oil of course has no intrinsic therapeutic value; it is an external symbol, as a flag is a symbol upon which we focus in exercising patriotism. In like manner the oil has a therapeutic value only because of what James reminds us of: "and their prayer, if offered in *faith*, will heal him, for the Lord will make him well." Jesus, when he healed the man who was lowered through the opened roof, "saw their faith" — that is, the corporate faith of the family members who brought the paralyzed man to Jesus. Added to this is the power of a spiritual healing in the anointing: "and if his sickness was caused by some *sin*, the Lord will forgive him" (James 5:15 LB).

During this time of anointing, those who are waiting

and those who have returned to their seats after being anointed should be using that time, ideally, to pray for others in the assembly; while speaking of anointing, James says: "Pray for each other that you may be healed" (James 5:16). This mutual prayer is also advisable during the post-Communion period of the Eucharist when Jesus is exquisitely sensitive to the presence of faith, and especially corporate *(family)* faith in a healing context. (Grouping of people for a healing service is to be preferred to a private prayer for healing, since it involves a liturgical "ecclesial" public prayer form, and also the plural component that Jesus said gives efficacy to prayer — even "two or three gathered in my name" [Matt. 18:20].)

Q Does the healing service need to be repeated?

A Jesus said, "Always pray, and don't give up" (Luke 18:1).

It is often helpful to repeat the Eucharistic service for the healing of the family tree, perhaps even several times, particularly for families in which the wounds and ailments and aberrant behavior, etc., are deeply ingrained. The deeper the injury, the more love is needed to heal it. Repeating the sacrament of love and participating lovingly with a loving yearning for the union with Jesus in Communion is the surest way of dissolving the bondage that infects one's family tree.

Q Can family members be healed without being present at the healing service? Can they be healed even when they don't know they're being prayed for?

A The Eucharist may be celebrated for members of one's family, living or dead, with or without the consent or knowledge of the persons for whom it is intended. However, it is certainly to be preferred that all living members of the family would be present at the Eucharist and receive Holy Communion devoutly; if not all members are able to participate, as many as possible should endeavor to do so.

Q **Is there any deliverance prayer in the Eucharistic family healing service?**

A In the Eucharistic service it is customary to recite together the Lord's Prayer. The last petition of the Lord's Prayer — "deliver us from the evil one" — is the essence of "deliverance prayer." The intention of the petitioners at this point should be to ask God to free both living and dead persons in their families from the power of the Evil One and then to give subsequent protection from the Evil One. The prayer should include an intention of binding the power of evil, for Jesus said "to bind the strong man" (Matt. 12:29). At this point, the Evil One should be remanded to the power of Jesus, for him to dispatch the demon or demons as he sees fit.

In the context of the Eucharist, the deliverance prayer has special significance because of the total incompatibility of demon forces with the healing presence of Jesus in the Eucharist: "One can't drink the cup of the Lord and the cup of demons, too; you cannot have a part in both the Lord's table and the table of demons" (I Cor. 10:21). Among the many reasons for the Eucharist being the most perfect vehicle for healing the family tree, this reason stands out preeminently.

Q **Are the heredity factors affected by the Eucharist in this healing service?**

A In healing the family tree, there is a "cleansing of the bloodlines" by the blood of Christ in the Eucharist. We could ask for a healing or cleansing of "bad blood" of the genetically transmitted defect, but also the deliverance from the evil forces that have been superimposed on those hereditary factors.

Q **I know that giving and receiving forgiveness are**

important for the healing process. Is there a place for this in the Eucharistic celebration for healing?

A In preparation for the celebration of the Eucharist, there is usually some form of a "penitential rite" to receive the Lord's forgiveness by repentance. At this point we should go beyond the simple act of repenting for our sins and include also with them the confessing of the sins of our ancestors, living or dead, as mandated by Leviticus 26:40 (cf. Jer. 3:12-15; 14:20; Ps. 106:6; Neh. 9:2).

At the same time that we seek forgiveness for our sins and those of our ancestors, we must also consider the other side of the forgiveness coin, giving the Lord's forgiveness to others, especially during the "sign of peace" ritual within the Mass (Matt. 5:23) acting as channels of his mercy (II Cor. 2:10). Without this, our prayers would be useless (Mark 11:25). It is important at this time to experience as deep a level of forgiveness as possible for all who have offended us, whether they be living or dead. Our dead relatives may be eagerly awaiting our forgiveness, if we have been withholding it from them. The importance of loving forgiveness can hardly be overemphasized. Read Luke 6:27-38, if you find it hard to forgive anyone, living or dead.

Q Are there any special preliminary prayers or anything to make the service more effective?

A In the opening prayer of the Eucharist, it is helpful to express a petition silently, or publicly where appropriate, that we, *first*, may be freed from all controlling forces outside of ourselves, causing personal phobias, demonic domination of other persons, etc. *Second*, the petition should also be that we be made free of sinful habits in ourselves; and *third*, we should pray that the bondage be broken that recurs from generation to generation as we visualize the blood of Jesus interspersed "vertically" between each generation and also "horizontally" in the consanguineal lines between brothers, sisters, uncles, aunts, etc. (The general content of this prayer is also appropriate in the post-Communion period, usually in silence.)

Q How does Jesus, received in Communion, become a source of healing for living and dead members of the family tree?

A In two ways: among the living, and between the dead and living.

First, by the *unifying* (corporate healing) effects of his Eucharistic physical body among *living* members of his mystical body: "Is not the bread we break a participation in the Body of Christ? Because there is one loaf, we [the living] who are many, are one body, for we all partake of the one loaf" (I Cor. 10:16-17). In early Church assemblies, one loaf was broken and shared, symbolizing the unity of the Body of Christ, the Church, nourished by himself, the one Bread of life (cf. John 6:33-58).

Second, by his *living* body *dying* symbolically and "proclaimed" as such by our Communion (I Cor. 11:26), he becomes the link between ourselves and our deceased relatives. "Christ died and returned to life so that he might be the *Lord of both the dead and the living*" (Rom. 14:9).

We "see the goodness of the Lord in the land of the living" (Ps. 27:13), that is, among our *living* relatives, by his releasing us from the bondages derived from our *dead* relatives, as Aaron stopped the transmission of the plague (that had killed 14,700 people), by standing between the contaminated dead and the living. The trans-generational bondage transmitted from the dead ancestors to us, the living, is broken by Jesus' stance, as the plague was broken by Aaron's stance between the two (Num. 16:48).

Q After the sought-for healing is attained, is there something I need to do to preserve it?

A Once the freedom from bondage has been attained, the perseverance in this newfound freedom has a double requirement: (1) God's ongoing power to preserve us and (2) our exercise of faith in him. These two requirements are epitomized by Peter: "Through *faith* shielded by God's *power,* we are thus caught up in God's *protective* loving embrace" (I Pet. 1:5). This, in turn, will foster within us a tenderhearted love among our family members (I Pet. 3:8) also in God's "protective embrace."

As a corollary of this, Peter then quotes Psalm 34 to show how this results in a gratifying, holy life blessed by God who is eager to answer the prayer of such a family: "For the eyes of the Lord are on the righteous, and his ears are attentive to their prayer."

Q Is there any brief prayer that would ensure a lasting healing and encompass all that I should pray for in the healing of my family tree?

A Any prayer is helpful. The formulation of the words is not all that important, but the firm purpose of amendment for our own sins and the remorse for the fact that God was offended by the sins of our ancestors is the most perfect private prayer for this healing. It would be much more effective if this were conjoined with, or in the context of, the celebration of the Eucharist. However, as a suggested private prayer, the following may be found helpful:

Dear Heavenly Father,
We praise and glorify you for your love and mercy that you have bestowed upon us and for the spirit of revelation working within us to reveal all hidden sins — both our own and those from former generations. We now take authority in the name of Jesus Christ over all familial spirits, all generational bondage, all hereditary defects, genetic or of blood, or wrong inclinations that may have been transmitted to us from within our family tree or within spiritual families to which we belong, including the defects within the church that have had their effects

upon us personally. By the faith that you give us, we rebuke all sin and the forces of evil that lead to sin. In the holy name of your Son, Jesus Christ, we take authority over *all* familial spirits and bondage, and their manifestations within our lives. By that same power of Jesus, we break the power of evil from ourselves and our families and destroy what otherwise might be transmitted to our descendants. We implore you to help us accomplish your perfect will and fill our hearts and minds with praise of you as we acknowledge your tender mercy. Thank you, Lord, for total healing and deliverance, in Jesus' precious name. Amen.

To make this prayer far more effective, ask any priest to reserve the stipendiary intention of a Mass for your family, living and dead (even if he is not familiar with the family tree healing program). Arrange for as many family members as possible to attend that Mass — or a simultaneous Mass elsewhere — and to receive Communion devoutly while praying for all living and deceased relatives, especially ancestors to the third or fourth generation, including in-laws, as well as future generations as yet unborn for preventative healing. Especially at the time of the Consecration and Communion, each person should ask that Jesus' precious blood be applied to dissolve any bondage linking the generations, and to remit the sins of the ancestors (Lev. 26:40), as well as one's own sins (v. 41).

Depending on the faith involved in the persons attending such Eucharistic celebrations, and the number of family members cooperating in the healing plan, more than one such Mass may be necessary to bring about a thorough family healing. Yet, even one person can be an instrument for the healing or even salvation of an entire household; witness Aaron (Lev. 16:6), Noah (Gen. 7:1), and Cornelius (Acts 11:14). With doubt-free faith *anything* can be accomplished (Mark 11:24; Matt. 21:21).

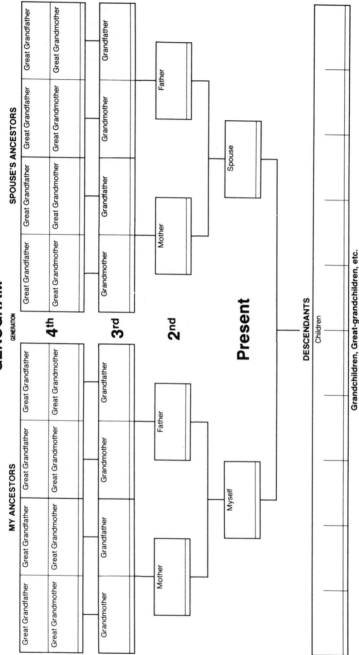

GENOGRAM SYMBOLS

The following symbols may be used—or any others of your personal preference—with names or initials of persons in the family tree that can be remembered. This very simplified genogram lists only the vertical lines from one's ancestors through oneself to the descendants. This may be expanded on a separate larger paper to include also horizontal relationships of consanguinity, or even adoptive relationships (more remotely connected with healing the family tree). In the horizontal relationships, one may include brothers, sisters, cousins, uncles, aunts, step-brother or sisters, half-brothers or sisters, etc. Question marks may be used for unknown persons, forgotten names, even possible ancestors of whose existence you may not be sure. Since this is not a scientific genealogy, but only a prayer-focusing tool, its completeness is not particularly relevant. God knows the individuals in the family tree, especially those who may need our prayerful help for release from bondage.

If you like to supply more detail, you might add numbers to signify present age or age at time of death. Color codes may be used for various personality characteristics or publicly known disorders, like addictions, practice of witchcraft, invalid marriages, etc. or diseases or abnormalities.

Remember that the genogram is meant only to help you specify your prayer intentions—thus also helping to intensify your faith. It can provide a visual framework for you to call the blood of Jesus upon individuals, living or dead, to help them, and to be applied, as it were, between each generation to block the transmission of sins' effects. It can also help to recognize situations in which there are repeated behavioral patterns or disorders.

☐ MALE   ○ FEMALE

△ Miscarried baby, stillborn, or one who died   ⊿ Aborted baby. Provide a name for the baby.
  at birth or in early infancy. Give name to child.

☒ ⊘ Deceased male or female   ☒ ⊘ Male or female having had violent or accidental death.

⊟ ⊕ Suicide of male or female   ☐─○ Male and female spouses

☐─○ Spouses having experienced divorce   ☐─⊘ One spouse (here female) deceased, leaving other spouse
   ╱ (Look for deep lingering hatred, etc.)   widowed. (Look for bondage in long-sustained *morbid*
                                                         grief, etc.)

PERSONAL NOTES

PERSONAL NOTES

PERSONAL NOTES

PERSONAL NOTES

PERSONAL NOTES

PERSONAL NOTES

PERSONAL NOTES

INDEX

Send for Free Catalog of Audiotapes, Videotapes, and Books by Same Author

(U.S. funds only, prices subject to change)

Available on Same Subject:

Healing Your Family Tree **videotape** (four one-hour TV programs on this subject on a two-tape album: $79.95 plus $5 postage — California residents add $5.40 tax)

Healing Your Family Tree **audiotape** (six-hour four-tape album: $18.00, plus 10% postage — California residents add $1.20 tax)

Books — *Faith: Key to the Heart of God* and *Key to Inner Peace*
$6.95 each, plus $1.00 postage — California residents add $0.45 tax)

Audiocassette Tape Albums — Audiotapes are available in fifty titles in various album sizes; the number after each title indicates number of tapes in album; 1 tape = $5.00; 2 tapes = $10.00; 4 tapes = $18.00; 6 tapes = $28.00; 8 tapes = $35.00, plus 10% postage (alifornia residents add 6.5% tax).

1 Healing of Memories (short version) (2)
2 The Mass in Slow Motion (6)
3 Prayer — A Response to God (4)
4 New Insights into Marriage (2)
5 Understanding Teenagers (2)
6 Role of Love-Sex in Marriage (2)
7 How to Cope (4)
8 God's Love in Your Life (2)
9 Riding High (Testimony Rev. John Hampsch) (2)
10 Spiritual Warfare (2)
11 Healing Through Forgiveness (4)
12 When It's Hard to Forgive (4)
13 Fruits of the Spirit (8)
14 Reflecting Christ (1)
15 Where Do I Go from Here? (8)
16 Using Your Gifts (1)
17 Deepening Love in Marriage (4)
18 Communicating Love in Marriage (1)

19 Power in Prayer (4)
20 Elements of a Happy Marriage (4)
21 Sharing Christ's Love (2)
22 Rooted in Faith (4)
23 Open to the Spirit (4)
24 Getting Close to God (2)
25 Joy -- The Sparkle of Life (2)
26 Healing of Memories (long version) (6)
27 The God-Encounter Experience (1)
28 The Man from Galilee (4)
29 In Search of God's Will (4)
30 Perseverance in the End-Times (1)
31 Guide Through Darkness (originally Art of Suffering) (4)
32 Chosen by God (8)
33 Persons God Uses (1)
34 What Makes You Lovable (2)
35 Coping with Worry (4)
36 The Why of Suffering (1)
37 Healing Your Marriage (2)
38 The Gift of Tongues (2)
39 Discernment of Spirits (2)
40 The Art of Listening (2)
41 Scriptural Basis for Devotion to Mary (2)
42 God's-Eye View of Suffering (2)
43 Discerning the Will of God (2)
44 God's Word — Springboard to Prayer (2)
45 Making Prayer Groups Come Alive (2)
46 Achieving Inner Peace (4)
47 The Touch of the Spirit (2)
48 Applying Scripture in Your Life (4)
49 Healing the Family Tree (4)
50 Glad You Asked (Questions and Answers) (2)

CLARETIAN TAPE MINISTRIES
P.O. Box 19100
Los Angeles, CA 90019-0100
Phone: (213) 734-1234